# Google™ For Dummies

**Cheat Sheet**

W9-DIT-757

## Standard Search Operators

**+ (AND)** Use before a keyword that must be included in search results. In the absence of any other operators, Google assumes that keywords are preceded by the *AND* operator. Example: *french +fries*.

**- (NOT)** Use before a keyword that must be excluded from the search results. Example: *soup stock -market*.

**" "** Use around keywords that must be matched as an exact phrase. Example: *american revolution "one if by land"*.

**OR** Use to match either one keyword or another. When *OR* is placed between two keywords, Google is forced to include one of them. Example: *cheese cheddar OR swiss*.

## Google URL Operators

**link** Finds incoming links to whatever URL you provide after the operator. The search displays sites that contain links to the specified URL. Example: *link:www.blogcritics.com*.

**info** When paired with a URL, this operator displays links to further information about the specified site. Example: *info:www.nytimes.com*.

**cache** Displays Google's cached (stored) snapshot of whatever URL follows the operator. Good for taking a short hop back in time. Example: *cache:www. usatoday.com*.

**site** One of the most important operators, this one restricts search results to a specified URL. Works with top-level domain extensions such as .edu and .gov by themselves in place of a specific *site* URL. Example: *yankees red sox site:www.nytimes.com*.

## Google Keyword Operators

**intitle** Matches the following keyword against Web page titles in Google's index. Dramatically narrows results and makes them more relevant. For example, *intitle: dog training*, displays Web pages with *dog* in the title and *training* in the title or page.

**allintitle** Forces all the following keywords to match against Web page titles in Google's index. Narrows results even more than *intitle*. For example, *allintitle: dog training* displays Web pages with both *dog* and *training* in the title.

**inurl** Matches the following keyword against URLs (addresses) in Google's index. Severely narrows results and makes them highly relevant. For example, with *inurl:fleet online banking*, the results would have *fleet* in the URL and *online* and *banking* in the URL (not likely) or the page (likely).

**allinurl** Forces all the following keywords to match against URLs in Google's index. Ferociously restricts search results. For example, with *allinurl:yankees tickets*, the results would have both *yankees* and *tickets* in the page URL.

**filetype** Restricts the keyword search to results of a certain file type, such as Adobe Acrobat .pdf files or Microsoft Word .doc files. Excellent for conducting research. Example: *speed of light filetype:pdf*.

## Alternative Googles

Google these and try them out!

- Googlebar
- TouchGraph Google Browser
- Google Ultimate Interface
- GooFresh
- Googlert
- Google Smackdown
- Googlism
- Elgoog

# Google™ For Dummies®

**Cheat Sheet**

## Google For Dummies Googly Awards

A subjective selection of superlative search support.

### Best appliance
The Google Toolbar at `toolbar.google.com`

### Most addictive index
Google Groups at `groups.google.com`

### Most important Webmaster tool
Google AdWords at `www.google.com/ads`

### Newest Google juggernaut
Google News at `news.google.com`

### Most used Google operator
The *site* operator (example: `site:www.anydomain.com`)

### Most fun Google game
Googlewhacking at `www.googlewhack.com`

### Most glamorous alternative to Google
TouchGraph Google Browser at . . . Google it! (Or see Chapter 14.)

## Searching with Keyboard Controls

Try browsing and selecting Google search results without using your mouse — keyboard controls only. Go to this page for a specialized Google search engine:

`labs.google.com/keys/index.html`

| | |
|---|---|
| k | Places balls (cursor) next to first result, and then moves the cursor down the search results list |
| i | Places cursor on previous result |
| Enter | Links to selected result page |
| c | Displays cached page |
| s | Searches for pages similar to selected |
| l | Moves cursor to AdWords column |
| j | Moves cursor from AdWords to main search results |
| n | Displays next page of results |
| p | Displays previous page of results |
| a | Highlights the keyword box |
| ? | Displays keyboard controls on results page |

## Google Information Operators

| | |
|---|---|
| stocks | Preceding a stock ticker symbol, this operator bypasses the search results page, sending you to Yahoo! Finance to see a price quote for your requested symbol. Example: *stocks:intc msft*. |
| phonebook | When followed by a name (last name only) and either a state abbreviation or a zip code, Google displays the full address and phone number when available. Example: *phonebook:jones nj*. |
| rphonebook | Limits phone book results to residential listings. |
| bphonebook | Limits phone book results to business listings. |

**For Dummies: Bestselling Book Series for Beginners**

# Google™ FOR DUMMIES®

## by Brad Hill

**WILEY**

Wiley Publishing, Inc.

**Google™ For Dummies®**

Published by
**Wiley Publishing, Inc.**
111 River Street
Hoboken, NJ 07030
www.wiley.com

Copyright © 2003 by Wiley Publishing, Inc., Indianapolis, Indiana

Published by Wiley Publishing, Inc., Indianapolis, Indiana

Published simultaneously in Canada

For general information on our other products and services or to obtain technical support, please contact our Customer Care Department within the U.S. at 800-762-2974, outside the U.S. at 317-572-3993, or fax 317-572-4002.

Wiley also publishes its books in a variety of electronic formats. Some content that appears in print may not be available in electronic books.

Library of Congress Control Number is available from the publisher.

ISBN: 0-7645-4420-9

Manufactured in the United States of America

10 9 8 7 6 5 4 3 2 1

1O/QV/QZ/QT/IN

**WILEY**   is a trademark of Wiley Publishing, Inc.

# About the Author

**Brad Hill** has worked in the online field since 1992 and is regarded as a pre-eminent advocate of the online experience. As a best-selling author of books and in his columns, Hill reaches a global audience of consumers who rely on his writings to help determine their online service choices.

Brad's books include a *Publishers Weekly* bestseller and a Book-of-the-Month catalog selection. Brad's titles in the *For Dummies* series include *Internet Searching For Dummies*, *Internet Directory For Dummies*, and *Yahoo! For Dummies*. In other venues, Brad writes about cybercultural trends, digital music, virtual investing, and all sorts of online destinations.

Brad is often consulted in the media's coverage of the Internet. He appears on television and radio Webcasts and is quoted in publications such as *Business Week*, *The New York Times*, and *PC World*.

Brad doesn't get outdoors much. Sunshine baffles him. As compensation, he is listed in *Who's Who* and is a member of The Authors Guild.

# Dedication

To my wife, Ann, whose loving support made this book possible.

# Author's Acknowledgments

Every book is a partnership of author and editor. Susan Pink is the editor of this book and a collaborator in other projects as well. Her keenness, careful reading, and incisive comments shine through every paragraph . . . except for the one that I hid from her. You'll know it when you see it. Besides being an unusually fine editor who makes me look a lot better than I would without her, Susan has a gift for remaining calm during the most intense deadline crises. She also laughs at all the right times.

Allen Wyatt had the challenging job of technical editor. His insights, in this and other books, are invaluable.

Melody Layne at Wiley Publishing nursed this project from the start, getting it off the ground quickly and helping shape its focus. I'm very thankful.

Mary Corder pulled me into the *For Dummies* family several years ago, and is a delightful friend. She is so sick of seeing her name pop up in my acknowledgments. But I am forever grateful, so she'll have to deal with it.

Many thanks to all the copy editors and production experts who pored over every page of the manuscript.

Finally, I'd like to thank the Academy and my directory, Steven Spielberg, without whom — oops, wrong speech.

## Publisher's Acknowledgments

We're proud of this book; please send us your comments through our online registration form located at www.dummies.com/register/.

Some of the people who helped bring this book to market include the following:

**Acquisitions, Editorial, and Media Development**

**Project Editor:** Susan Pink

**Acquisitions Editor:** Melody Layne

**Technical Editor:** Allen Wyatt, Discovery Computing Inc.

**Editorial Manager:** Carol Sheehan

**Media Development Supervisor:** Richard Graves

**Editorial Assistant:** Amanda Foxworth

**Cartoons:** Rich Tennant, www.the5thwave.com

**Production**

**Project Coordinator:** Kristie Rees

**Layout and Graphics:** Jennifer Click, Seth Conley, Joyce Haughey, LeAndra Hosier, Lynsey Osborn, Jacque Schneider, Shae Lywn Wilson

**Proofreaders:** John Tyler Connoley, Andy Hollandbeck, Dwight Ramsey

**Indexer:** TECHBOOKS Production Services

**Publishing and Editorial for Technology Dummies**

   **Richard Swadley,** Vice President and Executive Group Publisher

   **Andy Cummings,** Vice President and Publisher

   **Mary C. Corder,** Editorial Director

**Publishing for Consumer Dummies**

   **Diane Graves Steele,** Vice President and Publisher

   **Joyce Pepple,** Acquisitions Director

**Composition Services**

   **Gerry Fahey,** Vice President of Production Services

   **Debbie Stailey,** Director of Composition Services

# Contents at a Glance

Introduction ..................................................................... 1

*Part I: Taming Google* ........................................ 7

Chapter 1: Discovering All That Google Can Do ..............................9
Chapter 2: Better Googling: Finding the Right Stuff .......................19
Chapter 3: Directory Trolling and News Browsing ..........................47
Chapter 4: 800 Million Messages at Your Fingertips: Google Groups ........61

*Part II: Specialty Searching* ............................ 87

Chapter 5: Shopping with Froogle and Google Catalogs .....................89
Chapter 6: Searching the Specialty Categories ...........................107
Chapter 7: Searching for Answers ........................................115
Chapter 8: Experimenting in Google Labs .................................135

*Part III: Putting Google to Work for You* ..... 157

Chapter 9: Google on Your Browser .......................................159
Chapter 10: Googling in Tongues .........................................185
Chapter 11: Using Google AdWords ........................................197
Chapter 12: Bringing Google and Its Users to Your Site ..................217

*Part IV: Tricks, Games, and Alternatives to Google* ..... 225

Chapter 13: Hosting a Weblog with Google's Blogger ......................227
Chapter 14: Alternatives to Google ......................................241
Chapter 15: Twisted Googling and Google Games ...........................275

*Part V: The Part of Tens* ................................ 295

Chapter 16: Ten Google Tricks ...........................................297
Chapter 17: Ten More Google Tricks ......................................311
Chapter 18: Ten Sites about Google ......................................323

Index ......................................................................... 333

# Table of Contents

*Introduction* .......................................................... **1**

About This Book ..........................................................1
Conventions Used in This Book ...................................2
What You're Not to Read ...........................................2
Foolish Assumptions ..................................................3
How This Book Is Organized .......................................3
    Part I: Taming Google ...........................................3
    Part II: Specialty Searching ....................................4
    Part III: Putting Google to Work for You ..................4
    Part IV: Tricks, Games, and Alternatives to Google .........4
    Part V: The Part of Tens .........................................5
Icons Used in This Book ..............................................5
Where to Go from Here ...............................................5

*Part 1: Taming Google* ...................................... **7**

## Chapter 1: Discovering All That Google Can Do ...............9

Beyond Keywords ......................................................10
The Mythical Internet Library .....................................11
    Finding all sorts of stuff .......................................11
    Hidden strengths ...............................................12
    Answers from real people ....................................13
    And now . . . Weblogs .........................................14
    Portable information butler ...................................14
Google the Business Partner ......................................15
The Open Index .........................................................16
The Greatness of Google ...........................................17

## Chapter 2: Better Googling: Finding the Right Stuff .............19

Setting Preferences ...................................................19
    The international Google ......................................21
    Searching for non-English pages ...........................23
    G-rated searching ...............................................24
    Opening the floodgates ........................................24
    New windows .....................................................25
Basic Web Searches ..................................................25
Understanding the Google Results Page .......................28

Breaking Down Web Search Results ..............................................30
    Page description ................................................................30
    Directory category ............................................................30
    The Google cache ..............................................................31
    Similar pages ....................................................................32
    Indented results ................................................................33
Using Advanced Search ..............................................................34
    Using multiple keywords ....................................................35
    Other Advanced Search features ..........................................36
Searching Shorthand: Using Operators ........................................38
    Typing standard search operators ........................................39
    Understanding special Google operators ..............................40
A Picture Is Worth a Thousand Keywords ....................................42
Advanced Image Searching ..........................................................43

**Chapter 3: Directory Trolling and News Browsing** ...............**47**
Relaxing into Browsing Mode ......................................................48
Understanding Google Directory ................................................49
Submitting a Web Page to the Directory ....................................53
Googling the Day's News ............................................................56
Searching for News ....................................................................59

**Chapter 4: 800 Million Messages at Your Fingertips:**
**Google Groups** .........................................................**61**
Welcome to the Pre-Web ............................................................62
Browsing and Searching Google Groups ....................................66
    Using the group operator ....................................................69
    Understanding related groups ............................................72
    Sorting search results ........................................................73
    Interpreting search results ................................................73
Reading Messages and Threads ..................................................74
Posting Messages through Google Groups ..................................80
Advanced Searching ..................................................................84

*Part II: Specialty Searching* .................................**87**

**Chapter 5: Shopping with Froogle and Google Catalogs** ..........**89**
Google's Approach to Online Shopping ......................................90
Searching and Browsing in Froogle ............................................91
    Search results in Froogle ....................................................92
    Froogle search operators ....................................................94
Froogle Advanced Search ............................................................98
About Google Catalogs ..............................................................99
Searching Google Catalogs ......................................................100
Advanced Catalogs Searching ..................................................105

**Chapter 6: Searching the Specialty Categories** ...................107

    Finding the Specialty Searches ..................................................108
        Knowing the specialty URLs ...........................................108
        Specialty searching from the Google Toolbar ...............109
    U.S. Government Searches ......................................................109
    Linux and BSD Searches ..........................................................111
    Mac and Microsoft Searches ...................................................112
    University Searches ..................................................................113

**Chapter 7: Searching for Answers** ...........................115

    Paying for Google Expertise ....................................................115
    Creating an Account and Logging In ......................................116
    Posting and Canceling Questions ...........................................118
    Comments and Conversations .................................................124
    Evaluating Answers and Clarifying Questions .......................127
        Clarifying and modifying a question ...........................128
        Fine-tuning and rating answers ....................................128
        Adding a comment .........................................................129
    Good Questions at the Right Prices ........................................130
        Good questions = good answers ...................................130
        Putting your money where your query is .....................133

**Chapter 8: Experimenting in Google Labs** ......................135

    Sharing Your Computer with Science .....................................136
        Understanding how Google Compute operates ...........136
        Installing Google Compute ...........................................138
        Tweaking Google Compute ...........................................138
        Uninstalling Google Compute .......................................142
    Watching Google Viewer .........................................................143
    Breezing Through WebQuotes .................................................146
    Getting It Defined in Google Glossary ....................................148
    Building Google Sets ................................................................150
    Voice Searching ........................................................................152
    Fingering Through Results: Keyboard Shortcuts ...................153
    The Labs Upshot ......................................................................155

*Part III: Putting Google to Work for You* ......................*157*

**Chapter 9: Google on Your Browser** ...........................159

    Installing the Google Toolbar .................................................160
    Choosing Toolbar Options ......................................................163
        General Toolbar options ...............................................164
        Button options ...............................................................165
        Experimental features ...................................................170

Google Toolbar 2.0 (Beta) ........................................171
    The Toolbar Options dialog box ........................174
    The Search Country button ...............................175
    The Blog This! button ......................................176
    AutoFill ...........................................................177
    Pop-up blocker ................................................179
Pushing Google's (Browser) Buttons ...........................180
Putting Google Under Your Browser's Hood ..................182

## Chapter 10: Googling in Tongues ........................185

Google in Your Native Tongue ...................................186
Searching Around the World ......................................189
Translating on the Fly ..............................................191
Non-English Google Toolbars .....................................194

## Chapter 11: Using Google AdWords ....................197

Understanding the AdWords Concept ..........................198
Creating an Account and Your First Ad .......................201
Activating Your Account ............................................206
Managing Your Campaigns .........................................207
    Viewing your campaign reports .........................208
    Editing your campaign .....................................210
    Starting a new campaign ..................................211
More About Keywords ...............................................212
    Keyword modifiers in AdWords ........................213
    The Keyword Suggestion tool ..........................213
    The Power Posting tool ....................................216

## Chapter 12: Bringing Google and Its Users to Your Site ..........217

The Google Crawl ......................................................218
Getting into Google ...................................................218
    Luring the spider ............................................219
    Spider-friendly tips .........................................221
The Folly of Fooling Google .......................................222
Keeping Google Out ..................................................223

## Part IV: Tricks, Games, and Alternatives to Google .......225

## Chapter 13: Hosting a Weblog with Google's Blogger ...........227

Starting Your Blogger Account ...................................228
Creating a Blog at BlogSpot .......................................229
Creating a Blog at Your Own FTP Server .....................231
Running Your Blog .....................................................232
    Writing, posting, and publishing ......................233
    Adjusting your blog settings .............................235
    Formatting your blog .......................................238

**Chapter 14: Alternatives to Google** . . . . . . . . . . . . . . . . . . . . . . . . . .241
  Bare-Bones Results ................................................................243
  Finding the Freshest Google ...................................................244
  The Amazing TouchGraph ......................................................246
       Visualizing related sites ..................................................246
       Visual keyword sets ........................................................252
  Google by E-Mail ...................................................................255
       Searching by e-mail ........................................................256
       Google e-mail alerts ........................................................256
  Dancing the Google Dance ....................................................259
       My Google-Dance-Machine ..............................................259
       Google Dance Tool ..........................................................262
       Two more Google dance sites ...........................................263
  Very Advanced Searching: The Google Ultimate Interface ..........264
  GAPS, GARBO, and GAWSH .................................................266
       Proximity searching with GAPS ........................................266
       Relation browsing with GARBO ........................................268
       Search by host with GAWSH ............................................270
  Chatting with Google ..............................................................271
  Flash with Floogle ..................................................................272
  Two Final, Frivolous Alternatives to Google .............................273

**Chapter 15: Twisted Googling and Google Games** . . . . . . . . . . . . . .275
  In Pursuit of the Googlewhack .................................................275
  The Random Googlelaar ..........................................................278
  Googlism ...............................................................................280
  Squabbling Keywords .............................................................281
  More Random Searching .........................................................284
       Mangle ...........................................................................285
       Random Bounce Me .........................................................286
       Random Google page ......................................................287
       Random imagery .............................................................287
  Google Backwards .................................................................289
  Google Art .............................................................................290

*Part V: The Part of Tens* ..............................................**295**

**Chapter 16: Ten Google Tricks** . . . . . . . . . . . . . . . . . . . . . . . . . . . . . .297
  Searching within Search Results ..............................................297
  Mapping It .............................................................................299
  The Google Phone Book ..........................................................300
  Opting Out of the Phone Book .................................................302
  Seeing (and Erasing) Previous Searches ...................................303

Word Meanings ............................................................303
Negative Search Operators ....................................305
Searching by Date .....................................................305
Quick Stock and Company Information ................307
Double- and Triple-Clicking Keywords ................308

**Chapter 17: Ten More Google Tricks** ...................**311**
The Google Zeitgeist ................................................311
Including the "Stop Words" ....................................313
The Google Toolbar as Spellchecker ....................313
Operators First, for History's Sake ......................314
Post Factum Toolbar ................................................315
The Google Library ..................................................316
Talking with Other Googlers ..................................316
The Toolbar Headline Generator ...........................318
The Google Store .....................................................319
Google Logos .............................................................320

**Chapter 18: Ten Sites about Google** ....................**323**
Google Watch ............................................................324
Webmaster World: Google ......................................324
Google PageRank ......................................................325
Google Weblog ..........................................................326
Elgoog.nl ....................................................................327
The Founders' Home Pages ....................................328
Googlepress ...............................................................328
Google Review ..........................................................329
gooGuide ...................................................................330
Something Awful (Logos) ........................................331

*Index* ...............................................................*333*

# Introduction

· · · · · · · · · · · · · · · · · · · · · · · · · · · · · · · · · · · · · · · · · · · · ·

*T*here has never been an Internet phenomenon like Google. Not even Yahoo! of 1994 and 1995 could claim the importance in so many lives that Google can claim. Amazon, eBay, Napster — all have been milestones, but Google is a uniquely big wheel. It has been adopted quickly, its user base is of global scope, and it has influence on society at large. (A recent marketing survey reported that Google was a more recognized brand than Coca-Cola and Starbucks.) No online activity has become as deeply embedded in our culture and language as Googling.

Google is far more than just a search engine and has become more important than other general search engines. Google's value is partly due to its amazingly accurate search results, which sometimes seem almost as if Google were intuiting your information needs. Part of Google's appeal lies in its reactionary divergence from search engine portal design and its no-fluff presentation. (As of this writing, the English version of Google's home page contains 36 words.) Not to be forgotten are Google's supporting services — all of which are covered in this book — which elevate its usefulness to the level of indispensability. Want to find out something? Google it.

After I wrote three editions of *Internet Searching For Dummies*, Google was unleashed and started gaining traction. At first I thought that if I were to write another edition of *Internet Searching*, it might contain one sentence: "Go to Google." Then, after digging deeply, I realized that Google warranted — needed, demanded! — its own book. You are holding the result.

## About This Book

My intent in these pages is to reveal the inner depths and hidden features of the Googling lifestyle. Previous search engines attempted to become home bases and launching pads to the Internet by dint of overwhelming and varied content. These gigantic, customizable portals still scream with colors, facts, advertisements, stuff to read. Google's power is all under the hood, where it counts. And quietly surrounding the astonishing Google index and its superlative search results are a host of unpromoted services that you might not be aware of. Even in the core service — the Web search engine — Google silently and without hype implements features that, when known, make daily Googling faster, more powerful, and more targeted.

People get excited when I talk to them about Google. While writing this book I discussed Google's hidden power with veteran and beginning Googlers alike. Most people were astonished at the many brilliant Google features they didn't know about. Getting fast stock quotes; searching through every page in thousands of mail-order catalogues; finding files on government and military sites; Googling over the phone; navigating search results without using the mouse; searching only the titles of Web pages; playing Google games at innumerable Google fan sites; plumbing the amazing Google Groups (one of the most remarkable reference resources in the world); using Google as a phone book; highlighting a word on any Web page and launching a Google search from that page; using the Google Toolbar to block pop-up ads . . . I could go on. And, in fact, I do for the next few hundred pages.

So, what is this book about? It's about the most important online service of our time. Without conceit, I can tell you that these pages are about your virtual life, your online intelligence, and your informed citizenship in the Internet nation. Whichever translation of this book you are reading, whatever country you live in, the beneficent informational power of Google belongs as much to you as to anyone.

# Conventions Used in This Book

I despise conventions. All that walking; the bad food. Fortunately, that has nothing to do with the conventions used in this text, which are layout styles and typefaces designed to identify certain kinds of information. To make following along easier, this book is consistent in how it presents these items:

- ✔ Web addresses, also called URLs, look like this:

    www.google.com

- ✔ When I use an unusual term for the first time, I *italicize* it.

- ✔ Google keywords appear *italicized* when embedded in text, and sometimes appear below a paragraph like this:

    keywords google search

# What You're Not to Read

This book is not technical, so I don't need to warn you away from difficult parts. But don't feel as if you must read straight through from start to finish. This isn't a novel. Google's many services fall naturally into distinct chapters, and it's natural to be interested in some things more than others.

For the Google beginner, Chapters 1 and 2 are probably the most important. But if you have lots of experience with basic Googling, those two chapters might be the least important. Pick and choose from the Table of Contents.

# Foolish Assumptions

Google has so few requirements that, in writing about it, I don't need to make many assumptions. Which is a good thing, because I have a long track record of mistaken assumptions. For example, right now I'm assuming that you're eating Krispy Kreme donuts. That's probably wrong, but I can't get the image out of my head.

I do assume that you can get on the Internet and operate a Web browser. Occasionally it's helpful to check which browser you're using, including the version number of that browser, and I blithely assume you can do that. Basic Internet navigation skills — such as visiting a Web site, filling in online forms, and following on-screen download instructions — are useful when exploring Google's many services. I'm quick to assume that you know all that stuff.

So I guess I am assuming a fair amount about your ease of movement online, but honestly, nothing in this book is difficult. If Google were hard, it wouldn't be so popular.

# How This Book Is Organized

This book employs a new and startling organizational system by which words are gathered into sentences, which in turn form paragraphs, and the whole shebang is printed on pages. Just turn the page, and . . . more words! I've collected thousands of the finest words in circulation, and strung them together in a manner that occasionally approaches coherence.

The book's chapters are organized into five parts, as follows.

## Part I: Taming Google

The four chapters in Part I present a detailed look at Google's basic services — the ones you reach from the home page. Here you learn about Web searching, image search, the Google Directory, Google News, and Google Groups. This part is not merely an overview. To the contrary, I get very detailed about search operators (they can improve your life, trust me), finding certain types of document, trolling through newsgroups, and explaining how the directory works. Don't skim past these chapters if you know basic Googling! This part is stocked with tips and little-known facts about Google's under-publicized features.

## Part II: Specialty Searching

Part II goes somewhat further afield to Google's fringe services. Chapter 5 describes how Google provides a product database for virtual window shopping. Chapter 6 explores several specialty search engines that Google operates in parallel to the main Web engine. Google Answers, a for-pay research service, gets the next chapter. Finally, Chapter 8 examines several search-lab experiments that Google throws open to the public.

## Part III: Putting Google to Work for You

The chapters in Part III describe four uncommon ways in which Google can be put to work. First, and for many most importantly, Google can attach to Web browsers in various ways, offering one-click searching from anywhere on the Web. I venture to say that the Google Toolbar is the single most important Google service beyond the basic search engine, and I strongly recommend that you read Chapter 9. Google's translation services are covered in the next chapter. Chapters 11 and 12 are of special interest to site owners. The complex AdWords service takes over Chapter 11. Chapter 12 explains how Google searches the Web and how anyone with a Web page can get into Google's search results.

## Part IV: Tricks, Games, and Alternatives to Google

Part IV is almost all recreational. Google's Blogger.com service, which provides Weblogs free of charge, is in Chapter 13. If you're new to blogging, a whole new world awaits you. The next two chapters take you all over the Web, trying Google-related sites developed by individuals who took advantage of Google's standing invitation to build alternate search interfaces. Google's index is available to any programmer, and some of the results are spectacularly successful — improvements, even, on Google's own pages. Fun and games are in Chapter 15. If you've heard of Googlewhacking and wondered what it is, this is the chapter for you.

## Part V: The Part of Tens

In the traditional *For Dummies* list-of-ten chapters, I stashed the miscellaneous features, tricks, and tips that didn't fit into other chapters. Chapters 16 and 17 together contain twenty tips for more effective Googling that I find essential. The book's final chapter points you to ten sites *about* Google — pages that explain Google exotica and even sites that are openly, loudly critical of Google's success.

# Icons Used in This Book

See how big these pages are? We have to put something in these wide margins, so we came up with icons. Figuring that they might as well be more than just decorative, we assigned meaning to the pictures you see marking some paragraphs:

This book is full of these things. They remind you to tip your waitress. Also, these icons indicate that the paragraph contains an especially usable nugget of information.

I throw in a lot of these, too, but I forget why. It'll come to me.

Rarely, I slip into the kind of technobabble that makes people avoid me at parties. Just slap me when I get like that. And feel free to ignore these paragraphs if you're not interested — they don't contain anything you need to know.

Using Google is considerably safer than leaping out of an airplane with a sack full of bowling balls, so I don't often have reason to issue warnings. But when I do, get the kids to a safe place and board up the windows.

# Where to Go from Here

I don't know about you, but I'm going to lie down. It's 2:00 in the afternoon, for goodness sake, and time for a nap. If you're in the mood to keep reading, do it quietly.

Starting at the beginning never hurts, but if you're ready for the advanced stuff, I suggest leaping to the section on search operators in Chapter 2. Jumping to Chapters 14 and 15 can be fun, too. If you do nothing else with this book, look in Chapter 9 and make sure you're up to speed with the Google Toolbar.

Wake me up for dinner, and happy Googling.

# Part I
# Taming Google

The 5th Wave — By Rich Tennant

"I think you're just jealous that I found a community of people that worship the yam as I do, and you haven't."

# In this part . . .

In the first part of *Google For Dummies,* I introduce Google's main search areas — which, of course, anybody can see by going to the Google home page. Ah, but by *introduce,* I mean that this part lovingly peels back layer after layer of Google search functions to reveal dozens of ways to maximize your daily Google experience.

Google is good when you know just the bare minimum. Imagine how much better it can get for a laser-minded, Web-addicted power user who can blast apart a results page with a few simple search operators. Are you ready for this? Because that's what this collection of chapters is all about.

Chapter 1 sets you up with the overview; Chapter 2 goes way beyond basic keyword plodding; and Chapter 3 rebuilds your life around daily Google information feeds. Chapter 4 navigates the rocky shoals of the incredible Google Groups and spits you out safely on the other side — with your mind recalibrated to new realities. This isn't about sharing pictures of your kids on AOL. This is life-altering information designed to rattle your matrix and supercharge your relationship to the living global network writhing on the other side of your computer screen. So shift your eyes to the right and start the first moment of your new virtual life. [Editors' note: Brad Hill has promised to switch to decaf by the time you reach Part II.]

# Chapter 1

# Discovering All That Google Can Do

*In This Chapter*

▶ Getting an overview of Google's many services

▶ Understanding Google's many search realms

▶ Uncovering Google's hidden features

▶ Introducing Google's non-search services

▶ Understanding why Google's is better . . . much better

*Y*ou're about to embark on an adventure that will stimulate your mind and gratify the most urgent desires of your soul. Then, after you drink that triple cappuccino, you'll start discovering Google.

I know what you're saying: You've already discovered Google. Who hasn't? Not since the early Web days of 1994 and 1995, when everybody surfed through Yahoo!, have people flocked so unanimously to a single, dominant search engine as they do to Google.

During the time since Yahoo! got the ball rolling, many keyword-oriented search engines have come. Many have gone. Some remain, offering specialty searches or emulating Google. (Imitation and flattery — you know the drill.)

Now, with *Googling* a common term in the mainstream vernacular, general searching of the Web has become standardized into a universal ritual. Anybody wanting to find an online destination follows this three-step process:

1. Go to Google.

2. Type a few words related to the search goal.

3. Click the search results to visit relevant Web sites.

---

## Life without Google

In my life as an online citizen (no, I don't get out much), two destinations are indispensable. One is Yahoo!, a gargantuan domain that provides more free services than a sane person would try to count. The other is Google, which makes my virtual movements faster and more exact than ever. Online life without either is inconceivable. The amazing thing is that Google has been around only since the fall of 1999. Yahoo! has been building its reputation and service platform for nearly ten years. And it can be argued that Google has embedded itself into the lifestyles of ordinary Internet citizens and the business practices of companies more profoundly and securely than Yahoo! ever has. Whereas Yahoo! spent millions on the "Do you Yahoo!?" ad campaign, everybody started saying "Google this" and "Google that" with little or no formal advertising from Google.

I've written *Yahoo! For Dummies* and *Google For Dummies*. Each service is a cornerstone of the Internet. Prediction is a risky business, but when I'm in a divining mood, I can easily see Google becoming the most important online service in history, approaching the geek-idealist's dream of indexing every bit of network knowledge and virtual expression, with an awareness of the surrounding context, each contribution ranked by its peers and instantly accessible. A profoundly foolish vision? The surprising part is how closely Google is chasing it already.

Life without Google? With each passing day, the thought becomes more inconceivable.

---

All well and good. Google is lightning fast and devastatingly accurate. And the chapters in Part II dismantle general searching to help you maximize your basic Google experience. But as it turns out, general Web searching is just the tip of the Google iceberg.

# Beyond Keywords

The term *search engine,* so apt for the lumbering, early-generation monsters that crunched through the Web looking for sites, seems only fractionally fitting for Google. Rather, Google should be called an information engine. Or a knowledge life-form. The stuff you get from Google might come from its vast and smart index of Web pages, or it might come from other indices seamlessly woven into the core data dump. Some of the usefulness that you can pry out of Google, such as Weblogging, comes from autonomous companies that Google has acquired and put under its service umbrella. However you use Google, greater awareness of what's under the hood is certain to make your online life easier, better informed, and more fluid.

The following sections furnish a quick survey of Google's information engine, including and beyond general keyword searching.

# The Mythical Internet Library

The World Wide Web was developed to bring order to the chaotic Internet, which had been lurking in academia and the government since the 1960s. Because the Internet was regarded primarily as an information source — more than an entertainment medium or a community space — it was natural to imagine the quick construction of a universal, all-inclusive online library. Through the years, I often heard people mistakenly speak of the Internet as an information realm in which one could find anything, read any book, and access all knowledge.

But the truth splintered away from that ideal. First, the Web became a distinct and autonomous entity with its own content, disregarding for the most part the academic material that was already online. Second, regular folks who stormed into the new virtual playground were interested in other, more recreational pursuits than learning. So the mecca of unlimited access to knowledge withered away from reality — and even from the imagination.

I am not going to imply that Google single-handedly manifests an Alexandrian library of human knowledge. (Yet.) However, through the astounding accuracy of its search results, Google does ease access to an unprecedented breadth of knowledge. To whatever extent the Internet comprises the communal content of the human mind, Google illuminates the gray matter with clarity and usefulness. Want to know something? Google it. That's the modern recipe for learning in this information-saturated age.

## Finding all sorts of stuff

In Google, basic Web searching couldn't be simpler. The next chapter covers the basics, plus powerful ways of grabbing the information you want quickly. In addition to offering traditional Web searching, Google blends other types of searching into the basic keyword process:

✔ **Google Directory:** Yahoo! set the standard of integrated searching (through a keyword engine) and browsing (through a topical directory). In the beginning, Yahoo!'s search engine searched the directory, which was carefully hand-constructed by a staff of editors. Yahoo! still builds its directory manually and also contracts another search engine to generate its nondirectory search results. As of this writing, that other search engine is Google, which won an unprecedented two consecutive Yahoo! contracts. Google also presents a topical directory for browsing, and you can search it separately from the basic Web search. See Chapter 3.

✔ **Newsgroup reader:** Newsgroups make up the portion of the Internet called Usenet, which is far older (and probably still bigger in some measure) than the Web. It has more than 30,000 groups, organized by topic, covering everything from astrophysics to *ER*. Usenet is a hangout for academicians, pornographers, armchair pundits, and nearly everyone else. It's a wild-and-wooly realm that's normally accessed through a dedicated computer program called a *newsgroup reader*. Outlook Express and other e-mail programs contain newsgroup-reading features. Google got into the act by purchasing the old Deja News, the groundbreaking company that first put Usenet on the Web. Google presents a deep archive of newsgroup messages, entirely searchable. Furthermore, it lets you establish an identity and post messages to groups, all through your Web browser. See Chapter 4.

✔ **Image finder:** The Web is a picturesque place. Every photograph and drawing that you see on a Web page is a distinct file residing at a specific Internet location, and Google knows how to search that tremendous store of images. See Chapter 2.

✔ **International newsstand:** In one of the most dramatic additions to the Google spectrum of features, Google News has replaced Yahoo! News as the default headline engine on countless screens. Almost unbelievable in its depth and range, Google News presents continually updated links to established news sources in dozens of countries, putting a global spin on every story of the day. See Chapter 3.

These features hook into Google's basic search engine. At the same time, each one stands on its own as an independent search tool. Other features, sketched next, exist more in the background but are no less important than the high-profile search realms.

## *Hidden strengths*

You might be surprised to find what Google can tell you if prompted in certain ways. Active Googlers stumble across some of these features in the course of daily rummaging, because Google spits out information in unrequested configurations when it thinks (yes, Google does seem like a thinking animal sometimes) you need it. Other chapters describe exactly how to coax explicit types of search results from the site. Here, my aim is to briefly summarize what's under the hood:

✔ **A phone book:** You heard me, a phone book. Actually, it's both a phone book and an address book — it works in both directions. And in my experience, the Google address finder works better, faster, and with less clutter than similar services provided by Yahoo!, Switchboard, WhoWhere, and others. See Chapter 16.

- ✓ **A shopping portal:** This is one of Google's huge, hidden, under-appreciated strengths. Again, comparisons to Yahoo! Shopping are difficult to avoid, and again, Google shames its competitor with its depth of innovation and superb ease of use. The two services differ crucially, though, in that you don't actually buy things through a Google transaction system as you can in Yahoo!. (For example, Google has no Google Wallet for storing credit card information for one-click purchasing.) Google has two main shopping services, Froogle and Google Catalogs. You use Froogle to find shopping sites. Google Catalogs — arguably the more important of Google's two shopping services and certainly the more fun — gives you a paper-free sense of accessing a mail-order universe. See Chapter 5.

- ✓ **A document repository:** Most people, most of the time, search for Web pages. But many other types of viewable (or listenable) pieces of content are available on the Internet. For example, almost every modern computer comes with the capability to view PDF files, which are documents such as articles, white papers, research texts, and financial statements that retain their original formatting instead of being altered to fit a Web page. Google includes documents other than Web pages in its general search results and also lets you narrow any search to a specific file type. See Chapter 2.

- ✓ **A translator:** Google is ferociously multilingual. Its fluency is occasionally evident in search results and comes to life on special pages that invite you to dump foreign text into an on-screen box for instant conversion to the tongue of your choice. See Chapter 10.

- ✓ **A government and university tracker:** Not to get all paranoid on you, but if you're into watching your back, the first of these features could prove helpful. More benignly, Google reserves distinct portions of its search engine for university domains and another for government domains. This arrangement has uses explored in Chapter 6.

These and other new aspects of the Google experience came from a dedicated technology incubation project called Google Labs. Remember when entire businesses were built solely on cultivating online ideas? Most of them crashed and burned, adding to the rubble of the exploded Internet bubble. Google is modestly, but importantly, continuing the incubating tradition by continually evolving ways of enhancing its information engine. See Chapter 8.

## Answers from real people

One problem with the Web as an information source is the question of authenticity. Anybody can put up a Web site and publish information that might or might not be true. True expertise is difficult to verify on the Web.

Google Answers is . . . well, the answer. Staffed by a large crew of freelance researchers in many subjects, Google Answers lets you ask questions and receive customized answers — for a price. How much? That's up to you; an auction system is used whereby you request an answer for a specified price, and individual researchers either take on your question or not. (See Chapter 7.)

One nice touch: Google maintains a directory of previously asked and answered questions, sorted by topic. Browsing through the archives is a nice way to audition the quality of the service (it's good), and possibly find that your query has already been solved.

## And now . . . Weblogs

Are you ready for Weblogs? They're ready for you. Weblogs — *blogs* for short — aren't new, but awareness of them is still growing at a terrific clip, and I believe the phenomenon of blogging is still in the early stage of popularity and prevalence. Google thinks so, too, leading the company to acquire one of the most popular do-it-yourself Weblog providers: Blogger.com. With Blogger.com in the fold — and incorporated into the new version of the Google Toolbar (see Chapter 9) — this book treats that service as part of the Google suite of features.

Chapter 13 covers Blogger in some detail. For now, know that Blogger is free and even hosts Weblogs at no charge. Both the hosting and the basic blog service can be upgraded to more powerful versions for modest subscription fees. Blogger is not the fanciest Weblog tool around — in fact, it's one of the least fancy. Its simplicity is a selling point to beginners who like the idea of easy Internet publishing and don't want to surmount the learning curve other programs and services demand.

## Portable information butler

Google provides excellent results for the lazy, one-stop Internet searcher. And don't we all deserve a search engine that works hard on our behalf? Well, Google goes beyond the call of duty by following you around even after you've left the site. Only if you want it to, of course.

You can rip the Google engine right out of its site (so to speak) and take it with you while traipsing around the Web in three ways:

 ✔ **Wireless Google:** The most portable style of Googling possible, the wireless method works with Web-enabled cell phones (and, boy, is the built-in phone book handy then), on Palm handheld computers, and on Handspring PDA (personal digital assistants). See Chapter 16 if you're ready to Google away from your desktop or laptop.

✔ **Google Toolbar:** If you're aware of the Google Toolbar, you're probably using it. You should be, anyway. If this is the first you've heard of it, today is the first day of the rest of your online citizenship. Internet life will never be the same. The Google Toolbar bolts right into your browser, up near the top where your other toolbars reside. It enables you to launch a Google search without surfing to the Google site. I believe that in some dictionaries there's a picture of the Google Toolbar next to the definition of *cool.* (See Chapter 9.)

✔ **Google browser buttons:** Perhaps even snazzier than the Google Toolbar, the browser buttons attach to your browser's existing toolbar, where they inscrutably await your mouse clicks. By so clicking, you can highlight a word of text on any Web page and launch a Google search with that keyword. Another button takes stock of the page you're on and delivers similar pages. (See Chapter 9.)

Google's portable features insinuate the service into your online life more deeply than merely bookmarking the site. Google will take over your mind. But that's a good thing.

# Google the Business Partner

With the Google AdWords program, Internet advertising has been brought to the masses — and boy, people are eating it up.

AdWords (see Chapter 11) is a revolutionary system that lets anybody with a Web site advertise for a reasonable cost on the Google search results page. This exposure, on one of the Internet's most highly trafficked domains, was unthinkably expensive and inaccessible in the past.

AdWords is stunningly innovative but also complicated. Here's the gist: You hook a small ad to certain keywords and assign a price you're willing to pay. That price is based on *clickthroughs*, which occur when a Googler conducts a search with one of your keywords, sees your ad on the results page, and clicks the ad to visit your Web site. Other site owners might have hooked their ads to the same keyword(s); if they offered a higher price per clickthrough, their ads are listed above yours. No matter how much you pay, your final bill is determined by actual visits to your site, and you can set a limit to the total amount you pay.

All this is handled automatically, making AdWords a surprisingly sophisticated system. The complexities are all explained in Chapter 11. AdWords isn't a search service, but the program is definitely part of the Google lifestyle for entrepreneurial types with Web sites ready for increased traffic.

*Note:* You might be wondering whether the AdWords system destroys the famous integrity of a Google search. Have hordes of Internet advertisers purchased placement in the search results pages, warping the accuracy of Google's engine? It's a good question because other search engines have been in public-relations trouble over this issue. The answer, emphatically, is no — Google AdWords don't pollute the purity of search results. The ads are placed over to the side, easily visible but not mingled with search results. Higher-priced sponsorships are placed above the search listing, in a manner that clearly differentiates them from the objective results.

# *The Open Index*

All search engines operate by building an index of both Web pages and the content of those pages. This index is constructed with the help of *bots* (software robots), sometimes called spiders or crawlers. The index is every search engine's prime asset, the ever-shifting body of information that the engine matches against your keywords to deliver results. The formula that each search site uses to compile and search the index is a closely guarded secret.

Although Google doesn't breathe a word about its indexing formulas, it does do something else that's unprecedented and exciting. Google has released its application programming interface (API) to the public. APIs enable software programmers to incorporate one program or body of data into another program. For example, Microsoft releases its Windows APIs to authorized developers who write stand-alone Windows software. Google's API lets software geniuses write programs that can access Google's index directly, bypassing the familiar interface at Google's site.

The public API is more important than it might seem at first. In the short time that the API has been available, many alternatives to Google have sprung up, each a legitimate and authorized new method of Googling. A few people have created instant-message conduits to Google, so you can launch a search while chatting in certain IM programs. Some graphic presentations of Google search results are being developed that are, frankly, mind-blowing. These and many other Google stunts are explored in Chapters 14 and 15.

Google's expansion through third-party development lends variety to the search experience that is basically a rather drab chore — no matter how skillfully accomplished. And, like other Google innovations, the public API will probably serve to drive Google even deeper into the mass consciousness of the Internet community. Google will take over your soul. This, too, is a good thing.

# The Greatness of Google

In this chapter, I serve a sample platter of Google's buffet of services. But one central question remains: What makes Google so great in the first place? How did it become so rampantly popular that it nearly eradicated other general search engines? Those, of course, are two questions, not one, and my inability to count is one reason Stephen Hawking doesn't return my phone calls. (In typing that little quip, I wasn't sure how to spell Hawking's first name. Naturally, I Googled it.)

Google's success depends to some extent on the size of its index, which has long passed the billion-page mark — Google claims to have the largest Web search index in the world.

But the big index is hardly the entire story. More important is a certain intelligence with which the index interprets keywords. Google's groundbreaking innovation in this department is its capability to not only find pages but also rank them based on their popularity. The legendary Google PageRank is determined largely by measuring how many links to that page exist on other sites all over the Web. The logic here is simple and hard to refute: Page A links to page B for one reason only, and that is because page B contains something worthwhile. If pages C, D, E, F, and G also link to page B, odds increase that page B has something important going for it. If 500,000 pages link to page B, it is without question truly important in some way.

This explanation is grossly simplified, and Google isn't divulging details. But the back links feature is the advantage that makes Google search results so fantastic. It's nearly miraculous for people who have been searching the Web for years. To a large extent, the days of laborious, frustrating searching are gone. Google can still dish up a clunker from time to time, frequently because of poor keywords. And dead pages haven't been eliminated. But when it comes to finding basic information or Web destinations, Google delivers stunning results with incredible speed and accuracy.

And Google is busy! Every day Google answers more than 200 million search queries. Google calmly digests keywords in almost 90 languages. At this writing, only a third of Google's search requests come from the United States. Googling is the one activity that unites the entire Internet citizenry, and Google has forever altered the Internet landscape and the ease with which we move through it.

# Chapter 2

# Better Googling: Finding the Right Stuff

## In This Chapter

▶ Setting your Google preferences

▶ Choosing keywords and searching the Web

▶ Interpreting and using the search results page

▶ Understanding advanced searching

▶ Discovering the convenience and power of search operators

▶ Searching for images

*T*his is where we get down to business. Searching for sites, finding files, wrangling with results, and generally raiding Google for all it's worth. You might be thinking, "I know how to search Google. You type a few words, press Enter, blink rapidly, and view the results." I won't comment on disturbing facial tics, but that process is essentially correct. And if you're impatient to explore more esoteric stuff, feel free to skip this chapter. I won't be hurt, bitter, or resentful. (And if I *am* hurt, bitter, or resentful, you'll never know it, so don't trouble yourself over my misery.)

Now. For those of you remaining, I'm going to send you each a million dollars. Which pales beside the wealth of useful information that follows in these pages. I get the basics out of the way quickly, leading straight to the finer points of the search results page, advanced searching, narrowing your search results in various ways, and other life-altering techniques.

So read on. Your check is in the mail.

## Setting Preferences

Many people breeze through Google umpteen times a day without bothering to set their preferences — or even being aware that there are preferences to

set. A recent Internet study asked users whether they would rather set
Google preferences or get bathed in chocolate syrup. Sentiment was over-
whelmingly against setting Google preferences. But I'm here to tell you that
the five settings on the Preferences page (see Figure 2-1) enhance the Google
experience far more than the effort required to adjust them.

To adjust Google preferences, click the <u>Preferences</u> link on the Google home
page or go here:

```
www.google.com/preferences
```

If you set your preferences and later return to the Preferences page by
manually entering the preceding URL, your browser displays an unadjusted
Preferences page (without your settings). That's because *your* Preferences
page has a distinct URL with your preferences built into it. For example, after
selecting English as Google's default language for your visits, the URL
appears like this:

```
www.google.com/preferences?hl=en
```

Your best bet for reaching the Preferences page after first setting your
preferences (when you want to readjust them, for example) is to use the
<u>Preferences</u> link on the home page.

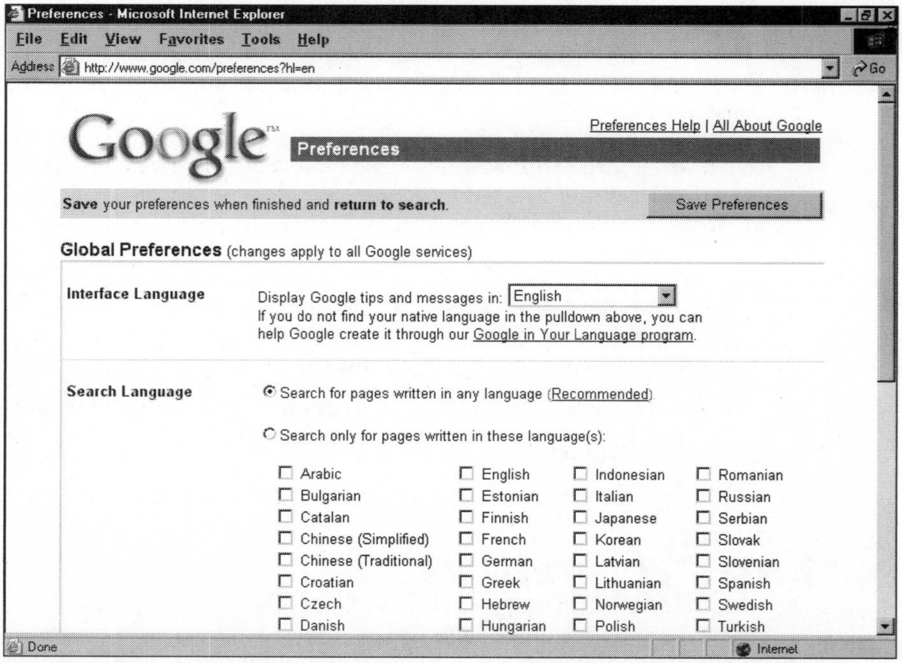

**Figure 2-1:**
Part of the
Google
Preferences
page. Its
settings
enhance
the Google
experience.

Preferences - Microsoft Internet Explorer

File  Edit  View  Favorites  Tools  Help

Address  http://www.google.com/preferences?hl=en

**Google**™  Preferences
Preferences Help | All About Google

**Save** your preferences when finished and **return to search**.
Save Preferences

**Global Preferences** (changes apply to all Google services)

**Interface Language**   Display Google tips and messages in: English
If you do not find your native language in the pulldown above, you can
help Google create it through our <u>Google in Your Language program</u>.

**Search Language**   ⦿ Search for pages written in any language (<u>Recommended</u>)

○ Search only for pages written in these language(s):

| | | | |
|---|---|---|---|
| ☐ Arabic | ☐ English | ☐ Indonesian | ☐ Romanian |
| ☐ Bulgarian | ☐ Estonian | ☐ Italian | ☐ Russian |
| ☐ Catalan | ☐ Finnish | ☐ Japanese | ☐ Serbian |
| ☐ Chinese (Simplified) | ☐ French | ☐ Korean | ☐ Slovak |
| ☐ Chinese (Traditional) | ☐ German | ☐ Latvian | ☐ Slovenian |
| ☐ Croatian | ☐ Greek | ☐ Lithuanian | ☐ Spanish |
| ☐ Czech | ☐ Hebrew | ☐ Norwegian | ☐ Swedish |
| ☐ Danish | ☐ Hungarian | ☐ Polish | ☐ Turkish |

Done   Internet

## How Google remembers your preferences

When you set preferences in Google, the site is customized for you every time you visit it, as long as you're using the same computer through which you set the preferences. To provide this convenience, Google must place a *cookie* (a small information file) in your computer. The site and the cookie high-five each other whenever you visit Google, and the site appears according to your settings. For this system to work, cookies must be turned on in your browser.

Some people are militantly anti-cookie, claiming that the data files represent an invasion of computer privacy. Indeed, some sites plant cookies that track your Internet movements and identify you to advertisers.

The truth is, Google's cookie is fairly aggressive. It gets planted when you first visit the site, whether or not you visit the Preferences page. Once planted, the Google cookie records your clicks in Google and builds a database of visitor behavior in its search results pages. For example, Google knows how often users click the

first search result and to what extent they explore results lower on the page. Google uses this information to evaluate the effectiveness of its service and to improve it.

As to privacy, Google does indeed share aggregate information with advertisers and various third parties and even publicizes knowledge about how the service is used by its millions of visitors. The key word is *aggregate*. Google's privacy policy states that individual information is never divulged except by proper legal procedure, such as a warrant or a subpoena, or by individual consent. The privacy policy is published on this page:

```
www.google.com/privacy.html
```

I have no problem with the Google cookie or with cookies in general. The convenience is helpful, and I don't mind adding to the aggregate information. It's rather comforting being a data droplet in Google's information tsunami.

A single basic process changes one or several preferences. Just follow these steps:

1. **Go to the Preferences page.**

2. **Use the pull-down menus, check boxes, and radio buttons to make your adjustments.**

3. **Click the Save Preferences button.**

4. **In the confirmation window (which merely says "Your preferences have been saved" and is unnecessary), click the OK button.**

The next sections describe what you can accomplish on the Preferences page.

## *The international Google*

If you're reading the English-language edition of this book, you probably enjoy Google in its default English interface. If you're reading the Icelandic edition of this book, please send me a copy — I want to see whether my jokes are any funnier in a chilly language. Whatever your native language, you should know that you can get Google to appear in one of dozens of languages unpronounceable by George W. Bush (besides English, I mean).

Interface Language is the first Google preference, and it adjusts the appearance of certain pages — specifically, the home page, Preferences page, Advanced Search page, and many Help pages and intrasite directories.

Changing the interface language does not alter the language on the search results page or the search results themselves. (To change the language on those pages, you use the Search Language preference, up next.)

Interface Language changes the Interface Language list in the pull-down menu. If you choose an obscure language that uses an unfamiliar alphabet while playing around (it's irresistible), you might have trouble finding your way back to the mother tongue. (English is the only language identified in its native tongue no matter which language is selected.)

Google is nothing if not occasionally silly, and Interface Language offers a few must-try languages:

- **Elmer Fudd:** First on the list, Elmer Fudd (or should I say Ewmew Fudd) capriciously changes all Rs and Ls to Ws. On the home page, Groups is now Gwoups, and Directory has been cartoonized to Diwectowy. Most hilariously of all, the I'm Feeling Lucky button is denatured to I'm Feewing Wucky. Before changing the language menu back to its original state, be sure to ponder the difference between Twaditional and Simpwified Chinese.

- **Pig Latin:** You nowkay owhay histay orksway.

- **Hacker:** Changes alphabet letters to numerals and symbols wherever possible (pretty much everywhere), rendering a semicoherent page best comprehended after several bags of potato chips and a six-pack of soda. (See Figure 2-2.)

- **Interlingua:** A vaguely Euro blend of tourism-speak roughly understandable by nearly everyone.

- **Klingon:** If I have to explain it, you don't watch enough *Star Trek*. In fact, the folks at Google should bone up on their reruns, too, because the term is Klingonese, not Klingon. (Have they no honor?)

All right, stop playing around with the languages. Let's move on.

**Figure 2-2:**
Google in
the mythical
Hacker
language.

## Searching for non-English pages

After you have the Google interface speaking your language, you can turn
your attention to searching for Web pages written in certain languages.

The language you search _for_ doesn't need to match the language you search
_in_. In other words, the first two preferences can be set to different languages.
Furthermore, you can select more than one language in the Search Language
setting, whereas the Interface Language preference, naturally, can be only one
language at a time.

Use Search Language to narrow your search results by language. Choosing
French, for example, returns Web pages written only in French. Use the check
boxes to select as many languages as you want.

If you don't select any languages, leaving the Search Language preference in
its default setting, your search results do not discriminate based on language.
You're likely to see an international array of pages if you rummage through
enough results.

## G-rated searching

Google uses a filter called SafeSearch to screen out pornography from Web-page and image searches. In its default setting (moderate), SafeSearch applies fairly strict filtering to image searches and leaves Web search results unedited. Change the setting to strict for harsher filtering of images and clean Web-page searches. You can turn off the filter entirely for an unbiased search session. You select the filtering strength on the Preferences page, as shown in Figure 2-3.

SafeSearch operates automatically but can be modified manually by the Google staff. They accept suggestions of sites and images that should be subject to the adult-content filter. If you come across any objectionable material through a Google search (with SafeSearch set to moderate or strict), feel free to send a link to the offending page or image to the following e-mail address:

`Safesearch@google.com`

## Opening the floodgates

You can increase the number of search results that appear on the page, raising it from the default 10 results. It's a good idea, I think; I keep my preference set at the maximum — 100 results per page.

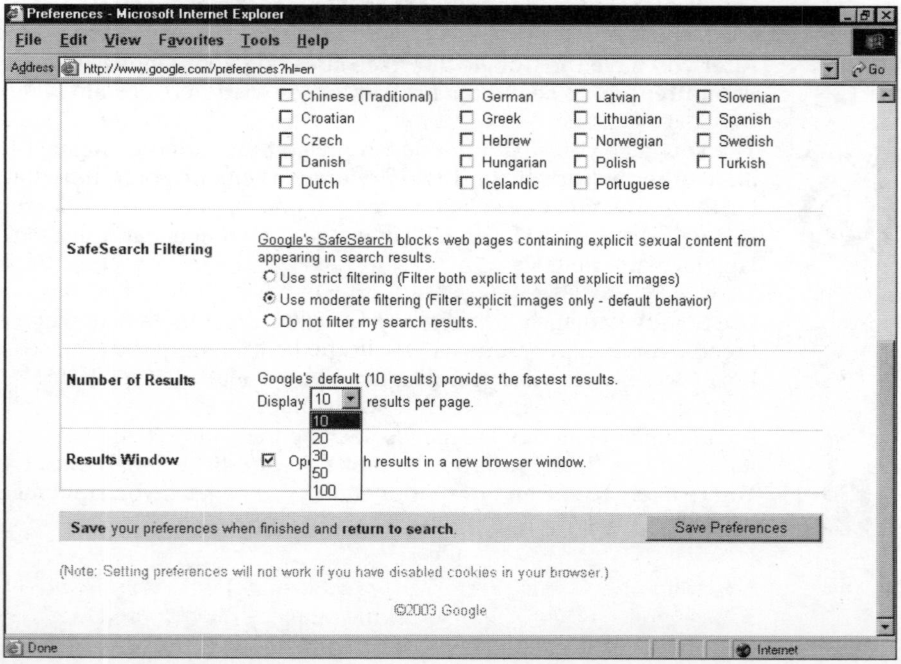

**Figure 2-3:**
The bottom portion of Google's Preferences page.

---

Preferences - Microsoft Internet Explorer

File    Edit    View    Favorites    Tools    Help

Address | http://www.google.com/preferences?hl=en

| ☐ Chinese (Traditional) | ☐ German | ☐ Latvian | ☐ Slovenian |
| ☐ Croatian | ☐ Greek | ☐ Lithuanian | ☐ Spanish |
| ☐ Czech | ☐ Hebrew | ☐ Norwegian | ☐ Swedish |
| ☐ Danish | ☐ Hungarian | ☐ Polish | ☐ Turkish |
| ☐ Dutch | ☐ Icelandic | ☐ Portuguese | |

**SafeSearch Filtering**    Google's SafeSearch blocks web pages containing explicit sexual content from appearing in search results.
○ Use strict filtering (Filter both explicit text and explicit images)
⊙ Use moderate filtering (Filter explicit images only - default behavior)
○ Do not filter my search results.

**Number of Results**    Google's default (10 results) provides the fastest results.
Display [10 ▾] results per page.
10
20
30
50
100

**Results Window**    ☑ Op[  ]h results in a new browser window.

**Save** your preferences when finished and **return to search**.    [ Save Preferences ]

(Note: Setting preferences will not work if you have disabled cookies in your browser.)

©2003 Google

Google reminds you that shorter pages are displayed more quickly, which is a good point for people who hit the site for lightning-quick searches many times a day. Google's results are so uncannily accurate that you might not often need more than 10 results. Still, I like the higher number because the long page of search results arrives more rapidly than shorter pages at competing search engines. Furthermore, I have the impatient attitude of a demanding Web surfer, and I never like calling up a second page of search results. If the content I want isn't on the first page of results, I usually try new keywords, so stocking the results page with 100 hits gives me a better chance of quick success.

You might not agree with my reasoning, in which case you should leave the number or results set to the default or choose a medium number of results from the drop-down menu.

Google is fast no matter how many results per page you request. The only thing that might hold you back is your modem speed. If you access the Internet using a high-speed connection (cable modem, DSL, corporate, or university connection), you might as well set the results number to 100 and be done with it.

## New windows

The Results Window setting is an important preference setting in my life. It consists of a single check box which, when checked, opens Web pages in new windows when you click a search result. This is a useful way of staying anchored in the search results page, from which you might want to sample several Web pages that match your keywords. Without this preference, your browser opens the Web pages in the same window that Google is in, forcing you to Back-button your way back to Google if you want to see the search results again. And if you drill deeply into a site, it becomes even more difficult to get back to Google.

If you dislike multiple browser windows cluttering your desktop, leave the Results Window box unchecked. If you prefer a hybrid experience in which you sometimes want to anchor at Google while exploring several search hits, leave the box unchecked and get in the habit of right-clicking search result links when you want a new window. Choose Open in New Window from the right-click menu that your browser displays.

## Basic Web Searches

Searching the Web is when you draw close to the life-form called Google. Entering a keyword is like venturing near the multilimbed Goddess of Knowledge and basking in the blazing glory of her wisdom. Or something. It's just a Web search, but with results so astute that you can't help wondering whether a person — a person who knows you very, very well — is lurking inside the machine.

The Google home page is a reactionary expression against the 1990s trend that turned search engines into busy, all-purpose information portals. (See Figures 2-4 and 2-5.) Yahoo!, Lycos, Excite, and others engaged in portal wars in which victory seemed to depend on which site could clutter the page with the most horoscopes, weather forecasts, news headlines, and stock market bulletins. This loud and lavish competition resulted from the failure of plain search engines to earn the traffic and money necessary to keep their businesses afloat. They piled more features into their pages and, in some cases, ruined their integrity by selling preferred placement in search results. During this mad gold rush, some specialty engines retained their primary focus on Web searching, and a few, such as HotBot, to this day keep their home pages clean of any distractions.

Google has embraced the purity of searching with an ad-free, horoscope-absent home page that leaves no doubt that searching is the task at hand. And its search results are so good that it has singly reshaped the search industry. Lycos, Excite, Netscape, and others barely register on anybody's radar as search engines, attractive though they might be as broad Internet portals. Some (Yahoo! and Netscape, for example) use the Google engine to deliver Web-search results. These days, for most people, to search is to use Google.

**Figure 2-4:** Yikes! The 1990s-style search portal is like an urban jungle. And you're not seeing the pop-up ads.

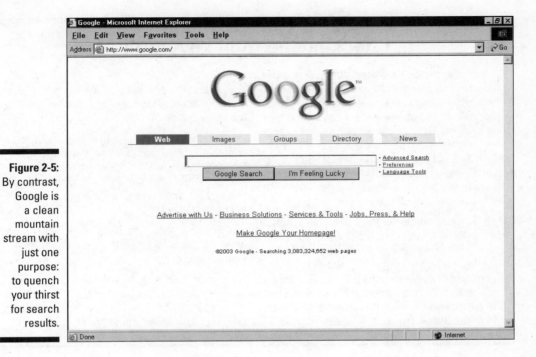

**Figure 2-5:**
By contrast, Google is a clean mountain stream with just one purpose: to quench your thirst for search results.

So let's get to it. A six-year-old would find the Google home page easy to use. When you log onto Google's home page, the mouse cursor is already waiting for you in the keyword search box. Type a word — any word. Or more than one. Or type a sentence in plain English. Press Enter or click the Google Search button. The results are on your screen within seconds.

Note the I'm Feeling Lucky button next to the Google Search button. Clicking it instead of the Google Search button takes you directly to the top search result's Web page instead of to the search results page. Only Google could dare to invite its users to skip the search results page and make it work out so well, so often. Try it. Remember: It's not a random-search button, and it works only when you've typed a keyword.

## How insensitive!

Rules dictating when to use uppercase or lowercase letters have taken a beating in the Internet's linguistic culture. The prevailing dialect of chat rooms, message boards, and e-mail discards the uppercase start to sentences as if it were an outgrown fad. Fortunately, nobody has to spruce up their typing habits for Google's sake because the search engine is oblivious to case issues — the technical term is case-insensitive.

## Choosing the right keywords

Google is possibly the most forgiving search engine ever created. You can type just about any darn thing into it and get good results. Sometimes you can even get away with sloppy spelling — Google often catches it and suggests the correct spelling. Much of the crafty keywording I wrote about in *Internet Searching for Dummies* goes out the window in Google, which turns vague hints and plain-English queries into gold. Still, some tips apply.

The golden rule in Internet searching is that more keywords deliver fewer results. So pile them on to narrow your search. With that technique, however, you run the risk of having conflicting or obfuscating keywords, creating a mixed bag of search results. Ideally, you want to concisely convey to Google what you need. I've found that two is the golden number of keywords to use in Google searches. At my Web sites, the tracking software tells me which search queries get to my pages, and invariably the two-word strings reach my best stuff.

On the other end of the pith spectrum, many people get good results by typing entire sentences in the keyword box. Google always eliminates certain little words such as *what* and *why,* which might seem to devalue questions but doesn't in practice.

Beware of words that have more than one meaning, especially if you search for one keyword at a time.

For power searching, in which the goal is not more results but fewer, better results, use the Advanced Search pages or the search operators, both described later in this chapter.

---

The tabs atop the keyword box — Web, Images, Groups, Directory, News — take you to the home pages of those sections when clicked. If you're on a search results page and click a tab, however, you get results for that tab (Web, Images, Groups, Directory, or News) instantly. So, the tabs shuttle between home pages when you don't have search results yet. The tabs shuttle between search results pages when you have one set of results in any area.

On to the search results page. That's where the action is.

# Understanding the Google Results Page

Every Google search results page for a Web search includes at least three basic types of information:

- A summary of the search results
- The search results themselves
- A few things you can do with the results

As you can see in Figure 2-6, the results summary is located in the shaded bar, above and to the right of the results list. The summary tells you how many total results for your keywords exist in the Google index and how long the search took. (Rarely does a Google search require more than two seconds.)

On the left side of the summary bar, your keywords are displayed as links. When you click one of those links, you go to Dictionary.com for a definition of the word. This seems a bit gratuitous — if you didn't know what a word means, why would you use it as a keyword? But don't underestimate the variety of ways that people use Google, including as a dictionary. Dictionary. com also functions as a thesaurus, so if a certain keyword isn't delivering good results, perhaps a synonym (derived from Dictionary.com) would. Note that the links to Dictionary.com appear only when Google's language is set to English — naturally enough, because Dictionary.com is an English dictionary.

The search results consist of the page name, which is hyperlinked to the page itself. Below that is a short bit of relevant text from the page. Below the text you can see the page's URL, which is there for information value and is not a link. Next to the URL is a number indicating the size of the page. Glancing at the page size helps you decide whether or not to visit it; pages more than 50K (that's 50 kilobytes) are too large for a quick visit if you don't have high-speed Internet access.

**Figure 2-6:**
A Google
Web search
results
page.
Notice the
suggested
spelling
correction.

The Google staff doesn't compose the page title nor the accompanying text, which explains why they're a little goofy sometimes and incoherent other times. The page title is created by the page developer as part of the HTML code underlying all Web pages. Some page designers forget how important the page title is, or they pack in lots of words to try and get the page higher on the search results pages of search engines such as Google. (The tactic generally doesn't work in Google, as I explain in Chapter 12.)

The text is not necessarily descriptive of the target page or even cogent. Google clips sentences and fragments that contain your keywords and presents them as evidence that you have a good hit. This is more useful than you might think. In fact, it's absolutely amazing how often a glance at the first few results and their accompanying text answers a search query without even visiting an outside page.

*Note:* The result link does not identify where on the target page your keywords are located. Not uncommonly, you link to a page and must then search in that page for relevant information — a headache when the page is long. Of course, you can always use your browser's Find feature to locate specific words on any Web page. The problem is solved more elegantly by the Google Toolbar, as described in Chapter 9.

# Breaking Down Web Search Results

Other elements on the search results page enable you to understand the result, continue the search, narrow the search, or avoid Internet traffic jams when seeing the target page. Some of these features are present on every search result, and some exist occasionally. Here they are.

## Page description

Remember when I said that the search result text wasn't composed by the Google staff? Well, sometimes part of the accompanying text *is* so composed. If the search result appears in Google Directory (which is built by humans), the brief description that appears in the directory is imported to the search result. It is set apart from the snippets of page text by the Description header.

## Directory category

Again, when the target page appears in Google Directory, its directory category is presented. The category is a link, and you can proceed directly to that page of Google Directory by clicking the link. Figure 2-7 shows a search whose first result is a directory listing.

**Figure 2-7:**
When a Web search result features a Google Directory listing, click the Category link to see that listing.

There's little difference between this method and starting your search in Google Directory. But the <u>Category</u> link on the Web search results page is helpful in a surprising way: When you want to see pages similar to the target page, Google Directory is better than the Similar Pages feature (described shortly). If your experience mirrors mine, the more you try the <u>Category</u> link, the more you'll come to rely on it for high-quality, related results. The hand-picked Google Directory houses more stable sites than an index search is likely to house.

## *The Google cache*

A *cache* (pronounced "cash") is a storage area for computer files. Google maintains an enormous cache of Web pages. Don't confuse the cache with the index. Actually, for practical purposes, it doesn't matter whether you confuse them or not, but they are different. The index is a database of Web-page content, stripped of its formatting. The cache contains the pages themselves. By and large, clicking the <u>Cached</u> link provides a quicker display of the target page because you're getting it from Google's computer instead of from the Internet at large.

So why would you ever *not* use the <u>Cached</u> link instead of the main page title link? Mainly because the cached page is not necessarily up to the minute, especially with pages that change frequently (such as Weblogs). If you view the cached version of a page that you know is changed frequently and dated, such as the front page of a newspaper site, you can see that Google's cache is about three days behind. For users without high-speed Internet access, it's more convenient to pull from the cache when looking for a big page (about 50K or so) that doesn't change much. Also, use the <u>Cached</u> link if the page title link refuses to display the page for some reason.

One disadvantage to pulling up a cached search result is the Google notice that appears atop all cached pages (see Figure 2-8). That is one bulky notice, taking up about two vertical inches of screen space on a screen resolution of 800 x 600. Besides being an eyesore, the notice sometimes makes additional scrolling necessary if you want to see the entire page. If you get tired of the notice, click its link to the uncached page.

## Similar pages

The <u>Similar Pages</u> link is interesting although not always tremendously useful. Clicking this link starts a new search for pages that somehow resemble the original search result. Sorry to be vague, but Google isn't very talkative about its Similar Pages formula.

The results are interesting and more diverse than you might expect. You'd think the search would yield a narrowed set of results, but my experience is to the contrary. Search for Kelly Clarkson, for example, and you get a solid set of results including fan sites and official *American Idol* destinations. Click the <u>Similar Pages</u> link under kellyclarkson.com and you get a far-ranging assortment of pages including sites dedicated to other singers and bands.

Searching with Similar Pages is a bit of a crapshoot — or perhaps I should say it's an adventure. Sometimes a pointless one. Let's get back to the Kelly Clarkson search results page. If you click Similar Pages for a fan site hosted by the Angelfire service, the ensuing results page contains nothing but links to the home pages of other hosting services similar to Angelfire. At this point, Google has taken you far away from Kelly Clarkson, *American Idol*, and the crass personality-manufacturing machine that propels reality TV to its unseemly impact on our cultural sensibilities. (That uncalled-for editorial rant was brought to you free of charge. And I'm a helpless *American Idol* addict.)

So when should you use Similar Pages? It's useful to get a sense of the network lurking around a Web page. Part of what the engine does with Similar Pages is explore outgoing links from the target page. On my site, for example, if I have a link going to an article I wrote on another site, <u>Similar Pages for</u>

bradhill.com will list that other site. Last time I checked, though, Similar Pages to my site also listed a Web page titled Amish Tech Support. There's no connection that I can see, though I respect the Amish and some day would like to try plowing a field. So, whenever you use Similar Pages, do so with a sense of adventure.

## Indented results

Some search results are offset from the main body of results with an indentation (look back to Figure 2-6). These indented sites are located in the same domain (such as bradhill.com or kellyclarkson.com) as the target page above them. They are indented to remind you that it might be redundant to click both.

Google refrains from listing all the pages in a single domain that match your keywords. But you can see more results from that domain by clicking the More results from www.*domain*.com link in any indented search result. Doing so is a great way to perform a minisearch within any domain that has already proved useful to you.

**Figure 2-8:**
Viewing a Google-cached page. Google's cache notice takes up a lot of screen space.

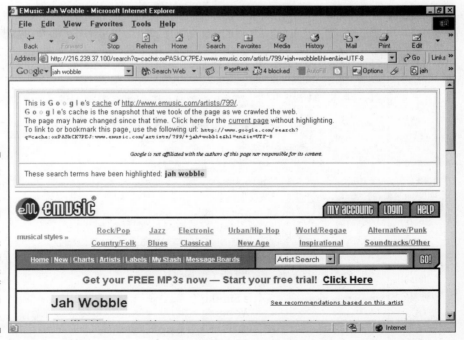

Searching in a large Web site (also called a domain) can be accomplished another way: by using a special search operator called the *site* operator. This operator tells Google to apply your keywords to a specified domain. You type the *site* operator, the domain, and the keywords in a single glop of instructions. For example, if you want to search my site for the *dummies* keyword, you could do so with a single entry:

```
site:www.bradhill.com dummies
```

You can reverse the order of the syntax by placing the keyword(s) before the *site* operator and domain, without affecting the search results.

# Using Advanced Search

Later in this chapter, I cover the use of special query terms (similar to the *site* operator just described), general search operators that can be used with keywords, and searching for specified types of documents. All these tricks and more are consolidated on the Advanced Search page, which is shown in Figure 2-9. To get to this page, you click the <u>Advanced Search</u> link on the Google home page.

**Figure 2-9:**
Google's
Advanced
Search
page
for Web
searches.
Image
search
has its
own advan-
ced page.

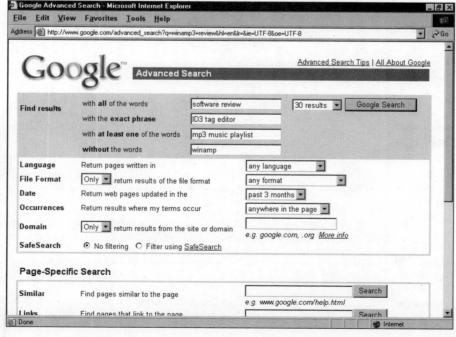

Use Advanced Search for any one of three reasons:

- ✔ You want to focus a search more narrowly than a general keyword search
- ✔ You don't want to bother with the complexity and thorny syntax of search operators
- ✔ You want to combine more than one search operation

As you see in Figure 2-9, the Advanced Search page bundles many keyword boxes and drop-down menus to launch a finely targeted search. You don't have to use everything this page has to offer. In fact, you may conduct a simple, one-keyword search from here, although that would be like using a race car to buy groceries.

Following is a review of the Advanced Search features. After setting any combination of these features, click the Google Search button to get your results.

## Using multiple keywords

At the top of the Advanced Search page are a series of keyword boxes grouped in a shaded area called Find results. (See Figure 2-9.) You use the four keyword boxes in this area to tell Google how to manage multiple keywords. If you have just one keyword, type it in the top box. The instructions next to each keyword box correspond to *Boolean operators*, which are typed shorthand instructions covered later in this chapter. The Advanced Search page gives you the laser exactness of Boolean searching without all the typing.

Use these keyword boxes in the following ways:

- ✔ **With *all* of the words:** Putting keywords here forces Google to scour for pages that contain every word, with no exceptions. It has the effect of narrowing search results. For example, if you type *alan greenspan federal reserve*, you won't see irrelevant pages that contain only *alan* or only *federal*.

- ✔ **With the *exact phrase*:** This is like using quotation marks in most search engines and delivers pages that contain your keywords in the exact order, and with the exact spelling, that you type. You might use this option for people's names (*david hyde pierce*), sport teams with their cities (*los angeles dodgers*), and colloquial phrases (*jump the shark*).

- ✔ **With *at least one* of the words:** This option is useful when you're less picky about matching your words. It has the effect of widening search results. For example, if you're conducting broad research about building string instruments, you might type *violin cello viola* in this box, with *instrument building* in the top box.

✔ *Without* **the words:** Much confusion can be avoided with this keyword box, which instructs Google to eliminate matches that contain certain words. This command is useful when one of your keywords is often (undesirably) associated with other words. It has the effect of narrowing search results and making them more accurate. For example, if you're looking for pages about giants in fairy tales, you can stack words into this box that would match with pages about certain sports teams, such as *new york san francisco baseball football*. At the same time, you'd need to place the *giants* keyword in the top box and *fairy tale* in the exact phrase box.

Here's an unprecedented truth to keep in mind: Google's general search results are so accurate that Boolean commands are usually unnecessary. It all depends on your level of searching. If, during a general search, you find yourself looking beyond the first page of results (given 30 or fewer results per page), the Advanced Search keyword boxes might speed your searches along. Using the Advanced page is also simply fun and helps focus the search goal in your mind.

You can see how your Find results entries translate into Boolean operators by looking in the keyword box atop the search results page (and also in the blue summary bar). In the preceding example about instrument building, the Boolean search string comes out as

```
Instrument building violin OR cello OR viola
```

Examining the search string on the results page is one way to get the hang of Boolean language on the fly. The appearance of the string also gives you a chance to adjust it for a new search without returning to the Advanced Search page.

## Other Advanced Search features

The central portion of the Advanced Search page contains six settings designed to narrow your results. They are

✔ **Language:** Similar to the Search Language setting on the Preferences page (see the "Setting Preferences" section earlier in this chapter), this pull-down menu instructs Google to return search results only in the specified language. The default setting is any language. Whereas the Preferences page has check boxes, allowing you to select multiple target languages, this menu limits your choice to a single language (or all languages). And whereas your Preferences setting affects all your Googling until you change it, the Advanced Search setting affects just one search at a time.

✔ **File Format:** Google recognizes certain distinct file formats, such as Microsoft Word documents (which end in the .doc extension) and Adobe Acrobat (.pdf) files. You can use the File Format setting to include or exclude selected file formats. Use the drop-down menu to select Only (to include your selected format) or Don't (to exclude your selected format). Then use the second pull-down menu to select the format. Feel free to ignore this setting if you're conducting a general Web search. When Any Format is selected in the second drop-down menu, your search results include all file types recognized by Google and will mostly consist of Web pages. When you get a search result in non-Web format, you can read it in its original form if you have the program associated with the file type. Or, conveniently, you can view Google's translation to Web-page format (HTML).

✔ **Date:** Google's index crawler can determine when a page was last changed. A page update might be as trivial as changing one word, or it might involve a massive content revision. The drop-down menu for this feature doesn't give you fine control over the update time — you may select pages updated in the past 3 months, past 6 months, and past year. That might seem useless, but one purpose of choosing the 3-month setting over the default (anytime) is to reduce the occurrence of dead links (pages that no longer exist) in your search results.

✔ **Occurrences:** This powerful and useful setting whisks away questionable search results and gives you control of how important your keywords are to the matched page. The purpose is not to determine where your keywords exist in the page's text (that is, how near to the top of the page they occur), nor is it to help you avoid scrolling the page. This feature culls pages in which your keywords appear in the page title, in the page URL, or — amazingly — in the page's incoming links. (Again, Google's capability to sense the network surrounding each page is astounding and helpful.) Using the title or URL choice powerfully narrows the search results, returning high-probability matches.

✔ **Domain:** Like the Occurrences setting, you can use this feature to include or exclude matches with certain properties. In this case, you're allowing or eliminating a certain domain, which is the portion of a site's URL after *www.* When typing the domain, you may type the *www* or leave it out. So, for the New York Times domain, you could type *www.nytimes.com* or *nytimes.com.* Use the first drop-down menu to choose Only (includes the selected domain and no others) or Don't (excludes the selected domain and admits all others).

✔ **SafeSearch:** The default position of this setting turns off SafeSearch if you have it turned on in your Preferences. You can activate SafeSearch on a per-search basis by using this feature of the Advanced Search page. No matter what you do here, it doesn't affect your Preferences setting for Google searches launched from the home page.

Following are the two page-specific Advanced Search features:

- **Similar:** Identical to the <u>Similar Pages</u> link on the search results page, this feature finds pages related to the URL you type in the keyword box.

- **Links:** This one is addictive and shows off Google's extreme network awareness. The *link* operator tells Google to find Web pages that contain links to a page that you specify. The URL of your specified page is the keyword you type in the box. Because most large sites link to their own home pages from every other page, these searches yield a lot of tedious results from within the domain. However, it's fun to try with an inner page from a site.

Google provides the Advanced Image Search page for fancy picture searching. I describe it later in this chapter, in the "A Picture Is Worth a Thousand Keywords" section. The Advanced Search page just described relates to Web searches, not image searches.

# Searching Shorthand: Using Operators

There's no need to detour to the Advanced Search page if you know about keyword modifiers called *search operators*. Standard search operators are not unique to Google; most search engines understand them and require the same symbols and syntax when typing them. Search operators are typed with the keywords right in the keyword box. You do have to type neatly and make sure you don't add spaces in the wrong places or use the wrong case (small letters instead of capital letters in some instances).

Standard search operators fulfill the same functions as the Find results portion of the Advanced Search page. (They are known as Boolean operators, or Boolean commands. Dr. Mellifluous Boolean was a 17th-century explorer who discovered the island of Quiqui, brought lemons back to the Old World, and prophesied the Internet. None of the preceding sentence is true.) You don't need to learn them to get advanced results. But they're not hard to master, and doing so saves you the trip to Advanced Search and the bother of finagling with all those keyword boxes. Using operators, you can quickly type an advanced search query in the simple keyword box on Google's home page (or in the keyword box in the Google Toolbar, as described in Chapter 9).

Google understands standard search operators that have been in common use for years, but it also provides special operators for Google only. These unique keyword modifiers take advantage of Google's extraordinary index and bring to life Google's under-the-hood power. The next section covers standard Boolean commands; the section after that details the unique Google operators.

# Typing standard search operators

If you're familiar with search operators and use them in Google or other search engines, feel free to skip this section. (Like you need my permission. By the way, be home by 11:30 tonight.) The four major Boolean operators work in Google's keyword boxes as follows:

- **AND:** The *AND* operator forces Google to match the search results against *all* your keywords. The operator is signified by a plus sign (+). The effect is to narrow search results, giving you fewer and more accurate hits. Place the plus sign immediately *before* any word(s) you want to force into the match, without a space between the symbol and the word, for example: *dog +chew +toy +slobber*. Keep in mind that Google naturally attempts to match all keywords without being commanded to. It always lists complete matches first, followed by Web pages that match fewer keywords. So the *AND* operator is best used in combination with other operators or in combination with words that are not preceded by an operator. An example of the latter is *recipe cookbook ingredients + vegetarian*. In this example, vegetarianism is the main focus, and every matched page must contain that word. Whether it's a page about recipes or cookbooks or ingredients is less important.

- **NOT:** The *NOT* operator excludes words that might otherwise bring up many undesirable page matches. The effect is to narrow search results. The symbol is a minus sign (-). Like the *AND* operator, place the symbol immediately before a word. In using it, you should think of anti-keywords that would thwart the mission of your pro-keywords. For example, you might type *kayak lake -canoe -whitewater*. (Nothing against canoes. But if you haven't tried kayaking, what on earth are you waiting for?)

- **OR:** Not as wishy-washy as you might think, the *OR* operator is helpful when using obscure keywords that might not return much of value if used singly. It also neatly divides a search along two concurrent avenues of exploration. There is no symbol for this one; simply type *OR* (use capital letters) before a keyword and leave a space between the operator and the following keyword. Google then accepts matches to the keyword preceding the operator or following the operator, such as *wintry climate maine OR antarctica*.

- **Quotes:** Identical to the Exact phrase feature of the Advanced Search page, the quote operator tells Google which keyword sequence or keyword phrase to leave untouched. Google can't assume you have misspelled something, and it can't change the word order to create a match. Whatever you type within the quotes is interpreted and matched literally by Google. It is best used with keyword groups in which each word could return its own set of irrelevant results, for example: *"old town" canoes prices*.

If you forget to close the quotation at the end of the quotes-applied keywords, Google will extend the quote operator to the end of your keyword string, possibly reducing your matches to zero.

Mix up search operators as much as you like. Here are a few examples:

```
television -cable -satellite "rural living"
"brad hill" +dummies -idiots
chocolate +dark OR bittersweet
stepdaughter +delinquent OR evil "why me"
```

## Understanding special Google operators

Now this is fun. Google has invented its own search operators that work only in the Google index. They enable fancy search tricks, some of which are also represented on the Advanced Search page. Knowing these operators takes a bit of memorization, and using them gives you power over the Google home page, circumventing Advanced Search.

Google-specific operators use a colon to separate the command from the keyword string. The format is like this:

```
operator:keyword string
```

Some Google operators require that you leave no space between the colon and the first keyword, as in the preceding. It doesn't matter with other operators. Because I don't want to remember which is which, I always crush the first keyword up against the operator's colon (this sounds like a medical condition).

You may use Boolean operators in the keyword string when the string is preceded by a Google operator, like this:

```
allintitle:new times -york
```

There are nine Google-specific operators:

✔ **stocks:** It seems cool at first, but this is the operator I never use because it doesn't reach into the Google index to do its work. Put one or more stock ticker symbols in the keyword string, preceded by the *stocks* operator, and Google throws you over to one of several financial sites to display the stock's quote. The default destination is Yahoo! Finance, and you can switch to one of four other sites represented by tabs near the top of the page. (See Figure 2-10.) Frankly, if I want stock quotes from Yahoo!, I'm inclined to go straight to Yahoo! to get them. However, there is some value in using the *stocks* operator in the Google Toolbar (see Chapter 9) — unless you also use the Yahoo! Companion toolbar. The Yahoo! Companion is described with breathtaking imagery in my book, *Yahoo! For Dummies.*

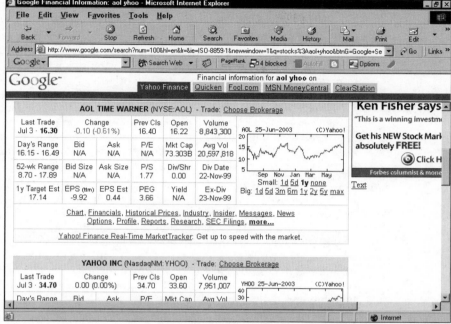

**Figure 2-10:**
Using
the *stocks*
operator
throws you
to Yahoo!
Finance,
with links to
four other
finance
sites.

✔ **cache:** If you know the Web page address, use this operator to pull up Google's cache of that page. By itself, not too useful. But the *cache* operator has an intriguing hidden feature. If you type a keyword after the page URL, Google highlights that word throughout the cached document that it displays. For example, try *cache:www.lycos.com music.*

✔ **link:** This operator performs the same function as the Links feature on the Advanced Search page, finding pages that contain a link to whatever URL you specify. For example, *link:www.dummies.com* displays sites that contain a link to www.dummies.com. If you operate a site yourself, running a search with this operator lets you check who is linking to you — a great tool if you operate a Blogger site (see Chapter 13).

✔ **info:** A nearly pointless operator, *info* is paired with a URL keyword. The result is the Google index entry for that page, plus links to view the cached page, similar sites, and pages that link to that URL. For information about the Google home page, for example, type *info:www.google.com.* I never use the *info* operator.

✔ **site:** Use this operator in your keyword string to limit results to a specified domain. It's a good way to search online newspapers, such as *alan greenspan site:www.usatoday.com.* Combined with the quote operator, you can get pretty specific results in a newspaper site, for example, *"axis of evil" site:www.nytimes.com.* This operator even works with domain extensions, such as *.gov* and *.edu*, without using a domain. Knowing this,

> you can search for keywords matching university or government pages, such as *"code orange" site:gov.*
>
> ✔ **intitle** and **allintitle:** These operators restrict your results to pages in which one or more of your keywords appear in the page title. The *intitle* command affects the single keyword (or group of keywords in quotes) immediately following the operator. All other keywords following the first might be found anywhere on the page. For example, *intitle:tiger woods golf* assures that result pages are about Tiger Woods, not Bengal tigers. The *allintitle* command forces Google to match all your keywords with page titles. This operator can severely narrow a search. For example, the last time I checked, the *allintitle:carrot top nobel prize* search string returned no results.
>
> ✔ **inurl** and **allinurl:** These function similarly to *intitle* and *allintitle* (see the preceding entry) but restrict search results to pages that contain one or more of your keywords in the page's URL (or Web site address). The result is a drastic narrowing of search results, but it's an interesting way to discover new sites with great domain names. For example, *inurl:diaper* returns *www.dog-diaper.com* as the first result. Another example is *allinurl:purple elephant*, which displays results, believe it or not. Note that using *allinurl* with two or more keywords is likely to match pages deep within Web sites with very long URLs.

Power Googling is all about knowing the operators and skipping the Advanced Search page. The more authority over the Google index you can wield on the home page, with its simple keyword box, the quicker you'll be on your way with great search results.

# A Picture Is Worth a Thousand Keywords

Image searching in Google is less complex than Web searching and is fun in different ways. For example, you can search for pictures of people you haven't seen in years, for postcard-like images of travel destinations, or for pictures of yourself.

Google's task is a tricky one. It must match your keyword(s) with pictures — a far harder task than matching words with text. At best, Google can make educated guesses about the identity or subject matter of a picture based on the file name of the picture, the URL address of the image, the surrounding text, and any caption. So the results are bound to be erratic. Fortunately, Google errs on the side of abundance, delivering truckloads of possible photos and other images in response to your keywords.

Simple searches are identical to Web searches. From the Google home page, click the Images tab, enter a keyword or two, and press Enter. You can even use the *site, intitle, allintitle, inurl,* and *allinurl* operators described in the previous section when searching for images.

It's in the search results that things differ from Web searches. Image results come in the form of *thumbnails* — small versions of images. Click any thumbnail to see a larger version of the image, along with the Web page on which it resides. As you see in Figure 2-11, Google reproduces the image above the Web page containing the image — arguably a big waste of space. (Click the Remove Frame link to get rid of it.) This second reproduction of the image is usually a thumbnail, too, albeit a somewhat larger one. You may click on this thumbnail to see a full-size version of the picture. Or you can scroll down the page to see the picture in context.

# Advanced Image Searching

As with Web searches, Google provides a collection of enhanced search tools on the Advanced Image Search page (see Figure 2-12) .Follow these steps to reach that page:

1. **Go to the Google home page.**

2. **Click the Images tab.**

3. **Click the Advanced Image Search link.**

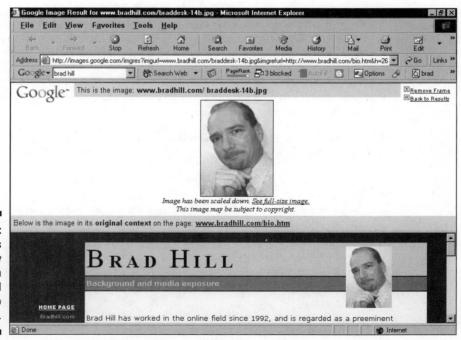

**Figure 2-11:** Google's display of a search image and its Web page.

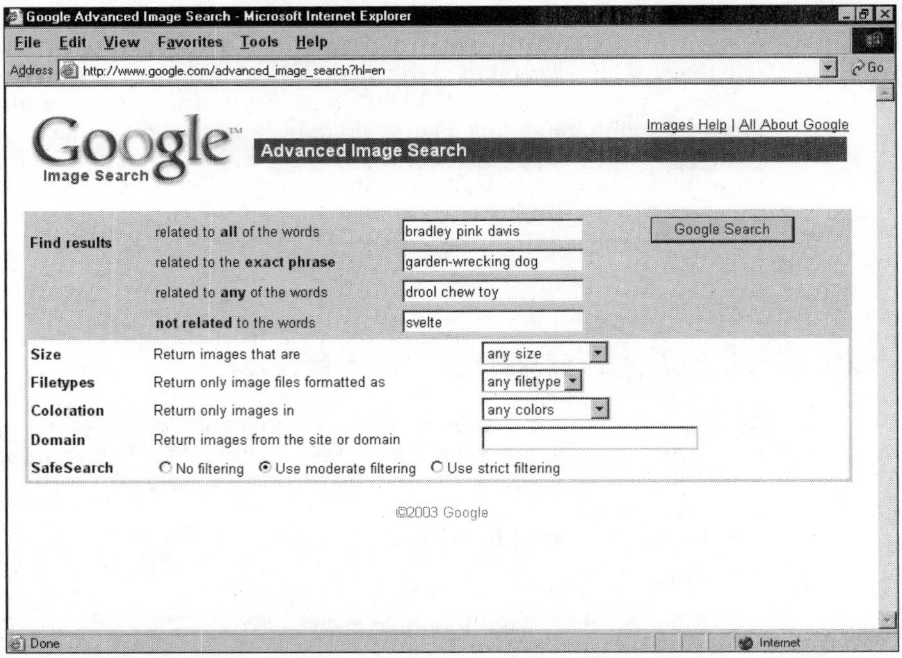

**Figure 2-12:**
The
Advanced
Image
Search
page.

The Find results portion of the Advanced Image Search page is nearly identical to the Advanced Search page for Web searches. (See the "Using Advanced Search" section earlier in this chapter.) The difference is that the keyword modifiers here relate to images by matching file names, captions, and text surrounding the images. Use the keyword boxes to add search modifiers to your keywords, but don't expect exact textual matches as with a Web search because images are not text.

Below the Find results portion of the Advanced Image Search page are five settings that determine the type and location of your sought images:

- **Size:** Use the drop-down menu to restrict your search to images of certain sizes. Admittedly, the choices are vague: icon-sized, small, medium, large, very large, and wallpaper-sized. By themselves, these choices are nearly meaningless. They refer generally to image dimensions, not file size. A wallpaper-sized picture can be contained in a smaller file size than a medium picture.

- **Filetypes:** Use this drop-down menu to select JPG, GIF, or PNG files. As a practical matter, these file formats are nearly interchangeable. Whatever you plan to do with your found images, you can probably do equally well with any one of those three types. Accordingly, I always leave this feature set to its default, which is any filetype.

- ✔ **Coloration:** Here you can choose to locate black-and-white pictures, grayscale images, or full-color art. Full-color images are usually the largest file sizes.

- ✔ **Domain:** Use this keyword box to specify a Web domain that you want to search for images. This is a helpful way to search online newspaper graphics.

- ✔ **SafeSearch:** With these three SafeSearch options, you can determine the level of filtering Google will apply to your image search. The choices are identical to the SafeSearch preference settings (see the first section of this chapter), but apply to only one search at a time.

In nearly all cases, the images you find through Google are owned and implicitly copyrighted by other people. There is some buzz among copyright scholars about the capability of search engines to display other people's property on demand. Google itself puts a little copyright warning about using the images dished up in its search results. If you're wondering whether you can download and apply a photo as desktop wallpaper, for example, the quick legal answer is no in most cases. The search results are meant to be informational, and Google is not intended as a warehouse of downloadable images.

How you choose to approach online intellectual property is your business, but respect for property of others strengthens the online community. Besides, in Google of all places, it's not too hard to find images whose owners invite downloads. Try using the keywords *public domain* or *free download* on the Advanced Image Search page to find images that you can legally reuse.

# Chapter 3

# Directory Trolling and News Browsing

· · · · · · · · · · · · · · · · · · · · · · · · · · · · · · · · · · · · · · · · · · · · · · · · · · ·

## In This Chapter

▶ Understanding Google Directory

▶ Browsing and searching the directory

▶ Visiting Open Directory Project

▶ Submitting a site to the directory

▶ Browsing and searching the astounding Google News

· · · · · · · · · · · · · · · · · · · · · · · · · · · · · · · · · · · · · · · · · · · · · · · · · · ·

Google is primarily known as a search engine, but it offers two services that provide superb browsing:

✔ **Google Directory:** A fastidiously crafted catalogue of good Web sites, broken into hundreds of topical categories

✔ **Google News:** The world's first international newsstand enhanced by Google technology

In a way, these two portions of Google are exactly opposed. Google Directory is completely hand-built, and Google News is completely automated. No site can be listed in the directory without human approval, whereas posted stories in Google News are untouched by human hands.

The directory represents the ultimate in human cooperation and virtual cataloguing. Google takes its basic listings from the Open Directory Project database, created by a large volunteer organization determined to assemble the largest and most useful classified index of Web sites. More than 20,000 real-life editors evaluate and select Web sites for this project, which was started in 1998. Listings created by the Open Directory Project are used by certain other Web directory sites, including Google Directory. To the raw Open Directory database, Google adds its PageRank formulas, creating an enhanced directory experience.

## Google versus Yahoo!

The comparison is inevitable. The two best-known Web directories pitted against each other in a titanic struggle to the death . . . in my imagination, anyway. A competitive atmosphere *does* surround Internet portals generally and Web directories in particular. Yahoo! essentially invented the directory format that became standard, and Google is now the foremost search-and-browse site. Hence the battle imagery. And in this case, it's a one-round knockout. Google is the new champion.

Don't get me wrong. I wrote *Yahoo! For Dummies* and I am the world's biggest fan of the Yahoo! experience. If Yahoo! disappeared, I'd turn off my computer and step outside for the first time in years. I pray it won't come to that. But when it comes to trolling Web directories, Google's brilliance casts Yahoo! into the shadows.

Google dominates for two reasons. First, Google's directory listings come from the Open Directory Project, a large Web directory maintained and updated by thousands of volunteer editors. Yahoo!'s in-house staff, diligent though it be, cannot crank the numbers competitively. The results are lots of dead links in the Yahoo! Directory and a famously long lead time (seems like forever) to get a submitted site included in their directory.

The second reason for Google's dominance is its PageRank system, which prioritizes the already stellar listings compiled by the Open Directory Project, enhancing its already stellar listings. And one more thing: Yahoo! Directory is nearly overwhelmed by ads and portal clutter, whereas the Google Directory page is clean as a cloudless day.

So, Yahoo! Directory, farewell. You gave me my first tours of the Web in 1994, during a thrilling time that is no more. Now, when the urge to troll comes over me, I head for Google Directory.

Google News employs computer algorithms to select and organize news stories from about 4,500 online news sources around the world. The news site is continually updated and organized by topic and news story, not by newspaper or news source.

This chapter covers both Google Directory and Google News. You might be less familiar with the directory than with the increasingly popular News section, but consider reading through both halves of the chapter. They contain tips that will turn your life around and save you from imminent perdition. Well, let me back down from that statement. The chapter contains tips for getting more out of Google. That seems safe.

## Relaxing into Browsing Mode

After a hard day of Googling, there's something comforting about putting on the slippers, lighting up the pipe, and cruising around Google Directory. And if that scenario isn't weirdly retro-tech enough for you, throw in a dog bringing you the newspaper.

Browsing *is* more relaxing than searching, though. Trolling the directory leads to unexpected discoveries as opposed to the routine precision of Google's Web search. Google's search index is so precise and uncannily helpful that it's easy to lose track of the directory entirely. Don't. The directory is truly fun.

If you liken Google searching to finding a needle in a haystack (and a whopping big haystack, at that), browsing the directory is like shining a giant spotlight on broad topic areas of Web content. Search the index to be productive; browse the directory for fun.

The directory has its productive uses, too. In particular, Google Directory serves as an alternate search engine for those who don't like using search operators (see Chapter 2) to narrow down the search field. The directory is all about narrowing down, from broad category to thin subcategory. Drilling into the directory, and then using the within-the-category search function, is a fantastic way to bring up high-quality sites with a minimum of hassle and technical search knowledge.

Here's an example of directory productivity. If you're searching for an online edition of your hometown newspaper, you could drill into the directory's News category, select Newspapers, select Regional, and search for your town's name in the Regional directory. This method avoids clumsy search operators in the Web index.

# Understanding Google Directory

First things first. Google Directory, like most other directories, is self-explanatory on the face of it. You just need to visit the front page to get started. Here it is:

```
directory.google.com
```

Alternatively, click the <u>Directory</u> link on the main Google home page, or use the Google Toolbar (see Chapter 9) to go straight there. Figure 3-1 shows the home page of the Google Directory.

Click any of the main category links or any of the subcategory links to get started. Many more subcategories exist in directory strata beneath the front page. However, you needn't dig deep before encountering results: Most main category pages list primary Web sites for that category in addition to the first level of subcategories for that topic. Figure 3-2 illustrates how this structure works; I have scrolled down the page a bit to show the subcategories and the first few primary site links.

**Figure 3-1:**
The Google
Directory
home page.
Start
exploring by
clicking a
category or
subcategory.

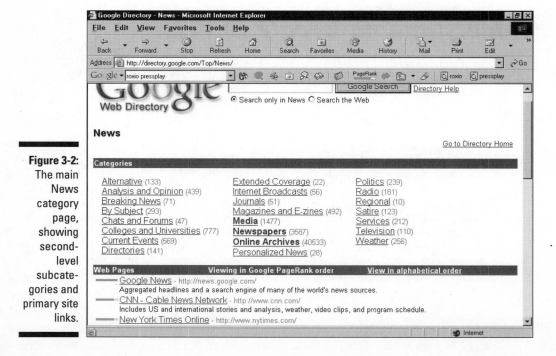

**Figure 3-2:**
The main
News
category
page,
showing
second-
level
subcate-
gories and
primary site
links.

## Open Directory Project

Google Directory is not an original work, but it's enhanced by original technology. The directory selections — that is, the categories, subcategories, and site selections — represent the work of Open Directory Project, a volunteer organization begun in 1998 and dedicated to cataloguing the World Wide Web. No Web catalogue can ever be complete, because of the nearly immeasurable size and ever-changing nature of the beast. Open Directory Project uses the zeal and talent of thousands of topical editors who select directory listings. About one-and-a-half million sites are listed as of this writing.

Open Directory is open to the extreme. Modeled on the open source software movement, in which resulting software programs are not owned and anybody can contribute to their development, Open Directory is distributed free of charge to many of the most important Web portals on the Internet, including Netscape (which acquired the Open Directory organization in 1998 and oversaw development of this free directory), Lycos, and of course Google. Accordingly, you can view the nearly identical directory (allowing for minor differences due to distribution time lag) at several online destinations, including the Open Directory home page (see the figure):

```
www.dmoz.org
```

Google adds unique value to Open Directory and makes it its own (as Randy Jackson would say on *American Idol*) by imposing its PageRank structure on the Open Directory template. That means the site selections in each category and subcategory are ordered by Google's popularity and importance formulas. In other locations, including its home site, Open Directory is organized alphabetically.

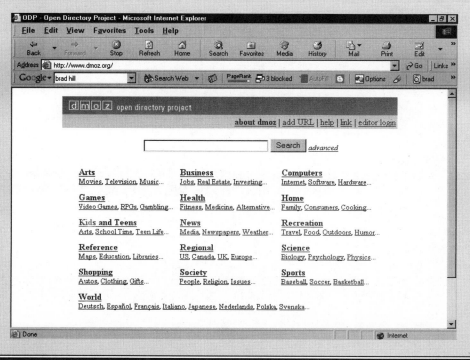

The directory runs deep — it's not hard to drill down six levels in many subjects. Don't give up early. Searching in a lower-level category yields interesting results.

When you search the Web within the directory, you're not searching the entire Google Directory. You're shifting your search over to the Web index, which is separate. To search the entire Google Directory, go to the directory home page and use that keyword box.

You might think that searching in a narrow subcategory is pointless because a quick scroll down the page shows you what sites are listed. But when Google searches a category, it doesn't match your keywords against only the words on the category page; it searches the *content* of the listed pages. This throws the door wide open, but in a small topic area. Searching in a narrow directory category results in extremely rewarding hits.

Figure 3-3 shows a subcategory page, in this case a second-level page in the News category. Two items on subcategory pages are worth noting:

> ✔ The directory path is displayed above the Categories banner. Figure 3-3 is a second-level page with a short path. Lower-level pages have longer paths, and each step you climb down is linked, so you can leap back upward along the path.

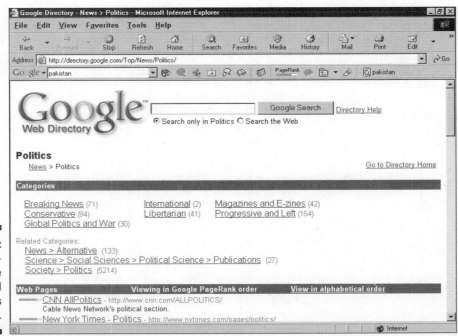

**Figure 3-3:**
A subcategory page with related categories listed.

> ✔ The Related Categories section, under the Categories banner, links to directory categories that share some degree of topicality with your current category.

# Submitting a Web Page to the Directory

Anyone may submit a site for inclusion to Google Directory or offer corrections of currently listed sites and their descriptions. When doing so, you deal not directly with Google but with Open Directory Project, from which Google obtains its listings. Google provides links for interacting with the Open Directory Project submission forms, but I think it's easier to operate from the Open Directory site.

Most people do not sit in front of their computers trying to find interesting sites that aren't represented in Google Directory. If you do find yourself burning hours that way, you might consider becoming an Open Directory Project editor. (Click the Become an Editor link at the bottom of any Google Directory page.) Site submissions are usually made by site owners hoping to get more exposure for their pages. Nothing wrong with that, but be aware that Open Directory Project is a hand-picked, edited directory, and they are not obligated to list a submitted site.

You submit a site by filling in an on-screen Open Directory Project application that asks for the site URL, a description, the proposed directory category for inclusion, and your contact information. Google provides links to this application at the bottom of some category pages. Look for the Submit a Site link.

---

## Directory preferences (not)

On the subject of preference settings for Google Directory . . . there aren't any. Lack of global settings isn't really a problem because directory browsing is a simpler matter than Web searching, which *is* subject to preference settings (see Chapter 2). On one point, though, you might expect the Web-search preferences to cross over to the Directory experience: Namely, the ability to open a new window when you click an outside Web link. This preference is extremely useful in the search engine, because it keeps one browser window anchored on the search results while you're off in another window exploring a result site.

Don't expect Google to open a new window when you click a directory link, even if your search preference is set that way. Instead, right-click any directory link and choose the option to open a new window.

# Searching and browsing combined

A degree of integration exists between Google's Web search results and the directory. On the search side, Google Directory listings sometimes appear on search results pages, naturally enough. When they do, an accompanying link takes you to the category page on which that listing resides.

The figure shows a search results page with two directory listings.

On the other side is the searching capability of Google Directory, covered earlier in this chapter. You can launch a category-specific search from any category page or initiate a Web search from the same keyword box.

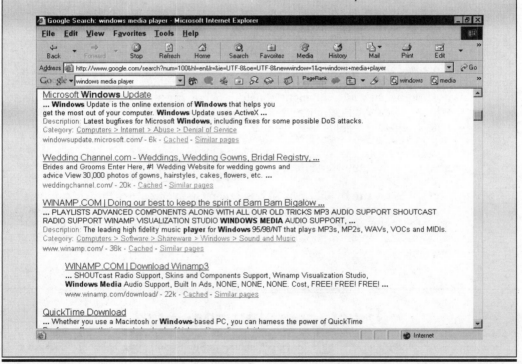

The <u>Submit a Site</u> link is convenient, but there's a problem. Open Directory Project is in charge of deciding which categories and subcategories are open to new submissions. Not all of them are — especially upper-level directory pages. Google doesn't distinguish between open categories and closed categories, so it places the <u>Submit a Site</u> link at the bottom of *all* pages. When you click that link on a category page open to new submissions, you get the application form with any special instructions that apply to that category.

When the category is closed, clicking the <u>Submit a Site</u> link displays the general information page about submitting to Open Directory Project.

Because of this confusion, I recommend starting your submission from Open Directory's home base. Go to this URL for the Open Directory's home page:

```
www.dmoz.org
```

Figure 3-4 shows the Open Directory main page with its top-level categories. They're the same categories as in Google Directory, but the layout is different.

As you drill into the directory, keep an eye on the upper-right corner of the page. Notice that some pages carry no reference to adding or correcting a URL, while other offer the <u>add URL</u> link, the <u>update URL</u> link, or both. Figure 3-5 shows a third-level directory page with both links. Click the <u>add URL</u> link to see the application for that subcategory.

Generally, the broad categories closer to the top of the directory are unavailable for new submissions. Open Directory is particular about where new listings are placed, and your submission is better received if you take the time to research appropriate categories.

**Figure 3-4:**
Home page
of Open
Directory
Project.
Start your
site
submission
project
here.

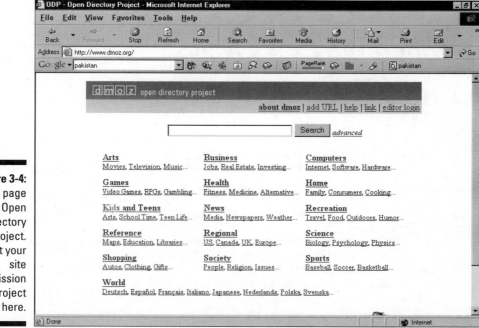

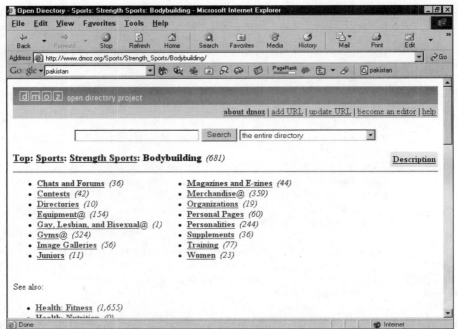

**Figure 3-5:**
Check for
links to add
or update in
Open
Directory.

# Googling the Day's News

Google News is simply incredible. There's a good reason why the Google Toolbar (see Chapter 9) contains a dedicated button linking to the News section. After you get a taste for Google's news delivery style, you'll go back for more throughout the day. The front page (see Figure 3-6) is the first place I turn for headlines or in-depth current events. And I don't mean just among Web sites. I prefer Google News to TV, radio, newspapers, and magazines. Nothing on the planet approaches its global scope, intelligent organization, and searchability.

Start at the beginning — the front page. It contains five main features:

✔ **Searching:** As in each of Google's main information areas, Google News presents a keyword box for searching. (More on this in the next section.) Use the Search News button to confine the search to Google News. Use the Search the Web button to toss your keywords over to the Web index.

**Figure 3-6:**
The Google
News home
page. It is
updated
every few
minutes.

✔ **News categories:** The left sidebar contains seven main news categories: World, U.S., Business, Sci/Tech, Sports, Entertainment, and Health. Each of these subject divisions has its own portion of the front page — scroll down to see them. Clicking a sidebar link takes you to a dedicated news page for that news topic.

✔ **Top story categories:** Top current event items crowd the entire front page, throughout the categories. The first section is devoted to Top Stories. The seven main news sections have their top stories further down the page. At the bottom, a More Top Stories section lurks.

✔ **Headlines:** When you click a headline, the source page opens. This method differs from Yahoo! News, Google's main competitor, which reformats its sources in the Yahoo! style. Google does not pursue the same type of licensing arrangement as Yahoo! does, preferring to simply link to a large pool of online newspapers and magazines. Accordingly, your browser's performance when displaying Google News stories varies depending on the source's capability to serve the page when you click it. Slowdowns can also be the result of attempting to display a publication from halfway across the world.

✔ **Related stories:** This is where the scope and thoroughness of Google News shines. Click any <u>related</u> link after a headline to see an amazing range of publications covering that story. The related articles are listed simply on as many pages as it takes to fit them all (often there are hundreds), and each listing includes the first line or two of the published story. Figure 3-7 shows a portion of one of these pages. Observe the timing notes; Google News indicates how fresh the story is by calculating how long ago it was posted. Links in the upper-right corner invite you to sort the list by relevance or date. My experience is that the most recent hits are usually the most relevant.

Unlike Google Directory, your Google Preferences apply to Google News. This means that if you have Google Web search set to open a new window when you click a search result (recommended in Chapter 2), Google News likewise opens articles in new windows.

If you prefer a less graphic presentation of news, find the <u>Text Version</u> link on the left side of the front page. This format has the same features as the graphical version, but without any photographs or columns, as shown in Figure 3-8.

**Figure 3-7:** Browsing related stories reveals divergent coverage of a story from all over the world.

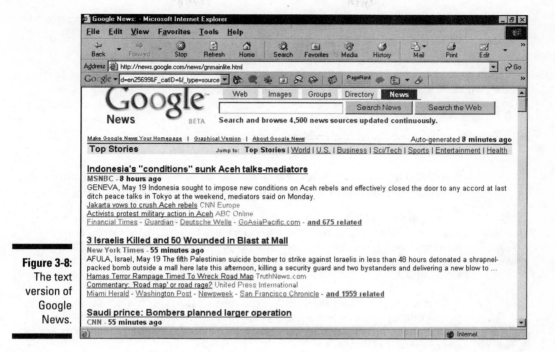

**Figure 3-8:**
The text version of Google News.

# Searching for News

You search Google News with the same set of tools described in Chapter 2 for searching the Web. Keywords go in the keyword box. (Click the Search News button or press Enter to begin the search.) Google attempts to streamline your results by filtering similar articles and presenting the top-ranked hits for your keywords.

## Tracking a story over time

Using the related stories feature, you can track the evolution of a current event. Here's how:

1. **On the Google News front page, click the related story link after any headline.**

2. **On the next page, click the Sort by Date link.**

3. **After the page reloads, scroll to the bottom and click the last result page listed.**

4. **On the last page, view the oldest headlines related to the story.**

   Move forward in time by clicking the Previous link at the bottom of each page.

## Submitting a news source

If 4,500 news sources just aren't enough, or if your favorite offbeat publication never seems to be represented, you can suggest a news source to Google. The submission method is informal.

Just send your suggestion by e-mail to this address:

`news-feedback@google.com`

Figure 3-9 illustrates a News search results page. Note that at the bottom of the page, Google offers to repeat the search without filtering.

Although Google News searching is nearly identical to Web searching in its use of operators, note that the site operator doesn't work correctly as of this writing. Don't beat your head against that wall. There is no way to force Google to return news stories from a particular site or top-level domain. (See Chapter 2.)

A final word about Google News. If the default U.S. version doesn't pertain to your geography or nationality, try one of the five other national editions linked at the bottom of the front page. More country-specific versions are in development.

**Figure 3-9:**
Search
results in
Google
News.

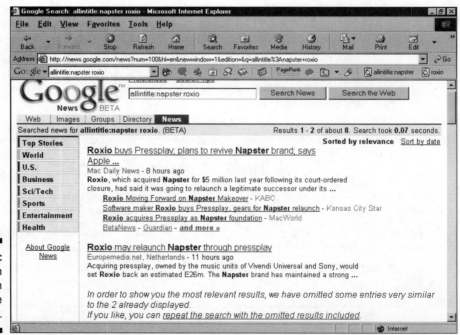

# Chapter 4

# 800 Million Messages at Your Fingertips: Google Groups

### In This Chapter

▶ A brief history of Usenet newsgroups, the Internet's bulletin board system

▶ A glossary of essential Google Groups terms

▶ Browsing and searching the Groups archive

▶ Using standard and Groups-specific search operators

▶ Advanced searching in Google Groups

*W*hen I wrote *Internet Searching For Dummies*, I devoted quite a bit of space to a unique search engine called Deja News. Deja, as it was affectionately called by its devoted users, maintained a growing catalog of messages posted to Usenet newsgroups, which make up the native bulletin board system of the Internet. You could look up messages posted years ago, relive old flame wars, track down participants in e-mail, review somebody's entire Usenet output across all newsgroups, and perform a slew of other newsgroup tricks. You could even use the site to post messages to groups — an innovative, if clunky, departure from the traditional use of a stand-alone newsgroup program.

Then, disaster. Deja News crumbled, a victim of the Internet boom-and-bust period. Much grief was felt across the online nation. But redemption was at hand in February 2001, when Google purchased Deja News and its catalog. The renamed Google Groups performs essentially the same functions as Deja News did, but with Google's advanced searching sensibility and lightning-quick page delivery.

If you are unfamiliar with Usenet, this chapter might seem like a big nuisance. I implore you to mellow any such harsh attitude and ease into these pages with an open mind. Usenet is incredible. Google Groups is magnificent. The encompassing newsgroup culture is, to my mind, an indispensable part of online citizenship. Let me tell you a little story.

Some time ago, one of my Internet service providers, a local cable-TV company that provided high-speed Internet access through a cable modem, sold my town's franchise to another cable company. There was no problem with my TV service after the transition, but I suddenly couldn't log on to the old company's Usenet service, naturally enough. I called the new company and asked for the new server address that would enable me to get my newsgroups. To my astonishment, the representative told me that they would not be offering Usenet service to their inherited customers. This was like hearing they wouldn't be providing e-mail service. So I immediately cancelled my account and got another ISP. Internet life without Usenet is inconceivable.

I won't do business with an ISP that refuses basic services such as Usenet, but the truth is I could have continued my newsgroup habit through Google Groups. So if this scenario happens to you, don't feel like you have to leave in a huff as I did. If you learn one thing from my tragic (well, annoying) experience, let it be to floss daily. Oh, and that Usenet newsgroups should be an important part of everyone's online lifestyle.

So, what the heck *is* Usenet and its newsgroups, anyway? Read on. This chapter gives you a bit of history, and then moves to the practical stuff of using Google Groups to begin — or, for the more experienced, to enhance — your Usenet participation.

# Welcome to the Pre-Web

Usenet is older than the World Wide Web and quite possibly bigger. It's hard to measure relative size in this case, because the Web consists of pages with text and pictures, but Usenet consists of posted messages. Usenet is more closely related to e-mail, which is why many e-mail programs (such as Outlook Express) read public Usenet messages as well as private e-mail messages.

Usenet is the original bulletin board system of the Internet. You're probably familiar with some type of online message board. If you use AOL, you've most likely seen or used AOL's private message board system. If a favorite Web site includes a discussion forum, you've probably read or posted messages in that format. Both examples are bulletin boards, but neither is Usenet. The crucial difference lies in back-end technicalities that are unimportant here. However, it *is* important to understand the three major differences between Usenet and specially built systems such as AOL and a Web site forum:

✓ **Usenet is public:** Anybody with Internet access, on any computer, can view and participate in Usenet. Google makes it easy to stay connected with Usenet even if your ISP puts up a barrier, you don't have Usenet software, or you're traveling and are away from your home computer.

✓ **Usenet is threaded:** Threading is a layout style that clarifies conversational flow. On a threaded message board, you can see at a glance who is responding to whom. AOL's message boards are famously primitive in the threading department, discouraging depth of conversation. Many Web-based forums are likewise flat and unthreaded.

✓ **Usenet is unregulated:** This is a whopper. Nobody owns Usenet and nobody even tries to regulate it. Message board behavior is uncontrolled. Usenet is not a place for children. I am not being critical; the simple fact is that Usenet reflects the scope of human nature, in conversational format, much as society does in offline formats. People are mean, kind, ill-tempered, good-humored, stupid, smart, inarticulate, eloquent — and you see it all on Usenet. Language is spicy. Hundreds of groups are dedicated to pornography. Fortunately, the Usenet realm is organized and avoiding undesirable newsgroups is easy.

The Usenet system contains more than 30,000 newsgroups. The Google Groups archive holds about 800 million messages and is expanding daily, even hourly. Size isn't everything, though, and the issue is really what value Usenet has, or could have, in your life. I find newsgroups irresistible in four major ways:

✓ **Community:** The online realm has long been prized for its capability to connect like-minded people without regard to geography, time zone, or any other factor that keeps people from meeting face-to-face. A newsgroup is created for practically every area of human discourse, from philosophy to specific television shows. Finding a home in one of these groups, and getting to know people from the inside out — without the distracting clues upon which we usually base our likes, dislikes, and judgments — is a unique experience. It is this quality of interaction that first drew me to online services many years ago, and it is still, despite the advances of the Web, the best thing about the Internet. Every morning I check my e-mail and my newsgroups, before setting foot on the Web. The *alt.* portion of Usenet is where most of the social groups reside.

✓ **Expertise:** When I have a technical question, especially about computers, Usenet is the first place I turn. Thousands of people hang out in the *.comp* groups (and others) for no purpose other than to help answer questions and share knowledge about computers. Some of those helpful souls are amateurs; others are professionals. A recent persistent glitch in my home network was solved by an expert at Microsoft, who posts dozens of newsgroup messages every day, outside his job, assisting people like me.

✓ **Recreation:** Newsgroups are just plain fun — the rants, the humor, the childishness, the astuteness, the complex threads. I browse through Google Groups sometimes, searching on various keywords that come to mind, just to get out of my well-worn newsgroup ruts and see what people are saying in other parts of the vast Usenet landscape.

✓ **Learning:** Besides getting technical questions answered, I regularly read certain newsgroups (especially in the *.sci* cluster) to eavesdrop on professional chatter. I have an amateur's interest in physics and cosmology — quarks and black holes and other unseemly phenomena — and it's fascinating to listen in on conversations among people who really know what they're talking about. Being a Usenet lurker in any knowledge field adds a dimension to learning that you can't find in books and magazines.

# A Usenet glossary

Know what you're talking about when the conversation turns to newsgroups. More importantly, know what I'm talking about in this chapter. Following are some essential terms regarding Usenet and newsgroups, in particular:

✔ **Alias:** see *Screen name*.

✔ **Article:** Traditionally, a newsgroup message is called an article. This terminology is a holdover from the days when newsgroups were about news and academic discourse. Now, messages are usually called messages or posts. This book doesn't refer to newsgroup articles, but the Help pages at Google Groups do.

✔ **Binaries:** Media files posted to Usenet. Discussion newsgroups usually discourage posting binaries such as pictures, music files, and video files. Even HTML posting is frowned on — plain text is the preferred format. But thousands of newsgroups are devoted to binary postings, from music to movies to software to pornography. These groups are usually identified by the word *binaries* somewhere in their Usenet address.

✔ **Cross-post:** A message sent to more than one newsgroup simultaneously. Although typically a low-level type of spam, cross-posting is sometimes used legitimately to ask a question or make a comment across related groups. Capricious or spammy cross-posts are loathed, partly because failing to notice the cross-post is easy, resulting in a developed thread running in several groups at once. Generally, cross-posting is bad form. If you do it, acknowledge the cross-post in the message.

✔ **Expired messages:** Usenet messages stay on their servers, available for viewing, for a certain time. Then they expire, which

is sometimes called scrolling off or just scrolling. The amount of time varies from server to server and even from group to group on one server depending on the group's traffic. When messages expire, Google Groups swings into action by archiving the content that would otherwise be lost.

✔ **FAQ:** Frequently Asked Questions. Many newsgroups maintain a *FAQ file,* which is a long message spelling out the customs and basic facts of the group. It's acceptable to post a message asking where the FAQ file is located. Google Groups can also locate FAQs for individual groups — just search for FAQ within a group. Ignore the FAQ at your peril.

✔ **Flame:** A message posted with the intent to hurt. Flames are personal attacks, launched sometimes in response to spam or other behavior contrary to community interests or just because somebody is in a bad mood. Flaming is an art form and can be funny or frightening depending on the practitioner.

✔ **Lurking:** Reading without posting. In any message board community, lurkers greatly outnumber active participants. There's nothing illicit about lurking; newsgroups are for recreational reading as well as conversation. Anyone can delurk at any time to post a message, and then slip back into lurker mode or stay out to talk.

✔ **Message:** Similar to an e-mail message and often composed in an e-mail program, a Usenet message is posted to a newsgroup, where it can be read by anyone in the group.

✔ **Newsgroup server:** Usenet newsgroups are distributed through a network of autonomous, networked computers called servers. That's how the entire Internet works, in fact, and newsgroup servers are a specialized type of Internet computer. Each newsgroup server administrator decides which newsgroups to carry as well as the duration of messages in the groups.

- **Newsgroups:** Topical online communities operating in message board format. Newsgroups don't necessarily have anything to do with news; many groups are purely social. Technology companies such as Microsoft often use newsgroups to provide customer service.

- **Newsreader:** A stand-alone program interface to Usenet, often paired with e-mail functions. Outlook Express, primarily an e-mail program, is the best-known newsreader. Some specialized programs deliver only newsgroups, not e-mail messages. Google Groups provides a Web interface to Usenet and needs no program besides your browser.

- **Post and posting:** Posting a message (often called a post) places it on the public message board. Usenet software, operating behind the scenes, positions the post in correct thread order as long as you don't change the thread title.

- **Quote-back:** Portions of a previous message repeated in a new message, to sustain continuity in a conversation. Google Groups provides quote-backs automatically, indicated by the > symbol before each line of the quote.

- **Screen name:** The online identity of a Usenet participant, the *screen name* is also called an *alias*. You find a great deal of anonymity in newsgroups — and also lots of real names out in the open. In Google Groups, you set your screen name when establishing a Groups account.

- **Spam:** One message, usually promotional in nature, posted (or e-mailed) to many destinations simultaneously. Less formally, any repetitive and self-serving behavior is regarded as spam. Spamming is considered a diabolical sin in Usenet and is met with flames.

- **Subscribe:** Bookmarking a newsgroup in a newsreader is called subscribing. Unlike a newspaper subscription, there is no charge and nothing is delivered to your screen. Subscribing is an easy way to keep handy the newsgroups you follow. There is no subscription feature at Google Groups, but you can use your browser's bookmark function to tag your favorite groups.

- **Thread:** A series of messages strung together into a single newsgroup conversation. Sometimes called a string. A thread might consist of two messages or hundreds. Initiating a new conversation on a newsgroup message board is called *starting a thread*.

- **Threaded:** Online conversations whose message headers are graphically displayed to clarify the evolution of the discussion. Threaded message boards make it easy to see who is responding to whom.

- **Troll:** Newsgroup disrupters, trolls post deliberately offensive or off-topic messages in an apparent desire to get noticed at any cost. Some practitioners have taken the art of trolling to a high level of imagination and are regarded with some admiration and even occasional affection. By and large, though, trolls are reviled by Usenet inhabitants.

- **Usenet:** A network of Internet-based bulletin boards called newsgroups, used primarily as discussion forums and secondarily as repositories of media files.

## Accessing newsgroups on and off the Web

Some people use Google Groups as their only interface to Usenet for reading and posting messages. They have no choice in some situations, such as when a user doesn't own a computer and accesses the Internet on a public computer. When there is a choice, though, my recommendation is to perform most of your active Usenet participation using a stand-alone newsgroup reader. This program might not be the same as your e-mail program. (They're not the same for AOL users.) Outlook Express, probably the most popular e-mail program, offers full newsgroup functionality. In addition, many dedicated newsreaders are available as freeware and shareware downloads. The Netscape browser/e-mail/newsgroup program is free and quite advanced. X-News is another good (and free) one.

It might seem strange to advise against using Google Groups for the daily Usenet lifestyle. Let's be clear about its strengths and weaknesses. Google Groups is best at archiving and presenting a searchable database of Usenet history. It functions also as an interface for posting and daily reading, but its interactive features fall way behind those of a stand-alone program. Also, importantly, your ISP's newsgroup server is likely to be more up-to-the-minute than Google's server, and that factor definitely affects the Usenet experience.

So, my advice is to use Google Groups for searching and when traveling or forced away from your own computer. Otherwise, use a desktop program for subscribing to, reading, and posting to the current day's Usenet.

Google provides an excellent introduction to Usenet, one of the most venerable portions of the Internet. The searchable archive throws open the doors to Usenet history. You might not choose Google as your primary interface when posting, subscribing, and reading every day. Stand-alone programs are quicker and sleeker, and they have better tracking features than any Web interface can. But every longtime veteran Usenet pilot I know occasionally uses Google Groups for searching or when traveling.

# Browsing and Searching Google Groups

Just as with the Web, Directory, and News portions of the site, Google Groups allows you to both browse its content in directory style or search it with keywords. You can merge the two approaches by searching in a single part of the directory. And with so many newsgroups named cryptically, searching for a group is part of the browsing experience.

Google organizes newsgroups by Usenet top-level address types. The largest and best-known of these is the *alt.* collection of newsgroups. Google Groups carries ten of these major divisions plus many minor ones that aren't represented on the Groups home page (see Figure 4-1) but can be found by searching.

Start browsing from the home page by clicking a newsgroup type. Each subsequent page lists fifty groups in alphabetical order. You can see one of these subsequent pages in Figure 4-2. It's interesting to note that Google applies its PageRank system to evaluating the popularity and importance of newsgroups. The familiar horizontal green bars indicate how populous a newsgroup is, saving you much trial and error.

However, PageRank or no PageRank, browsing is difficult. Google does its best to help you navigate through thousands of groups by providing a drop-down menu that leapfrogs ahead in the alphabetical list. That's fine, but at this point resorting to keywords is the way to go. In fact, you can safely skip this second-level directory page entirely and start with a keyword on the home page. The benefit of launching your keyword search from the *alt.* page (or whichever page you're on) is that you can restrict your search to the *alt.* division.

**Figure 4-1:**
The Google
Groups
home page.

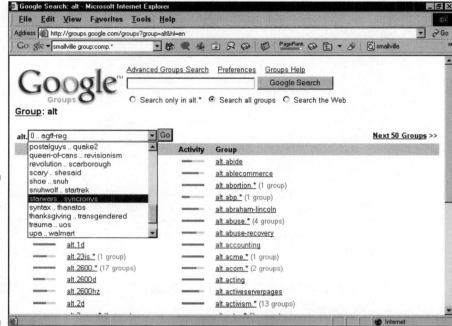

**Figure 4-2:**
The familiar
Google
PageRank
indicates
the
popularity
of news-
groups.

The following steps describe a Google Groups search:

1. **From the Google Groups home page, click the newsgroup link for the newsgroup division you want to search.**

   To follow along with the example, click the <u>alt</u>. link.

2. **In the keyword box, type your search words.**

   I'm assuming that you have a passion for anything related to Star Trek and want to read postings about the TV franchise *Star Trek*. So type **star trek** in the keyword box.

3. **Choose whether you want to search all groups or just a division.**

   These options appear below the keyword box. (Skip the Web option — let's stay in Groups.) To follow along, click the Search only in alt.* option. (The asterisk represents any words following the *alt.* division.)

4. **Click the Google Search button**

Figure 4-3 shows the result of this search. A few notable features of the search results page are itemized in the following sections.

**Figure 4-3:**
A search results page in Google Groups. In addition to individual messages, Google gives you related groups.

## Using the group operator

Notice in Figure 4-3 how the keyword string is now presented in the search box on the results page:

```
star trek group:alt.*
```

This syntax is an introduction to a new search operator specific to Google Groups: the *group* operator. Using it forces Google to match your keyword(s) against newsgroups in one division. You can use this operator to ferret out newsgroups in minor divisions that don't appear on Google's home page. For example, when searching for a Windows 95 support group in the Microsoft newsgroups, this keyword string is effective:

```
windows 95 group:microsoft.*
```

The result of this search is illustrated in Figure 4-4. Under the Related Groups banner, there is no direct match to the keywords (*windows 95*) in the newsgroup names — but Google determines that win95 and windows95 (without a space) are relevant hits. Google's capability to make smart choices on your behalf, based on comprehensive searches of content, is as pronounced in the Groups sections as in the Web search section.

When using the *group* operator, always place a period and asterisk after the division name you're searching for, if you know (or are guessing) an exact division. Neglecting the period-wildcard combination leads to quirky and less specific results. And another tip — use this operator only when searching all Google groups. If the search engine is set to search only the *alt.* division, for example, and you use the *group* operator and specify the *soc.* division, your computer will shoot lasers into your eyes. Kidding. Google handles the confusion rather well by simply adding the two divisions. But you shouldn't tempt the wrath of the Googlebeast.

Operators usually work in reverse as well (see Chapter 2). Such is the case with the *group* operator and the *-group* operator. The *group* operator, immediately preceded by a minus sign (no space), tells Google to exclude groups in the newsgroup division that follows. Suppose you want to find discussions about Windows 95 and want to avoid Microsoft-sponsored newsgroups. The following string is productive:

```
windows 95 -group:microsoft.*
```

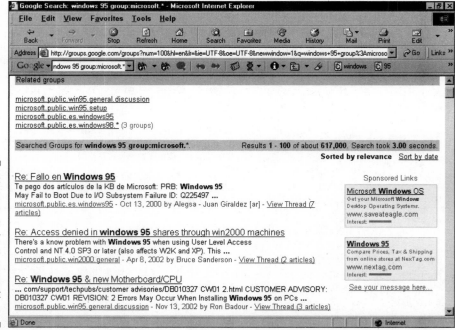

**Figure 4-4:** Searching with the *group* operator yields targeted and intelligent results.

I can't stop talking about the *group* operator. I want to make sure every reader understands that it's not just for defining top-level newsgroup divisions such as *alt., soc.,* and *microsoft.* You can use the operator to define a single newsgroup, if you know its name. Let's go back to the *windows 98* example. Perhaps you want to avoid Microsoft newsgroups, but you also don't want to trudge through a hundred miscellaneous groups in which your keywords might be mentioned. If you've received good results in the past from the newsgroup *alt.windows98*, your keyword string should look like this:

```
windows 98 group:alt.windows98
```

Note that there's no need for the wildcard asterisk because you're defining the entire newsgroup name. Now if the reverse is true, and you want to eliminate results from that particular newsgroup, here's your search string:

```
windows 98 -group:alt.windows98
```

## Search operators in Google Groups

Google Groups understands most of the same search operators that you use when searching the Web (see Chapter 2). The standard operators — *AND* (+), *NOT* (-), *OR*, and " " (exact phrase) — work fine in modifying your keywords in Google Groups. The exact phrase operator (quotation marks around the phrase) is especially useful when searching Usenet, which is full of colloquial speech. Suppose you want to look back at Usenet posts about the famous *Seinfeld* episode that introduced "master of your domain" into the vernacular. This search string is productive:

```
"master of your domain"
     group:*seinfeld*
```

In addition to specifying the exact phrase, you are defining a *Seinfeld*-related newsgroup, even if you don't know any exact names of such newsgroups. The two wildcards (asterisks) allow Google to search for newsgroup names containing *seinfeld*. The result I got shows 259 highly targeted messages, mostly from the *alt.tv.seinfeld* newsgroup and posted between 1993 and 1998.

One of the Google search operators discussed in Chapter 2 also works well in Google groups. It is the *intitle* operator, which forces Google to find only search results whose titles contain your keywords. The *intitle* operator includes only the first keyword after the operator. Use *allintitle* to include all your keywords in the title. The simpler *intitle* operator also allows you to include entire exact phrases with quotes surrounding them.

Working with the Seinfeld example again, you can narrow down the first search with the *intitle* operator, like this:

```
intitle:"master of your domain"
     group:*seinfeld*
```

That search string narrowed down the original 259 results to a trim, extremely relevant 59 results, each of which contained the specified phrase in the thread title. I should mention that Google always attempts to find keywords in the thread title, assuming that they are the most relevant hits, and groups those results toward the top of the search results list. Using the *intitle* operator gets rid of all extraneous results.

## *Understanding related groups*

Many search results pages, typified in Figure 4-3, contain a Related groups banner under which are newsgroups that Google has determined contain relevant search results. You can see those groups represented if you scroll through all the search results. The list is for reference only; you may click any group in that list, but doing so does not carry your keyword search into that group. Instead, you merely see the display page for that group, with the most recently posted message at the top.

In some cases, Google uses the wildcard in the Related groups list to indicate clusters of related newsgroups. Again, Figure 4-3 illustrates this, showing two clusters with a wildcard (*). Click the *alt.startrek.** cluster to see a new page containing the complete list of groups that fulfill the wildcard. (See Figure 4-5.) Note that wildcards can be found in this list, too, representing newsgroups whose names contain yet another dot-extension — that is to say, another period followed by another word. Newsgroup names can be quite long and cryptic.

When confronted with a long list of related groups, glance at the PageRank indicators to quickly determine which groups might be the best to browse.

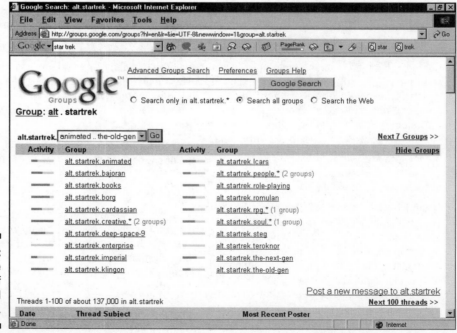

**Figure 4-5:**
A complete list of related newsgroups.

Whenever you're on a directory or results page for a single newsgroup or a cluster of groups, you have the option of restricting your next search to that group or cluster. This option doesn't exist on a search result page showing posts from many groups; naturally, Google wouldn't know how to restrict subsequent searches. When in doubt, just look below the keyword box for options that enable you to search all Google Groups or a subset of groups.

One beautiful feature Google presents in the related groups list (shown in Figure 4-5) is the capacity to search within those related groups. Click the leftmost option below the keyword box to activate this search restriction.

## Sorting search results

There's not too much to report on the subject of sorting. Search results are usually sorted by relevance, according to Google's mysterious and profound formulas. Use the <u>Sort by date</u> link to switch to a chronological order of posts. The chronology goes in reverse, with the most recent result at the top of the list.

## Interpreting search results

If you flip back to Figure 4-3, you can see a typical Groups search results page. Search results contain six elements:

- ✔ **Thread title:** Every message title carries the name of its parent thread. All message titles in a thread (except the first one) are preceded by Re:. The Re: prefix is standard practice in most newsgroup readers. Click the message title to read the message and see how it fits in the thread. (More on this in the next section.)

- ✔ **Message excerpt:** Google snips sentences that contain your keywords. The small excerpt is sometimes enough to determine whether it's worth clicking over to the full message.

- ✔ **Newsgroup name:** Click this link to see a straight, unmatched display of the newsgroup.

- ✔ **Date:** The date represents when the message reached Google's newsgroup server. If you display the entire message (by clicking the thread title), Google shows you the time — down to the second — that the message hit the server and was archived.

- ✔ **Screen name:** This is the screen name of the message's author.

- ✔ **View thread:** Clicking this link, which indicates how many messages await you in the thread, displays the entire single message and links to others in the thread. Understanding that page is the subject of the next section.

## Up to the minute, more or less

Google puts a *time stamp* on every message it displays and every message it archives. The time stamp indicates the date and time (in Pacific U.S. time, regardless of where you're located) when the message traveled through Usenet and hit Google's newsgroup server.

Keep in mind that time stamps for the same message differ from server to server. Also, Google has a reputation for being slower than ISP (Internet service provider) servers.

AOL users complain vociferously about the newsgroup server flaking out entirely for large stretches of time — sometimes days go by during which Usenet service is disrupted and inadequate. Google rarely, if ever, falls down on the job to that extent. But it's not uncommon for posts to show a delay of an hour or three before reaching Google's display. By contrast, my ISP's Usenet server shows me my posted messages within two seconds most of the time, and I almost never notice the sort of thread discontinuity that happens when a server isn't getting posts from elsewhere.

Although Google is superlative at cataloguing Usenet and making it available for searching, it gets average marks for its performance as a dynamic newsgroup server.

# *Reading Messages and Threads*

When you click a message title, Google throws you into a different sort of page that shows an entire newsgroup message (finally!) and various options that affect how you perceive and interact with the entire thread. It's from this page that you can post a message (see the following section for posting).

Figure 4-6 shows a full Usenet post from a search on the keyword *borg* in the group *alt.startrek.* *. Note that the keyword is highlighted throughout the message.

Just poking around might be the best way to get acquainted with the message page. Besides the message text itself, you should understand the following major elements:

- ✔ **Keyword box:** As always, the box sits atop the page, ready to launch a new search in the current newsgroup or in all newsgroups. (Searching the Web from here is also an option, but rather beside the point for our purpose.)
- ✔ **Sponsored links:** These are advertisements.
- ✔ **Message header:** In the large gray banner, you see details about the message. These details include the author, his or her e-mail address, the thread title, the newsgroup(s) to which it was posted, the date and time,

the position of this message on your search results page, and links for seeing an alternate format and the entire thread. You find out about many of these items shortly.

✔ **Post a reply:** Click the <u>Post a follow-up to this message</u> link to compose a message in response to the message you're reading. The next section covers composing a message (and creating a Google Groups screen name).

If you look more closely at the gray message header in Figure 4-6, you see several elements and links. Following is a breakdown of their functions:

✔ **Author:** The message author's screen name is linked to a list of that person's Usenet posts in Google's archive (see Figure 4-7). In some cases, the author is responsible for many thousands of posts. The author archives are organized by e-mail address, which is changeable. Sometimes people change e-mail addresses but keep the same screen name, leading to different archives of their posts. When researching a person's Usenet history, it's not uncommon to encounter multiple archives, and you need to know (or discover through Google) the e-mail address of each archive.

✔ **Author's e-mail:** This bit of information is also linked. Clicking it displays a window (called New Message or something similar) in your default e-mail program. This makes it easy to contact Usenet authors privately. Use this feature with discretion. It's generally considered rude to invade a stranger's e-mail box (you know how everyone feels about spam) without a very good reason. Don't respond to a Usenet message "off the board" (that is, by using the e-mail link) unless you have a compelling reason to make a private comment.

✔ **Newsgroups link:** Click this link (or one of these links, if the message was cross-posted) to see a straight, unmatched view of the newsgroup. You probably don't want that display right now, in the middle of exploring your search results.

✔ **Original Format link:** Click this link to see the message in raw text format, without any Web page formatting around it. Figure 4-8 illustrates what an unformatted Usenet message looks like. Usually this view is useful only when you want to see the complete Usenet header.

✔ **Complete Thread link:** This link leads to the most comprehensive view of the message and its place in the thread. Figure 4-9 shows this view, which is split into two frames. The left frame displays a link to every message in the thread, in a format that makes it clear who responded to whom. Rather than use message titles in this list (they would all be the same), Google shows us the author screen names and posting dates.

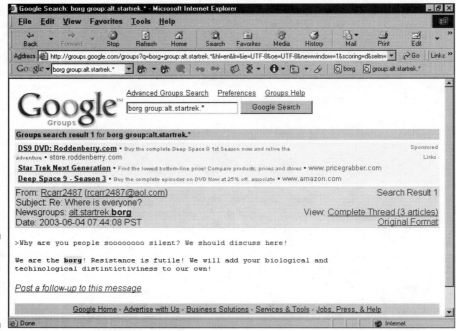

**Figure 4-6:**
A Google
Groups
message
page.

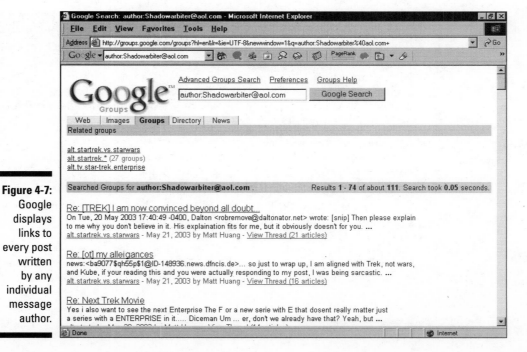

**Figure 4-7:**
Google
displays
links to
every post
written
by any
individual
message
author.

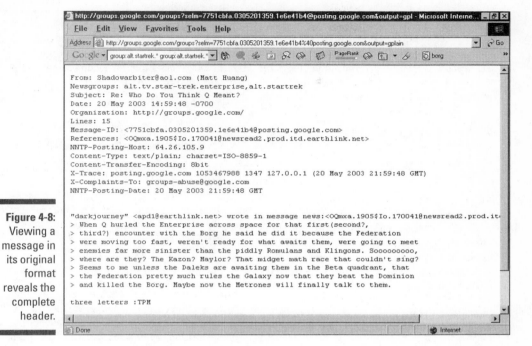

**Figure 4-8:**
Viewing a message in its original format reveals the complete header.

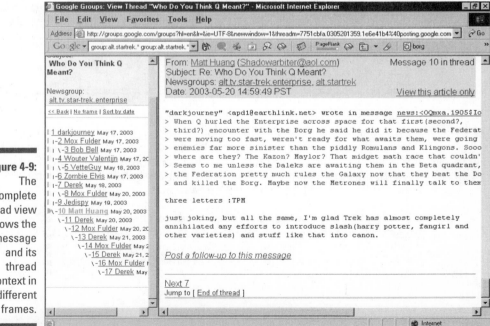

**Figure 4-9:**
The Complete Thread view shows the message and its thread context in different frames.

# Keeping your own stuff out of the archive

You can restrict Google from including your Usenet posts in the Groups archive in two ways: prevent Google from archiving a post to begin with or remove an archived post.

You can use the Usenet software to prevent archiving by typing a single line of code either in the message header or in the first line of the message body:

```
X-No-archive: yes
```

The line must be typed exactly as it appears here, with a single space between the colon and yes. Placing the line in a message header is less conspicuous than positioning it in the message body but much harder for most folks to accomplish. So, when posting a message that you want to keep out of the archive, just place that line in the message itself. Make sure it is the *first* line, above the quote-back that Google places in all response messages.

Removing an already archived post is more complicated. Follow these steps:

1. **From the Google Groups directory, click the Groups Help link.**

   The Google Groups Help page appears.

2. **Click the question, How can I remove articles from Google's archive?**

   An *article* is a posted message.

3. **Click the Automatic Removal Tool link.**

4. **Create an Automatic Removal Tool account.**

   Yes, another account. Please note that this one is not the same as the Google Groups account that establishes your screen name. After creating your Automatic Removal Tool password (which can be the same as your Groups password), Google sends you a confirmation e-mail.

5. **Click the link in your confirmation e-mail.**

   A browser page pops up showing the Automatic Removal tool. Note that you can use it to remove not only Usenet posts from the Groups index but also URLs from Google's Web index.

6. **On the Remove your URL or Google Groups Post page, click the Remove your usenet posts from Google Groups link.**

In the Complete Thread view, the relative sizes of the frames are adjustable. Position your mouse cursor over the border between the two frames until the double arrow appears, and then click and drag to the left or right. When dealing with long and complex thread that are sharply indented, the left frame needs to be widened to view the entire thread.

By the way, if you want to get rid of the thread view entirely, click the No frame link near the top of the thread frame. Doing so takes you back to a simple message view, without the graphical display of other messages in the thread. To return to the thread view, click the View with frames link at the top of the page.

Another toggle you can apply to the thread view is the choice between <u>Sort by date</u> and <u>Sort by reply</u>. The latter is the default view, and displays the thread with indentations that clarify who replied to whom. Clicking the <u>Sort by date</u> link removes the threaded indentations (which present the thread in conversational logic, which doesn't necessarily transpire in strict chronological order) and displays a chronological list of messages. (See Figure 4-10.) The oldest message is on top.

Yet another special Google search operator lets you troll the Groups index for messages written by a single person. The operator in question is the *author* operator. This one is useful when searching within a single newsgroup or across Usenet globally. The operator needs to be paired with an e-mail address, *not* with a screen name. (You can, however, search for a screen name without any operator.) As usual with Google operators, don't put a space between the operator and the address. Here's the correct syntax:

```
author:name@email.com
```

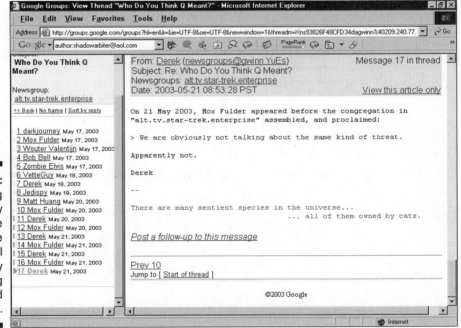

**Figure 4-10:** Viewing threads by date removes the graphical display showing who replied to whom.

# *Posting Messages through Google Groups*

Google allows posting to newsgroups, but you must register as a Google Groups user to do so. This necessary step is not the typical Web site registration forced upon you to get an e-mail address which is then sold to Internet marketing companies. The main reason you must register is to establish a screen name that is then used to identify your posts.

Registration is not required to browse, search, or read newsgroups through Google Groups. In fact, Google does not encourage or even display a path toward registration until you first attempt to reply to a newsgroup message or start a new thread.

Follow these steps to register:

1. **On any newsgroup page, click a message header link.**

2. **At the bottom of any message to which you'd like to respond, click the <u>Post a follow-up to this message</u> link (see Figure 4-11).**

3. **On the following registration page, enter a screen name and a password.**

   Note that if you created another Google account before this (in Google Answers, for example), Google prompts you for just a screen name — not a screen name. Your previously created password works in Google Groups. Your screen name can be any combination of characters that isn't already registered at Google Groups. Pause here to think. The first choice is whether to use your real name or some variant of it that doesn't hide you. Many people keep their identities out in the open. The other choice is to make up an alias.

4. **Read the terms and conditions, using the scroll bar to see the entire document.**

   You must agree to the terms and conditions, but you don't actually have to read them. They stipulate that Google doesn't own the content of Usenet, but it does own the formatting of that content and the page elements surrounding it; that you may not sell the content (at a garage sale, perhaps?); that Google does not endorse the content; that Google does not monitor Usenet or make any attempt to protect your privacy when you post; that you are responsible for your own bad self when romping through the newsgroups; and that you must behave civilly and legally when posting. If you have any questions or concerns about your rights and Google's obligations when using Google, take the time to read the terms and conditions.

5. **Click the Acceptance button.**

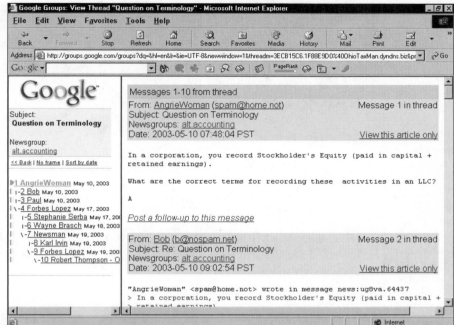

**Figure 4-11:**
Google refers to replies as follow-ups.

You are now registered, but look out. At the time of this writing, the Google registration process contains a confusing glitch. If you followed the preceding steps literally, going into the registration from an attempt to reply to a message, you find that Google presents you with a new message form. The newsgroup name is not filled in, nor is the original message referenced in any way. You fill in all that yourself, which is not how replying (what Google calls *posting a follow-up*) works. Instead, click the <u>&lt;&lt; Return to Google Groups</u> link to start over as a registered user. Awkward, I know.

Adding to the confusion, on this page (see Figure 4-12) Google recommends jotting down your username and password. Your username is your screen name (see Step 3 in the preceding list). But if this is *not* your first account at Google, you did not create a password with your Groups screen name. If you have registered somewhere else in Google — in Google Answers, for example — you have a Google password, and that is the password you should jot down with your newly-created Groups screen name.

Let's get back to posting. With an established Groups screen name, click the <u>Post a follow-up to this message</u> link, as described. The next page allows you to post your reply.

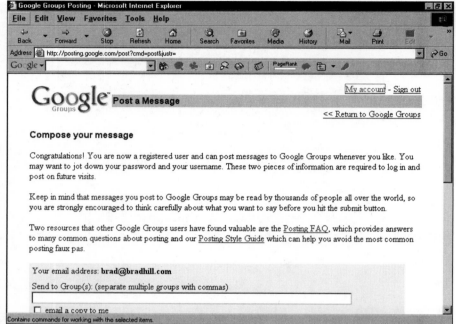

**Figure 4-12:**
Google
suggests
jotting down
your Groups
password,
which may
be the same
as another
Google
password.

As you can see in Figure 4-13, the newsgroup name and subject header are automatically filled in when replying to a message. (If you change the subject header, your message is posted as a new thread, disrupting the continuity of the current thread.) Notice, also, that the message you're responding to appears in the Your message box. This repetition is a standard Usenet practice called *quoting* or *quoting back*, and it reminds readers what you are responding to, exactly.

Due to the decentralized distribution of Usenet messages, not all threads are filled in at the same time for all readers, so quoting back fills in the gaps for anyone who's missing a message in their newsreader. Feel free to highlight and delete all but the most pertinent part of the quote, and then respond either above or below the quote (see Figure 4-14).

After you've composed your message, click the Preview message button to see what it will look like (and get one more chance to edit it), or go straight for the Post message — No preview button.

Your message might not show up in the group immediately. In fact, the question of when it shows up is meaningless because different readers see it at different times, depending on the erratic course of Usenet server distribution. Google Groups is hardly the fastest distributor in the world of posted messages, so don't be alarmed if you don't see your posted message right away or even in a few hours. That kind of delay is natural with a Web-based interface.

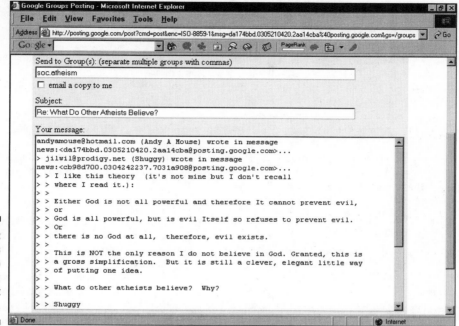

**Figure 4-13:**
Use this page to compose a Usenet reply.

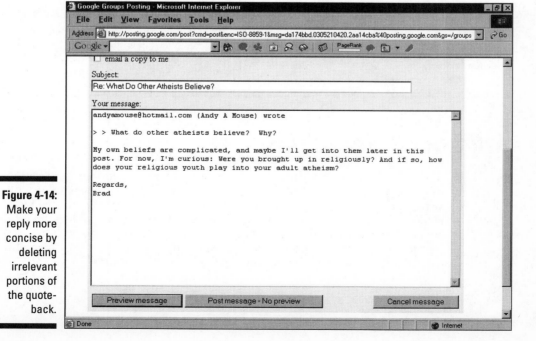

**Figure 4-14:**
Make your reply more concise by deleting irrelevant portions of the quote-back.

## Fun and flames: newsgroup etiquette

To a greater extent than other portions of the Internet (except perhaps chat rooms), Usenet embodies a distinct, autonomous culture. Embarking on a Usenet journey is not unlike visiting another country. You might know the language, but that doesn't mean you know the customs. It's easy to make gaffes. And unlike polite society in many countries, Usenet citizens don't hesitate to pound your virtual self to the ground when you make a mistake. Rudeness? Yes, but it's more than that; Usenet is ancient, by Internet standards, and proud of its traditions. An unspoken requirement is that newcomers learn the local ways before opening their mouths.

Perhaps the most important rule is this: Lurk before you leap. Even if you've been around online communities before, get to know any individual group before jumping in with your own posts. Read the board for a few weeks to get the flow of inside jokes, to understand its topical reach, and to learn the personalities and social power structures of the group. Google Groups can compress this process by allowing you to read back in time, covering a lot of ground quickly.

Always put the community first. Newsgroup stars develop through eloquence and intelligence, not by pushiness. Don't ever use newsgroups to promote products — even free products such as Web pages. (Placing a link to a personal Web page beneath your signature is perfectly acceptable.) Don't spam, cross-post, or generally attempt to mine Usenet's traffic for personal gain. Go there to contribute to the common good. If your contributions are worthy, attention will accrue to your entire online package.

Flame with discretion. I am not a Usenet peacenik who believes that all flaming represents an abuse of online anonymity. But nothing is more foolish (or worthy of reciprocal torching) than a misinformed flame attack. Make sure you have some standing in the newsgroup, and get your facts right. The most cogent and entertaining flames go after another poster's content, not the other poster's personality.

Overall, keep a giving attitude. No matter how you manufacture your Usenet personality — caustic, loving, intellectual, argumentative, whatever — make contributions that somehow enhance the group. It's all about community.

# *Advanced Searching*

Google provides an Advanced Search page for Groups as it does for its other indexes. And, as with the others, it offers a user-friendly way to employ search operator functions without knowing the operators. As you can see in Figure 4-15, the Advanced Groups Search page looks very much like the other advanced pages. The Find messages section works just as it does with a Web search (see Chapter 2). Use the four keyword boxes in this section in combination, forcing Google to treat your keywords in certain ways.

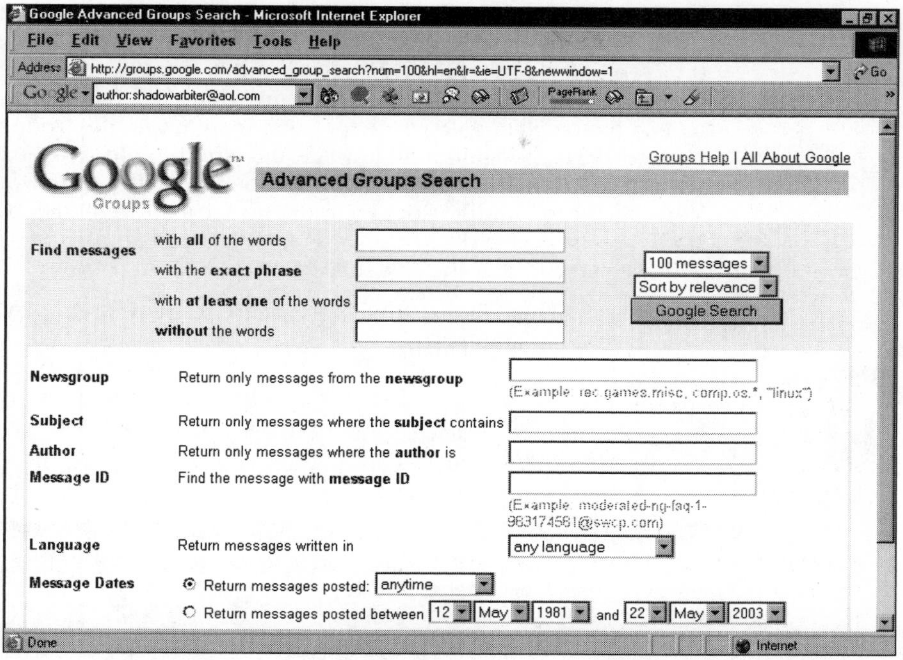

**Figure 4-15:**
The
Advanced
Groups
Search
page
resembles
Google's
other
advanced
search
pages, but
with
features
unique to
Groups.

The Advanced Groups Search page also includes the following search parameters exclusive to Google Groups:

- ✔ **Newsgroup:** Use this box to specify a particular newsgroup for searching, or even part of a newsgroup name. Feel free to include the asterisk if you don't know the entire name. This feature replaces using the *group* operator.

- ✔ **Subject:** Use this box for keywords that you want to appear in the thread title. This feature replaces using the *intitle* and *allintitle* operators.

- ✔ **Author:** Use this box to specify an author's screen name or e-mail address. In the latter case, this feature replaces using the *author* operator. Using the *author* operator with a screen name yields uneven results, which this advanced search page works out through fancy operator syntax.

- ✔ **Message ID:** This rarely used feature searches for a Usenet message ID, which you can glean from a message header.

- ✔ **Language:** Usenet is international, just like the Web. Use the drop-down menu to specify a language.

✔ **Message dates:** This is da bomb. Here's where the advanced action is in Google Groups. The Groups archive is precisely historical in a way that the Web index can't be because each one of the 800 million catalogued Usenet posts is stamped with a date and time. Use these drop-down menus to specify a date range for your search. Google Groups stretches back to 1981, though not all newsgroups are that old. This feature does not replace a search operator that can be typed into a keyword box. However, very handily, Google drags the drop-down menus over to the search results page (see Figure 4-16), so you can adjust the date range without returning to the Advanced Groups Search page.

✔ **SafeSearch:** This feature applies the same content filter as in Web searches. (See Chapter 2.)

You can throw a Web search into Google Groups by clicking the Groups tab above any Web search results list. It's a quick way to siphon the information flow in a new direction.

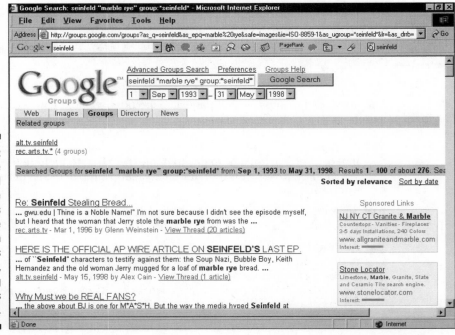

**Figure 4-16:**
The specified date range appears atop the search results page, allowing adjustments on the fly.

# Part II
# Specialty Searching

**The 5th Wave**      By Rich Tennant

"No Stuart, I won't look up 'rampaging elephants' on the Web. We're studying plant life, and right now, photosynthesis is a more pertinent topic."

# In this part . . .

This part moves to the fringe areas of Google, where the information can be even deeper and more personalized than at the core search engine. You might not be aware of Google's cutting-edge services because they aren't promoted on the sparse home page. In its outlying districts, Google becomes a shopping portal, a mail-order catalog browser, a government site tracker, a personal consulting company, and an open-door laboratory developing new online technology.

Nearly ten percent of Google's employees have a Ph.D., and in Part II, you get a glimpse of Google's extraordinary brain trust at work. Almost everything described here is an innovation, and I foresee the intersection of these chapters and your destiny. Take the cornerstones of these hidden services to build a new platform for your newly vivified, surprisingly diversified, tectonically empowered online immersion. [Editors' note: While our backs were turned, Brad Hill snuck some chocolate-covered espresso beans. We are now feeding him through a tube.]

# Chapter 5

# Shopping with Froogle and Google Catalogs

## In This Chapter

▶ Introducing the Google shopping portal

▶ Searching and browsing in Froogle

▶ Special Froogle search operators

▶ Advanced searching in Froogle

▶ Introducing the dazzling Google Catalogs

▶ Browsing mail-order catalogs with the Google Catalogs control bar

---

Google, the world's most intelligent search engine, has an academic, ivory-tower sheen. The science behind its index and the insightfulness of its results lend Google an other-worldly feeling. Except . . . shopping! Shopping is the common denominator of the Web — everybody likes to buy stuff. Google turns its all-seeing eye to the swarming, steamy jungle of e-commerce.

Yes, Google is a shopping portal, but not of the sort you might be familiar with in AOL and Yahoo!. Google provides two shopping directories and applies its insightful, destination-ranking intelligence to them. The result is a sharp, objective, results-oriented virtual window-shopping experience.

This chapter covers the details of Froogle, a keyword-empowered shopping directory, and Google Catalogs, an online mail-order browsing environment. Both are delightful — and more powerful than many people realize. The following sections cover basic keywords and clicks, and then introduce a few tricks I use in Froogle and Google Catalogs.

Froogle and Google Catalogs are still in *beta*, meaning they are still being tested by Google and its users. There's no danger here, because nothing new gets installed in your computer. My hope is that Froogle, cool as it is, gets significantly enhanced before the techies at Google stop working on it. (If, indeed, they ever stop working on anything, which I doubt.) If you have specific suggestions, complaints, or words of adulation about Froogle or Google Catalogs, use these two e-mail addresses:

- ✔ For Froogle: `froogle-support@google.com`
- ✔ For Google Catalogs: `catalog-support@google.com`

# Google's Approach to Online Shopping

The main difference between Google's shopping services and those in other major portals is that Google doesn't get its hands on the money. You don't buy anything through Google. Both Froogle and Google Catalogs function purely as directories to products, sending you elsewhere to get your hands on the goods. Google has no revenue-sharing association with e-commerce retailers (in Froogle) or mail-order companies (in Google Catalogs). The search results you get in both services are pure; preferred placement in the search results lists is not for sale by Google.

The inevitable comparison is between Froogle and Yahoo! Shopping. (Google Catalogs is unique and can't be compared to anything else online.) Yahoo! Shopping is a virtual mall whose directory and search results list Yahoo!'s stores. Banners for featured stores hog a portion of the front page. All this is useful, and Yahoo! houses many of the most important online retailers in the business. Yahoo!'s search engine shows off some smarts, breaking down many searches into brand listings. It also has a nice price-comparison engine.

Keeping all the stores under one virtual roof has other advantages, first among them being a shared shopping cart and payment wallet. You can load up products from multiple stores, and then pay for them all at once. You provide your credit card and shipping information just once; the information is then stored on Yahoo!'s computer. AOL and MSN have similar programs. Systems like this are purchase-oriented, whereas Google is search-oriented.

Google is not (currently) interested in handling purchase transactions, taking payment information, or hosting stores. There is no Google Wallet. The Google shopping portal is a search engine that separates products from stores to deliver targeted search lists. Furthermore, it uses similar evaluations as in its Web searches to determine which products matching your keywords are most important and should be listed first. The results aren't quite as startling as with a Web search, which often seems to know what you want before you do.

When it comes to buying through Google, *through* is the right word (as opposed to *from*). Froogle search results are like Web search results, insofar as they link you to target sites, in this case e-commerce sites with their own shopping carts and payment systems. Google Catalogs provides mail-order phone numbers and — where possible — links to Web sites.

# Searching and Browsing in Froogle

Your Froogle experience starts on the Froogle home page:

```
froogle.google.com
```

As you can see in Figure 5-1, Froogle presents a traditional combination of search engine and directory. You can leap right in with a keyword or two, or drill into the directory to see what you can find.

The directory extends several layers deep, each level delivering product listings in increasingly specific categories. This directory is an extremely picturesque one, displaying photos from the second level (see Figure 5-2).

After you get into the directory, your search options change. From the home page, your search encompasses all of Froogle. On any directory page, you may opt to limit your search to the subcategory at hand. The options below the keyword box (see Figure 5-2) default to limiting the search, but you can searching all of Froogle by clicking the other radio button.

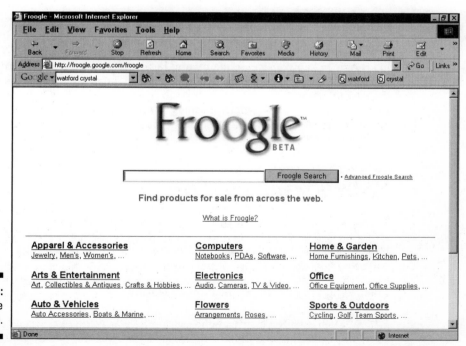

**Figure 5-1:**
The Froogle home page.

**Figure 5-2:**
A second-level page in Froogle, complete with product category photos.

In Froogle, a keyword search is by and large more rewarding than directory browsing. (The general Google Directory of Web sites, on the other hand, dishes out productive pleasures through browsing as well as keyword-targeted searches.) Presumably, when shopping, you have an idea of what you're looking for, and using a keyword gets you to that product page faster than pushing down into the directory.

## Search results in Froogle

Whether through browsing or keyword searching, you eventually reach a Froogle product page (see Figure 5-3). The product page is where you see individual items for sale. They are for sale only through their host sites — not through Google.

The product page contains eight main features:

✔ **Keyword box:** You may launch a new search from any Froogle directory or product page.

✔ **Summary bar:** This familiar feature tells you how long the search took and how items were found.

✔ **Narrow results:** The drop-down menu invites you to trim your results by applying the limits of a Froogle directory category. This menu appears only when you arrive at a product page through a keyword search — it isn't displayed on directory pages, naturally enough. I rarely find the menu useful, because searching by keyword usually gives the most targeted results in the first place.

✔ **Narrow by price:** Now *this* is useful. Specify a price range and click the Go button.

✔ **All products:** Froogle normally lists one search result per store. Click the <u>all products regardless of store</u> link for a more complete list. I find this option unproductive, because for any item you can drill into its store to see all matching products.

✔ **Product name:** The product name is the main link to its page in the host store. You may also click the picture.

✔ **Product description:** Here you find the basic stats: price, store name, and short product description.

✔ **All results from the store:** If the host store contains more product listings matching your keywords, click the <u>See all results from *store name*</u> link to display them.

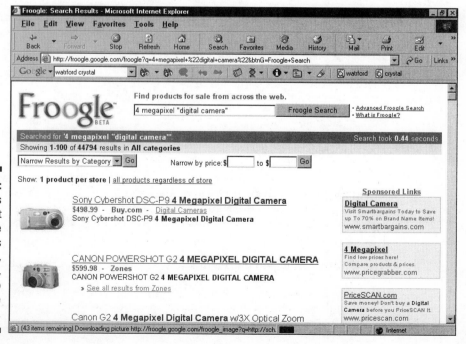

**Figure 5-3:**
Froogle's product page contains thumbnails, descriptions, and ways to narrow the search.

Froogle notices and obeys your general Google settings on the Preferences page (see Chapter 2). If you've set Google to display the maximum 100 listings per results page, Froogle will do so. Also, if you follow my recommendation and set Google to open a new browser window for the target page, Froogle will do so also when displaying an online store that carries the product you clicked. Doing so keeps you anchored at Froogle while you shop around in the target site.

This issue of loading 100 listings per page could be a problem for telephone modem users because Froogle results pages display thumbnail pictures next to nearly every product. A 100-item page is likely to contain 90 to 100 pictures, slowing down the page load considerably. Adjusting your Preferences just to use Froogle might not be worthwhile. My advice is to press the Esc key in Internet Explorer (or click the Stop button in any browser) when you get impatient with a page-loading delay. Doing so stops the page load where it is — in most cases, you will have loaded all the listings but only some of the accompanying pictures. You can always click the Reload button (Ctrl + R in Internet Explorer) if you decide you need the entire page with pictures.

Any so-called Sponsored Links that appear above or to the right of your search results are not part of Froogle's objective search. They are ads purchased by online retailers and information sites keyed to appear on certain search results pages. However, that's not to say you should necessarily ignore them.

## Froogle search operators

Froogle adds a new entry to Google's arsenal of search operators. Chapter 2 introduces Google-specific search operators: words in your keyword string that tell Google how to interpret your keywords. Standard operators that work in all search engines (*AND*, *OR*, *NOT*, and the exact phrase operator) mix with Google-specific operators listed in Chapter 2 to yield highly targeted search results.

In Froogle, three operators (one of them peculiar to Froogle) narrow your shopping search with great effectiveness:

- ✔ **store:** The *store* operator limits matches to particular stores.
- ✔ **allintext:** The *allintext* operator limits matches to product description text.
- ✔ **allintitle:** The *allintitle* operator limits matches to product names.

You look at the *store* operator first because it's special to Froogle and is one powerful little bugger. Using it, you can instantly browse one store's inventory in any product category. For example, type

```
"digital camera" store:bestbuy
```

That search returned 188 results, which can be narrowed by price or by model number. Figure 5-4 illustrates the results after narrowing the preceding search to a price range between $199 and $250. Searching this way saves you the effort of burrowing into the directory for results; you can leap from the Froogle home page directly to a list of items sold in a specific store.

The *store* operator is designed to work when the keyword following it is mashed up against it. Don't put a space between the operator and the keyword.

To effectively use the *store* operator, you must know the Internet domain name of the store. Froogle doesn't understand store names per se, if they differ from the domain names. For example, Home Shopping Network has an e-commerce Web site, and its URL is `www.hsn.com`. Froogle doesn't know anything about Home Shopping Network as a store name, but it does recognize *hsn* as a keyword related to the *store* operator.

You can use the *store* operator in a general way, without using keywords to define a product type, like this:

```
store:bestbuy
```

This search displays every Froogle listing for *bestbuy*, which isn't practical. However, now you can narrow the search, as if you were walking around the aisles of the store, by using Narrow Results by Category and Narrow by price.

**Figure 5-4:**
A tightly honed search in two steps: Use the store operator and then narrow by price range.

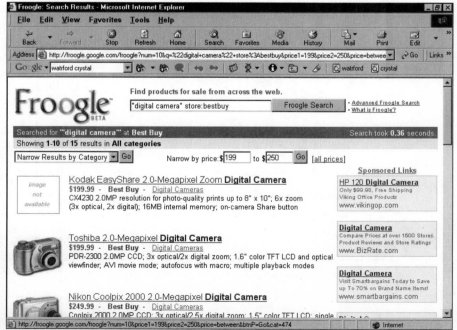

# Price comparisons in Froogle

Froogle can become a handy price-comparison search engine if you know the brand and model number of the item you're shopping for. Even if you don't know that information going in, Froogle can help you compare prices of any product you find while searching. Here's how it works:

1. **On the Froogle home page, start a search for some type of product.**

   In this example, search for *digital camera.*

2. **On the search result page, identify a product you're interested in.**

   Suppose that it's the first item listed in the figure, the Sony Cybershot DSC-P9.

3. **In the search box, type the product brand and model number.**

   To follow along with the example, type Sony Cybershot DSC-P9.

4. **Press Enter to launch your search and view the results, as shown in the figure.**

The search results list contained 968 hits on that product name. Scanning down the list gives you a good idea of the range of retail prices. You can further hone the results by identifying a small price range in the Narrow by price fields. Unfortunately, Froogle does not (yet) enable you to sort search results by price.

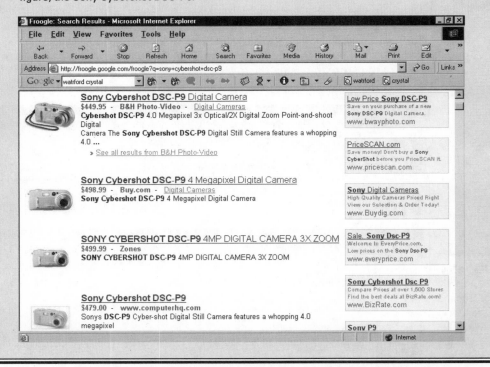

The *allintitle* operator forces Froogle to match your keywords to product names. I find this more useful when using descriptive keywords than when using identifying keywords. For example, the identifying keywords *digital camera* are likely to be in relevant results titles anyway. But if I'm searching for a certain type of digital camera, using this search string narrows the results beautifully:

```
allintitle:4 megapixel
```

In fact, the preceding search string is all you need to get a nicely target list of digital cameras because *megapixel* is a term so closely related to digital cameras. You can further narrow the search to a single store like this:

```
allintitle:4 megapixel store:zones
```

This string yields two 4-megapixel digicams currently on sale at Zones.com.

The *allintext* operator works similarly to *allintitle* but forces Google to look in the product description when matching your keywords. Going for the text instead of the title widens the search and lengthens your results. Use it when you're using keywords that describe product features and those features aren't likely to be part of the product name.

Note that many retailers squeeze lots of information into their product headers in an attempt to position higher on search results lists, because Google and other engines are swayed to some extent by whether keywords appear in titles. So when using *allintext*, your keywords might appear both in the text and in the title. Don't be frustrated — this reality merely encourages you to associate more esoteric keywords with the *allintext* operator.

Think in plain English when you're considering *allintext* keywords. Imagine you're talking to a salesperson in the store, describing features you want to see in a product. Here's an example that continues the digital camera expedition:

```
allintext:preprogrammed exposure mode
```

That search delivered 112 results, ready to be narrowed by price or store.

You may combine the store operator with *allintitle* and *allintext*. Doing so hones your results beautifully. Try this:

```
allintext:preprogrammed exposure mode store:officemart
```

At the time of this writing, that search string delivered the holy Google grail: a single search result (see Figure 5-5). Remember, though, that your search results with *allintext* are not conclusive of what's available. A lot depends on how stores describe their products and, therefore, how their listings appear in Froogle.

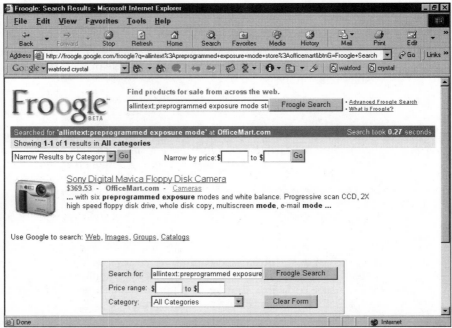

**Figure 5-5:**
Combining
Froogle
operators
narrows
searches
radically.

# Froogle Advanced Search

If you prefer avoiding the use of search operators typed by hand but want to make your searches more powerful, go to the Froogle Advanced Search page. (See Figure 5-6.)

The first section of the page, shaded in green and labeled Find products, operates identically to the Advanced Web Search page described in Chapter 2. This section employs standard search operators to include, exclude, and group keywords in certain ways.

The final three Advanced Search features jockey your keywords in ways described earlier in this chapter:

✔ Use the Price fields to define a price range within which products must fall to enter your search results.

✔ Use the Occurrences drop-down menu to specify whether your keywords should appear in the product name *and* description (the default selection), or just one or the other (the *allintitle* or *allintext* operator, respectively).

✔ Use the Category menu to limit searches to a single Froogle directory category.

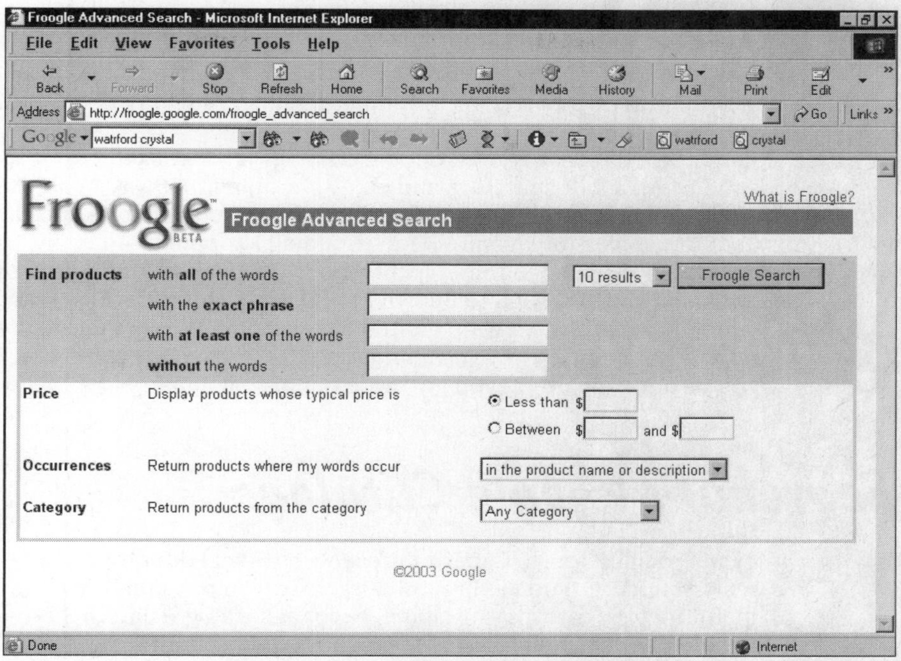

**Figure 5-6:**
Froogle
Advanced
Search
provides the
power of
search
operators in
keyword
and drop-
down
options.

# About Google Catalogs

Most of Google's great ideas depend on behind-the-scenes technology that works invisibly to precisely meet information needs. But one Google service relies more on hard work and continual maintenance than great programming: Google Catalogs, a searchable directory of mail-order catalogs, is brilliant in conception and execution. And keeping it going must require a monumental effort of scanning.

Unlike Google's Web index, which crawls through Web sites and reduces their content to a tagged database controlled by retrieval algorithms, the Google Catalogs index leaves the content in its original format. What you see in this directory are scanned catalog pages, laid out exactly as they would appear at home. Well, you're probably at home. But you know what I mean — you're reading the catalog magazine on the screen.

But there's more. Merely presenting scanned catalog pages would be interesting but ultimately frustrating and unproductive. Google can search every word of the scanned catalog pages, deliver targeted results, and even contrive to highlight your keywords when they appear on the pages. Google has also designed a control bar for thumbing through the catalogs, turning your browser into a specialized e-zine reader.

All in all, Google Catalogs is one of the most underrated features Google offers. You almost never hear people talking about it. Part of the reason is that Internet shopping is more sexy than old-fashioned mail-order. But mail-order is thriving, partly in reaction to the impersonality of e-commerce.

And here's the beauty of it: Google Catalogs is most useful to people who already get a lot of catalogs and enjoy shopping that way. Why? Because nobody gets the range of catalogs Google makes available. And Google Catalogs solves the one problem of catalog shopping — namely, the passiveness of an experience that depends on *waiting* for a catalog to arrive, and then reading it through to find what you want. Google brings searching to a realm that has always been limited to browsing. So whether you're using the Google Catalog viewer to examine a catalog that you regularly receive or one you've never heard of, you get more out of that catalog.

## Searching Google Catalogs

As in Froogle, Google Catalogs presents a topical directory and keyword searching. After you get into the directory, you can limit further searching to that directory category or launch a global Catalogs search. Start at the Google Catalogs home page (see Figure 5-7):

```
catalogs.google.com
```

The directory tempts by listing a few mail-order companies in each main category. Feel free to leap into the directory by clicking either a catalog or a topic on the home page. Figure 5-8 shows the directory page for Photography in the Consumer Electronics category. Note that each catalog is represented by its cover, title, short description, date, and Web link. Google maintains an archive of past catalogs, which can gum up the works when browsing the directory. The Advanced Search page (described shortly) lets you specify current catalogs, but some of them are a bit dusty, too.

Click any catalog cover to see its directory page (Figure 5-9). You get miniature presentations of each two-page spread. Notice, also, the viewer control bar atop the page. Some control bar features appear dimmed in Figure 5-9, but they spring into action when you click one of the pages to see a full-screen representation. I get to that in a minute.

Searching by keyword provides a somewhat different experience. Starting at the home page and entering the keyword string *digital camera* displayed the page shown in Figure 5-10. Here, for each result, you get the catalog cover, a thumbnail of the page matching your keywords, and a zoomed-in shot of the portion of that page containing your keyword.

**Figure 5-7:**
The Google Catalogs home page. Search by product keyword or browse by mail-order house.

**Figure 5-8:**
A Catalogs directory page, showing covers, dates, and Web links.

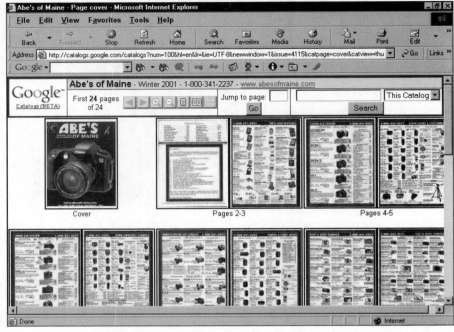

**Figure 5-9:**
Each catalog directory page contains thumbnails of that catalog's two-page spreads. Click a thumbnail to zoom in.

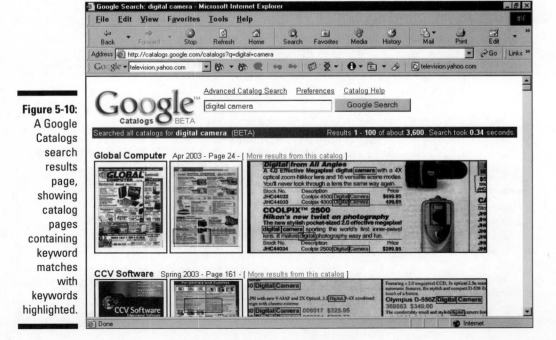

**Figure 5-10:**
A Google Catalogs search results page, showing catalog pages containing keyword matches with keywords highlighted.

Note the rectangular highlighting on the middle page, indicating the portion zoomed on the right. This, ladies and gentlemen, is fantastic search technology, blowing away the search engine for scanned documents at ProQuest, an expensive research service. Each of these three images is a thumbnail; click for a larger view. (The second and third thumbnails give you the same large view.)

Google normally display just one search result from each catalog. Click the More results from this catalog link above the items that *do* offer more hits to see a complete list.

Let's look at the larger view. Click either the second or third thumbnail to get the entire page, as in Figure 5-11. Things get really interesting on this page, because the Google Catalogs control bar kicks into action. This viewing assistant appears at the top of each page as you browse the catalog, allowing you to move from page to page, zoom, choose one-page, two-page, or four-page view, jump to pages, and conduct new searches.

Here's a rundown of the control bar's features:

- **Title bar:** Atop the control bar is a summary of where you are and how to purchase things. It includes the catalog title, its publication date, the company's mail-order phone number, and its Web URL. Remember that the Web sites for mail-order companies are not necessarily e-commerce sites. Even when they are, they sometimes carry different inventory and prices.

- **Page indicator:** To the left of the control buttons, this indicator tells you what catalog page you're currently viewing.

- **Page buttons:** Click the arrow buttons to move forward and backward by one page. (Or by two pages, if the two-page view is selected, or by four pages if the four-page view is selected.)

- **Zoom buttons:** Use these buttons to zoom in to, and out of, the page. Zooming in (the plus sign) magnifies a portion of the page. Clicking any portion of the page accomplishes the same zoom. You can zoom in twice.

- **Page view buttons:** You can view one page at a time, two-page spreads, or thumbnails of four pages at once. I prefer the two-page spread, zooming in as necessary. Large monitors running at high resolutions (at least 1024 x 800) are particularly suited to the two-page view (see Figure 5-12).

- **Jump to page:** Enter a page number and click the Go button. Using this feature is akin to flipping through a published catalog. If you're viewing in two-page or four-page thumbnail view, Google keeps that view, with your selected page as the first page of the spread.

- **Search:** Using the drop-down menu, you can launch a search of the catalog at hand or all catalogs — or you can leap over to a general Web search.

**Figure 5-11:**
An expanded catalog page with the Google Catalogs control bar ready for browsing.

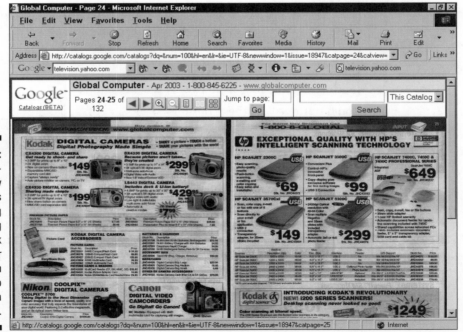

**Figure 5-12:**
The two-page view makes catalog browsing easier. Click a page or use a zoom button to magnify a page.

Google Catalogs recognizes your general Preferences settings that govern the behavior of Google Web search. If you set the number of results per page at 100 (the maximum), you'll get 100 search results in Google Catalogs, which is probably the most graphics-intense portion of Google. Even with a high-speed connection, loading a results page with 3 images per result can cause delays. The solution, as I suggested previously when describing Froogle, is to stop the page load before it's finished (press the Esc key in Internet Explorer), and reload the page if you end up needing the entire page of results.

You can request the addition of any catalog you don't find in Google Catalogs. Use the online request form located here:

```
catalogs.google.com/googlecatalogs/add_catalog.html
```

Or you can mail a request, using an archaic institution called the post office, to this address:

> Google Catalogs
>
> 171 Main St. #280A
>
> Los Altos, CA 94022

Before requesting additions to the Google Catalogs index, be sure your request doesn't already exist in the index. Don't count on browsing or haphazard search results — search directly for the catalog by name. In fact, searching for catalogs, not products, is a good way to review all recent issues of that catalog.

# Advanced Catalogs Searching

The truth is, advanced searching in Google Catalogs isn't as powerful as other Advanced Search pages. The reason for the simplicity of advanced searching is that the Google Catalogs search engine doesn't offer any special search operators. So the Advanced Catalogs Search page, shown in Figure 5-13, is useful mostly for invoking standard search operators without having to know them. Chapter 2 describes these operators (*AND*, *OR*, *NOT*, and the exact phrase operator) in detail.

The instructions in the Find results portion of the Advanced Search page might be self-explanatory; if not, please refer to the detailed description in Chapter 2.

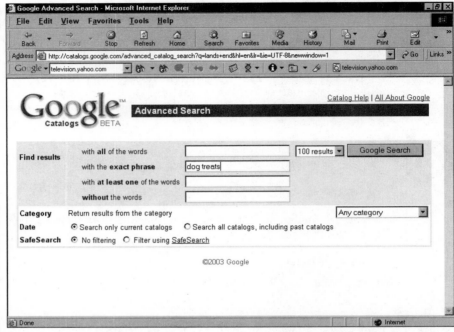

**Figure 5-13:**
The
Advanced
Search
page for
Google
Catalogs.

# Chapter 6

# Searching the Specialty Categories

## In This Chapter

▶ Finding your way to Google specialty searches

▶ Tips for using the U.S. government search engine

▶ Searching the Linux and BSD worlds

▶ Using the Apple Macintosh and Microsoft search engines

▶ University searching

*T*ake Google's hand and let it lead you into a specialized universe or two. Or three, or four, or five. Google has created alternate search engines whose results are limited to certain subject areas. Google accomplishes this topical restriction by choosing source sites that effectively contribute to search results. On the technical side, Google has isolated the worlds of Linux, BSD, Apple Macintosh, and Microsoft. Each of these areas enjoys a dedicated engine that searches sites provided by these organizations or related to them.

To me, the most interesting specialty search is the one devoted to the U.S. government and related fields of military, local government, and global government. Google playfully refers to this search engine as UncleSam.

Rounding out the specialty categories is a large group of university-specific search engines, each of which prowls through a single college or university Web site. This mission is less limiting than you might think, because students and professors stash all kinds of documents on the school's computers.

This chapter is mostly recreational, unless you have a professional interest in one of these subjects. The sites are Google experiments that you get to play with. Having said that, though, I find myself returning to the UncleSam engine over and over for truly productive specialty searches.

# Finding the Specialty Searches

Following its quiet tradition of refusing to promote its fringe features, Google buries its specialty services, perhaps discouraging regular use. You can get to the search engines described in this chapter through the main Google home page, but you have to know where to click and the procedure is tiresome. Your online lifestyle is too busy for excessive mouse clicks. You have virtual places to go and ephemeral people to meet. Chips to devour and soda to drink. This section provides some tips for quickly reaching the government, BSD, Linux, Mac, Microsoft, and university search pages.

## Knowing the specialty URLs

First, the URLs of the specialty search pages. The direct Web addresses are so easy to remember (with the exception of the university page) that your preferred method might be to simply type the URL in your browser's address bar. Here are the addresses, which point self-evidently to their respective search pages:

```
www.google.com/bsd
www.google.com/linux
www.google.com/unclesam
www.google.com/mac
www.google.com/microsoft
```

The university page is perplexingly more obscure, but if you have a good memory it doesn't pose much of a problem:

```
www.google.com/options/universities.html
```

Yes, you *do* need to type the .html at the end. Another option is to leap directly to the search page for a specific university by constructing a URL like this:

```
www.google.com/univ/princeton
www.google.com/univ/nyu
```

Notice that some universities are abbreviated, requiring some guesswork on your part. But most names are fairly obvious. Frustratingly, this address

```
www.google.com/univ
```

does not deliver the main university search page, though it is the basis of specific university pages.

## *Specialty searching from the Google Toolbar*

An easier way to get to the specialty search pages than typing URLs exists for Google Toolbar users. (See Chapter 9, which asserts that *everybody* should be a Google Toolbar user. That means you.) You need to put the Combined Search button on the Google Toolbar, if it isn't there already. That button's usefulness is described fully in Chapter 9.

For now, our purpose is just to find those specialty search pages. The following steps assume you have the Google Toolbar installed on your browser, but don't have the Combined Search button.

1. **Click the Google button on the Google Toolbar and choose Toolbar Options from the drop-down menu.**

   The Google Toolbar Options page appears.

2. **Scroll down and click the <u>experimental features</u> link.**

   The Google Toolbar Experimental Features page appears.

3. **Under Combined Search button, click the check box.**

   It's up to you to decide whether you want to click the second check box, which governs whether the Combined Search button remembers your last search destination. See Chapter 9 for more about this feature.

4. **Click the OK button.**

   The Combined Search button appears instantly on the Google Toolbar.

5. **Click the small arrow next to the Combined Search button.**

6. **On the drop-down menu, click one of the specialty search categories.**

   You don't need to enter a keyword into the toolbar's search box, though of course you may. Clicking the search category without a keyword displays the search page for that category. Using a keyword displays a search results page within that category. The specialty search category for universities does not appear under the Combined Search button.

# *U.S. Government Searches*

Arguably, the most useful of Google's specialty search areas is that devoted to the U.S. government. Actually, this distinct search engine is both larger and smaller than the name implies. This engine is global in reach. At the same time, it reaches below federal government sites to the state and municipal level.

You might think that this entire search engine merely replaces the *site:.gov* operator:keyword combination described in Chapter 2. Not so. In fact, *site:.gov* remains quite useful in the UncleSam search because the results pages dish up a hearty mix of *gov*, *mil* (for military), and *com* sites that bear some relation to government, public policy, law, defense, and other fields of administration, the judiciary, and the legislature. All domain extensions are represented here.

The best way to get a feel for the blend of results you get in the U.S. government search is to throw in some keywords and let it rip. Don't think too hard about it — any keywords will do. Try generic, common words that you'd use in a general Web search, such as *internet* or *music* or *paris vacation*. Or, choose newsy words such as *bush* or *terrorism* or *treaty*.

Use the results of your search to find Web sites that you can later search with the *site* operator. You can perform such a search in a general or UncleSam Web search. In fact, some of these discovered sites might make it to your bookmark list for regular visitation. The following are some examples of interesting sites that turn up in UncleSam searches:

```
speaker.house.gov
freedom.house.gov
democraticleader.house.gov
memory.loc.gov
gop.gov
```

Many related domains are too numerous and related to list, such as state government sites and the sites of individual House members.

Searching on issues and hot phrases can reveal who in the government (individuals, agencies, committees) is involved in that issue. Some examples include:

```
pledge of allegiance
fcc deregulation
abortion legislation
```

These searches display sites of agencies and members of congress, in addition to more general information pages.

All the specialty search engines recognize the same search operators you use in a normal Web search (see Chapter 2). I often use the *filetype* operator to search for PDF files in the U.S. government area, plumbing a rich trove of Congressional hearing transcriptions, court judgments, and other official documents that are customarily posted online in PDF format. Using *filetype:pdf* transforms any search; try adding it after any keyword string. For example:

```
music hearings filetype:pdf
housing starts filetype:pdf
testimony military filetype:pdf
consumer confidence filetype:pdf
```

The *intitle* and *allintitle* operators also work well in UncleSam searches. In fact, combining the power of those operators with the *filetype:pdf* combination is particularly fruitful because PDF files are usually titled so carefully — far more carefully than Web pages. Get specific with the title words. These examples have worked well to sharply narrow results:

```
allintitle:bush tax cut filetype:pdf
allintitle:social security future filetype:pdf
allintitle:iraq reconstruction filetype:pdf
```

The preceding examples also work nicely — and quite differently — without the *filetype:pdf* addition.

 Think about using keywords that are applicable to different fields of inquiry, such as *testimony* or *"congressional hearing"* or *policy*. Putting almost anything after one of those yields fertile results; try *music, movies, abortion, taxes, airlines* paired with one of them.

# Linux and BSD Searches

Linux is the open-source operating system that has been making waves for the past few years. Linux is much older than that, but it's only in recent years that developers have created ready-for-primetime versions of Linux and it has been loaded into computers selling in mainstream stores. Linux loyalists regard their operating system as a dynamic competitor of Microsoft Windows. Nobody owns Linux, though several companies own their respective operating system products based on Linux. Accordingly, Linux really refers to a family of operating systems, all built on the same foundation and with similar features.

BSD is also an open-source family of operating systems, based on Unix. BSD got its start at Berkeley, and the acronym stands for Berkeley Software Distribution. BSD has less prominence in the consumer marketplace than Linux does, but BSD servers (operating systems for Internet and intranet computers) are in fairly wide use.

 The term *open source* refers to any software authoring project operating in the public domain. Anyone may grab the code of such a project and alter it. Normally, open-source projects are organized to some extent, by volunteer programmers who work on the program either as a hobby or as a potential profession. By definition, open-source software code is not owned. But in most cases an individual or company is free to make a commercial product from a proprietary version of the software.

If you have no interest in Linux, BSD, operating systems, or the open-source movement, the Linux and BSD specialty search areas might not be of much interest. If you want to take an interest, either search site is a good place to find out about the history and current state of Linux or BSD. As with the U.S. government search site, the BSD and Linux engines both forage in a restricted universe of relevant Web sources.

One fun experiment, even for those with merely a passing interest in these subjects, is to search for *microsoft windows* in the Linux engine. One recent search turned up, as the first result, a source site for obtaining Windows refunds. (No bashing intended — I run a Windows-only household. I'm just easily amused.)

# Mac and Microsoft Searches

Apple Macintosh and Microsoft Windows: two operating system behemoths representing a fundamental polarity in the computer world. Nobody can claim that the Mac is a behemoth in terms of market share, because Apple sells less than 5 percent of all new computers. But when it comes to ferocious loyalty and PR stamina, Apple owns world-class clout. Google has assembled a trove of Web sources relating to each system and segregated them into distinct search engines.

A favorite game of mine (I am *very* easily amused) is to open two browser windows, one for the Mac search engine and one for the Microsoft search engine. Then I search both for the same terms. Try *internet explorer*, *ipod*, *"steve jobs"*, and *"bill gates"*. Compare results for mind-twisting alternative perspectives. Good times!

Because Apple and Microsoft both maintain substantial Web domains, those pages tend to appear disproportionately. Get around this by using a minus sign, which is the symbol for the NOT operator (see Chapter 2). When searching the Mac engine, blot out *microsoft.com*, and when searching the Mac site eradicate *apple.com*. Here are two example search strings:

```
itunes specifications -site:apple.com
windows 98 networking -site:microsoft.com
```

You can override the limitations of the Mac and Microsoft search engines by using the *site* operator, pointing it to any site. This is a marginally useful tip, granted, but there might be a time when you want to break out of Macland or Microsoftville by searching another site without tracking your way back to the Google home page. Of course, this point is superfluous if you use the Google Toolbar. Are you using the Google Toolbar? You should be. See Chapter 9 for more tiresome exhortations.

# University Searches

High school seniors take note: Google has your search engine. The University specialty searches let you rummage through a single university's Web site with the power of Google's search algorithms and operators.

University search operates differently than the other specialty searches described in this chapter. Google does not aggregate many university sites for searching. And this is not a search engine for getting information *about* universities in general. Instead, Google has actually created dozens of small search engines, each dedicated to a single university Web domain.

Useful? Well . . . this specialized search helps if you repeatedly search in a certain college site. Or, if you learn the URL syntax I divulge in the first section of this chapter, you can seamlessly surf around from one specialty university engine to another.

You can avoid the inconvenient trip to Google's university search pages by using the *site* operator, assuming you know a university URL. Virtually all university site domains end with the *.edu* extension, so you need to know the primary domain name, which is often easy to guess. Let's say you want to search for keywords matching inside Princeton's site. A simple (and correct) guess of Princeton's domain is *princeton.edu*. So this keyword string

```
admissions policies site:www.princeton.edu
```

gets you the links you want from the Google home page or Toolbar.

Remember, also, that you can conduct a search across all educational domains by using the *.edu* extension with the *site* operator, like this:

```
undergraduate stress site:edu
```

But let's not diverge too far from the straight and narrow. You can always approach the university specialty search sites the way Google intended:

1. **Go to the following page:**

   ```
   www.google.com/options/universities.html
   ```

2. **Click the university link you want to search.**

   All the universities links are contained on this single, long page. Scroll down or click an alphabet link to leap ahead.

3. **On the resulting search page, launch your search in the regular fashion.**

   All results links point to pages in that university's Web site.

Not all colleges and universities are represented in these search engines, by a long stretch. I sometimes visit Rollins College in Winter Park, Florida, and am disappointed that it's missing from Google's college list. But this is when using the *site* operator is handy; because I know the Rollins domain is `rollins.edu`, I can search it from Google's home page or the Toolbar at any time.

The university search engines are not affiliated with the universities. Go directly to the university Web site for a glossier presentation of the school.

# Chapter 7

# Searching for Answers

*In This Chapter*

▶ Creating a Google Answers account

▶ Posting and canceling questions

▶ Adding comments and joining conversations

▶ Clarifying questions and evaluating answers

▶ Writing effective questions and setting appropriate prices

As if Google weren't already a fount of knowledge, a service called Google Answers provides custom research. One of two Google services that isn't free (the other is AdWords, described in Chapter 11), Google Answers lets you set the price for expert advice, facts, and linkage.

This chapter covers every aspect of Google Answers — from creating an account to posting a question, from setting a price to rating the answers. Don't blow off this chapter, no matter how against the Google grain it might seem. Even if you're a veteran Googler who never needs research assistance, knowing your way around Google Answers (if only its directory archive of previously posted queries) can be invaluable. And if you're a budding researcher with no interest in paying someone else, this chapter shows you how you can sharpen your skills by observing Google Answers in action.

## Paying for Google Expertise

In the background, behind your screen, next to the heaving mass that is the living Google index, resides a freelance staff of human researchers approved by Google to track down the answers to specific queries. Whereas keyword search queries display automated search results — basically page after page of links — Google Answer queries result in conversations and expert answers.

This staff of researchers is screened rigorously by Google for informational agility and communicativeness. They are paid 75 percent of the fees assigned by users to their posted questions. Google gets the other 25 percent. Researchers are not assigned to certain questions; they claim them, based on area of expertise and willingness to tackle the query's needs.

The next section establishes how you create a Google Answers account. Creating an account allows you to participate in one free aspect of Google Answers: posting comments to questions. (Later in the chapter I offer guidelines for this type of participation.) Creating the account does not obligate you to pay a research fee or post a question. In fact, there's no need to provide credit card information until you post your first question, at which point you're prompted for it.

# Creating an Account and Logging In

The main purpose (at first, anyway) to creating a Google Answers account is to get an ID. The ID enables you to post a comment to somebody's question and be recognized by the system. Then, when you're ready, you can add payment information to your account and post your own question. To get the ID, follow these steps:

1. **Go to the Google Accounts page at this address:**

   `www.google.com/accounts/NewAccount`

2. **Enter your e-mail address and a password.**

   The password must contain at least six characters.

3. **Check the box indicating that you agree to Google's Terms of Service (TOS) statement and Privacy Policy.**

   The TOS is a standard set of agreements: you won't use Google for commercial purposes; you won't troll the index with automated software searchers; Google is not responsible for what you might find in a search; and Google is not responsible if a terrible heat wave causes your geraniums to wither.

   The Privacy Policy (also explained in Chapter 2) divulges that Google places cookies (software trackers) in your computer; that the cookies send anonymous usage data to Google; that Google shares or publishes the collected information but does not release personal information; and that Google promises not to rummage through your underwear drawer.

4. **Click the Create My Google Account button.**

   Google now sends an e-mail verification notice to the address you entered, to verify that it is indeed *your* e-mail address. You need to click a link in that e-mail. Note that (at this writing) the e-mail message comes with a confusing identifier: "accounts-noreply@google.com." Yes, it would be more easily recognizable as a crucial piece of e-mail if the From sender were simply "Google." As it is, the e-mail looks at first glance like a piece of spam, so be careful of your deletions when looking for it.

5. **Click the link provided in the body of the e-mail.**

6. **Back in the browser, which has changed to a different page, click the <u>Click here to continue</u> link.**

   Your e-mail program might open a new browser window, depending on your settings.

7. **On the Google Answers: Sign Up page, type a nickname and select your e-mail notification level.**

   Your e-mail choices are to receive a notice whenever any activity occurs on a question you've asked, a single daily notice whether or not any activity has occurred, or nothing. My choice is the first.

8. **Click the I accept box, indicating your agreement with the Google Answers Terms of Service.**

   This is a paid service, and you might want to read the TOS more diligently than you do those pertaining to free services. The statement includes warranty information, details on how your account is billed, the refund policy, a lot of disclaimers about the nonprofessional nature of the service's financial and medical information, and a declaration that, should you become stupider by using Google Answers, Google will not supply you with smart drugs. Click your browser's Back button to return to the Google Answers: Sign Up page.

9. **Click the Create My Google Answers Account button.**

   Your account is activated at this point, and you are deposited on the Google Answers: My Questions page.

The Google Answers: My Questions page (see Step 9) is accessible with the <u>My Account</u> link on any Google Answers page.

*Note:* Whenever your Google Answers nickname appears on the screen, the following hyphenated suffix is attached to it: -ga. So if your chosen nickname is mynkcname, your on-screen nickname is mynickname-ga. This alteration identifies you in the Google Answers portion of your Google Account, which covers a few different services.

Creating a Google Answers account does not authorize Google to collect fees from you. Note, in the preceding steps, that Google does not require your credit card information to establish the account. However, you can't post a question (see the following section) without providing payment information.

# *Posting and Canceling Questions*

Posting a question to Google Answers is simple enough, but never free. For putting a question in play, the minimum charges are

- ✔ A $0.50 listing fee
- ✔ A fee between $2.00 and $200.00, determined by you and paid to the researcher

So the least you can pay to get a question on the board is $2.50. The listing fee is credited to Google at the time of posting. The researcher's fee is charged when an expert answers your question — no answer, no payment.

Your credit card is charged on a schedule determined by your balance and the time of month. If you run up listing fees and researchers' fees come due of $25.00 or more, your credit card is hit for the full amount. If your due balance stays under $25.00, Google collects the dough once a month. Remember, researchers' fees come due not when you ask a question, but when you get an answer.

When you created your Google Answers account (see the preceding section) you did not provide credit card information or any other way for Google to bill you. Google Answers fees are always paid by credit card. You can't post a question without providing that information. There's no point in providing it *before* you ask a question, so the following steps assume that you've sat down at the computer, opened up your browser, and want to post your first question to Google Answers.

1. **Go to the main Google Answers page at** answers.google.com **or use the Google Toolbar (see Chapter 9) to select Google Answers under the Google button.**

2. **Click the <u>Log in or Create a Google Account</u> link.**

3. **Assuming you have created a Google Account (see the preceding section), log in with your e-mail address and password.**

4. **On your account page, click the <u>Ask a Question</u> link.**

   You can also begin setting up your payment information by clicking the <u>My Profile</u> link. But proceeding directly to Ask a Question takes you through the credit card process, too.

5. **On the Ask a Question page (see Figure 7-1), fill in the Subject, Question, and Price fields, and select a Category.**

   This seems a lot like work, doesn't it? It's worth it. For more about how to fill in these fields and maximize your chances of getting the answer you need at the price you want to pay, see the next section of this chapter.

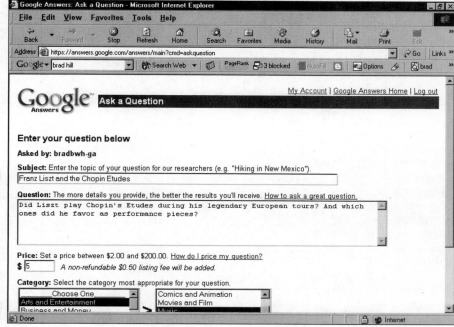

**Figure 7-1:**
Ask your question, title it, set a price, and choose a category all on this page.

6. **Click the Continue to payment information button.**

   You might be asked to enter your Google Account password again. No need to include the -ga suffix.

7. **On the Google Answers: Enter Payment page, fill in your credit card and billing information.**

8. **Click the Pay listing fee and post question button.**

   If you click this button, the listing fee of 50 cents immediately becomes collectible by Google. You may also use the Go back and edit question button to reword your query or set a different price. The preview posting of your question as currently worded and priced is displayed below the buttons.

That's it — your question is immediately posted. Click the <u>View your question</u> link on the confirmation page to see what you did. Figure 7-2 shows a posted question. Note that the time of posting and the expiration date are both listed. Questions remain posted, unanswered, for one month. Answered questions remain in the Google Answers directory permanently.

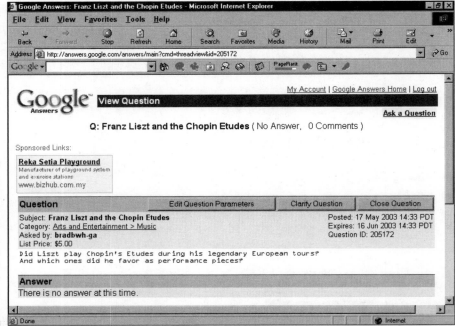

Figure 7-2:
A question
posted to
Google
Answers,
viewed on
the poster's
View
Question
page.

The View Question page contains enough features to warrant a closer look:

- ✔ You might see sponsored links on your View Question page (see Figure 7-2). Other Googlers see them, too. Google's AdWords program (see Chapter 11) positions these paid links throughout the service, not just on the search results page, where they are prevalent.

- ✔ Use the Edit Question Parameters button to adjust the wording of your question or the price you're offering for an answer. You may continue to tweak your words and price until the moment a Google researcher claims the question. Once claimed, the question is locked in place — Figure 7-3 shows what you see when you click the Edit Question Parameters for a claimed question.

- ✔ Use the Clarify Question button to add information to your question that would help a researcher better answer it. You can do so at any time.

- ✔ Use the Close Question button if you change your mind and no longer want to receive a paid-for answer. On the following page, simply click the Yes, Close Question button. Or if you're truly indecisive and now want to keep your question alive, click the No, Keep Question button.

If you close the question, it remains posted, but researchers can't claim it. And although you don't have to pay for an answer, you do still owe Google 50 cents for posting the question in the first place.

✔ Below your posted question is space for the answer (which, when it comes in, is as publicly viewable as your question) and space below that for comments from other Googlers. You don't pay for comments from the peanut gallery.

You may post as many questions as you like. Manage your questions, billing profile, and invoice information on your Google Answers account page, which is available through the My Account link on every Google Answers page.

A fair amount of dialogue can ensue between the person who posted a question and the researcher(s). In some cases, a second researcher joins the party. Researchers may seek to clarify questions, just as users may seek to clarify answers, so more than one researcher might be attempting to clarify a question before one of them finally claims and answers it.

Figure 7-4 illustrates a posted question with a researcher's request for clarification.

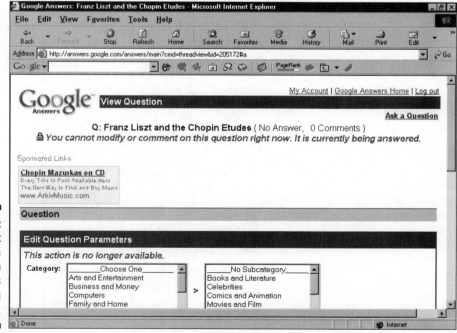

**Figure 7-3:** You can't modify a question in the process of being answered.

## Locked questions

A posted question is *locked* when a researcher has claimed it and is working on the answer. The lock remains in place for two hours, during which time a small padlock icon appears next to the question in the Answers directory. If the researcher doesn't post an answer after two hours, the question reverts to open status.

Locked questions do not prohibit comments, though, so if you have something worthwhile to contribute to a posted and locked question, go for it. Just click the question, and then click the Add a Comment button to display a form in which you type your comment. More on this later in the chapter.

Further down the page (Figure 7-5), the user clarifies the question, and the clarification is met with two more requests for clarification, from two researchers. This back-and-forth continues a bit, until one of the researchers (the second one to ask for clarification) claims the question and posts an answer (Figure 7-6).

Satisfied with the answer, the user rates the answer and tips the researcher (Figure 7-7).

**Figure 7-4:** An exchange begins with a posted question and a researcher's request for clarification.

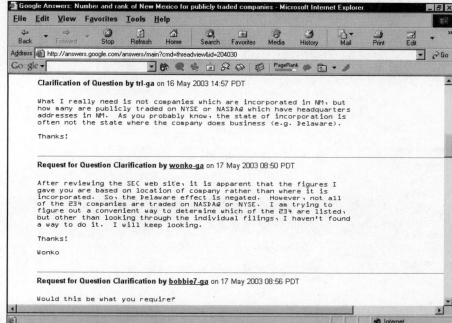

**Figure 7-5:**
A second researcher joins the conversation with a new request for clarification.

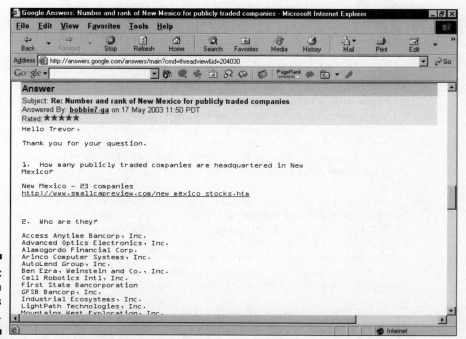

**Figure 7-6:**
Finally, an answer is posted.

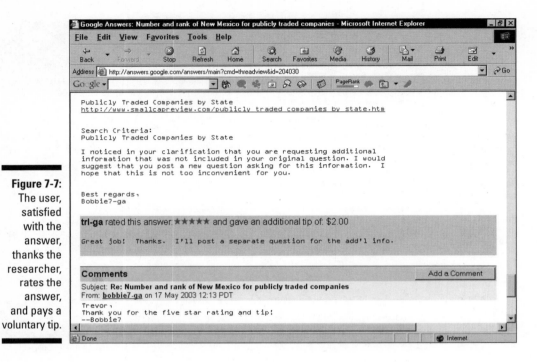

**Figure 7-7:**
The user,
satisfied
with the
answer,
thanks the
researcher,
rates the
answer,
and pays a
voluntary tip.

# Comments and Conversations

A lot of clarifying goes on in Google Answers, both before and after a researcher gets hold of your question. The system is devised to encourage conversation and cooperation between user and researcher. It's not Jeopardy. Flexibility is built into the system to increase the chance of satisfaction on both sides. Because of the conversational nature of the Google Answers system, combined with the eagerness to share knowledge shown by Google researchers and other users browsing posted questions, you can often find the information you want (or some of it) without getting a formal answer to your posted question.

Anybody can add a comment to a posted question, and the authors of added comments are not identified as researchers or regular users. The result is an information milieu in which everyone is sharing what they know. The trick is to distinguish between good information and bad information — an issue that can be universally applied to the Internet. Many Google Answer comments, and nearly all official answers, are documented with links to research sites, which helps establish their authenticity.

Figure 7-8 shows an open question followed by a comment. The illustration cannot be large enough to reveal that, in fact, four comments were posted to the question, which still doesn't have an official answer. The question is a historical one and difficult to answer definitively, preventing any researcher from finding a quick, definitive answer and claiming the payment. Still, the comments furnish much useful, fascinating information, plus links for questioners to explore on their own.

It might sometimes happen that your question gets essentially answered by comments, without an official researcher's answer. This development is somewhat rare in the case of specific, data-oriented questions, which researchers jump on with dizzying speed. But it's not so uncommon when a question requires deep research or has multiple answers. (Figure 7-8 illustrates such a situation with the Franz Liszt historical question.)

If you're satisfied with the posted comments your question has attracted and no longer need an official answer, feel free to close the question by following these steps:

1. **Click the <u>My Account</u> link on any Google Answers page.**

2. **Click the link to your question.**

   You might have more than one posted question. Use the drop-down menu to narrow your list, if necessary, by choosing Questions Awaiting Answers.

3. **On your questions' page, click the Close Question button (see Figure 7-2).**

   The page reloads with a confirmation notice at the top, asking whether you are sure that you want to close the question.

4. **Click the Yes, Close Question button.**

   After closing a question, that question appears on your Google Answers account page, with CLOSED in the Status column (see Figure 7-9).

All the back-and-forth discussion following a posted question can make Google Answers seem almost like a message board. Almost. The conversations are not *threaded* as a message board is, meaning you can't see at a glance who is responding to whom in Google Answers. However, the similarity to message boards brings up an interesting point: If you can get good information from informal comments in Google Answers, maybe you can likewise get questions answered on message boards elsewhere. That, in fact, is partly what Usenet newsgroups are all about, and Google provides the preeminent Web interface to Usenet newsgroups. Chapter 4 dives into Google Groups in excruciating detail. The point here is that, in general, informal knowledge sharing on the Internet can be as good as paid expertise, and there are many venues in which to get it.

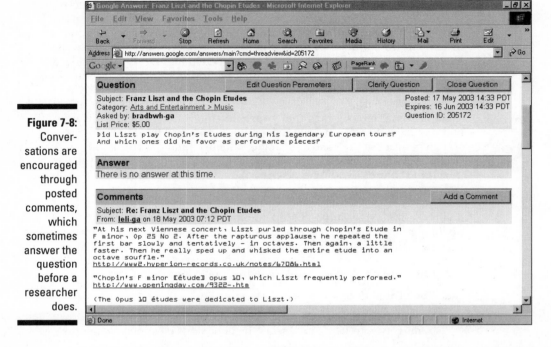

**Figure 7-8:**
Conver-
sations are
encouraged
through
posted
comments,
which
sometimes
answer the
question
before a
researcher
does.

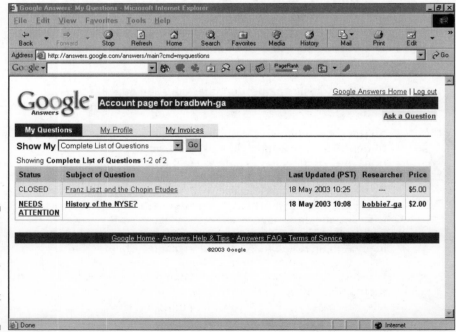

**Figure 7-9:**
Closed
questions
still appear
on the
account
page.

## Improving your own research

Although Google Answers is used by people who — due to lack of time, expertise, or interest — don't want to perform their own research, the service provides a sort of tutorial on research as a side benefit. Even if you never post a question, just reading the questions, comments, and answers of others can furnish great researching ideas. The researchers tend to use Google as a starting point (hardly a surprise), and they often divulge their search strings, complete with operators, at the bottom of the answer. A bit of study, especially directed toward some of the long, detailed answers, can improve anyone's search skills.

The great values of Google Answers are these:

✔ **Speed:** Google staffs the Answers section with hundreds of researchers, each waiting to pounce on a question and claim its payment. Most questions, unless they are hopelessly obscure, start drawing information within hours — sometimes minutes.

✔ **Accuracy:** Google Answers pops into my mind when I have an extremely detailed question. Surfing the Answers directory, you can see that such question receive hard work and good results from researchers, who seem to enjoy sinking their teeth into a sharply defined information challenge.

Newsgroups can also be fast and accurate, but they yield a more slapdash experience, replete with conversational sideshows and a generally impatient and grumpy attitude. Google Answers is a cleaned-up, more polite, and far more literate arena for extracting information than Usenet newsgroups. You get what you pay for, I suppose, with the bonus that sometimes Google Answers does its best work for nothing more than the 50-cent listing fee.

# Evaluating Answers and Clarifying Questions

You can interact with the Google Answers service on three levels:

✔ **Waiting for an answer:** You've posted a question and await a researcher's answer.

✔ **Received an answer:** You've posted a question and a researcher answered it.

✔ **No question:** You're browsing questions posted by others.

Each level offers options, covered in this section.

## Clarifying and modifying a question

Earlier in this chapter I described how to formulate and post a question. Doing so is the first of four options available to the Answers user requesting expertise:

- **Ask:** Posting a question is always the first step.

- **Modify:** You may change the wording, title, category, or pricing of your question while it's still in open status. Click the question title on your account page, and then use the Edit Question Parameters button.

- **Clarify:** You may adjust your question while it's still in open status. Click the question title on your account page, and then use the Clarify Question button.

- **Comment:** You may respond to comments posted to your question, as long as the question's status remains open. Click the question title on your account page, and then use the Add a Comment button. This button appears only after somebody comments on your question.

## Fine-tuning and rating answers

When you receive an answer to a posted question, your have four options:

- **Request clarification:** If an answer isn't satisfactory, you may request further work from the researcher. Use this option with great discretion! Its purpose is not to squeeze out more information than you originally asked for. If your question was unclear, you can acknowledge such and ask for a bit more writing from your expert. Likewise, if the answer is unclear, you have every right to ask for a clarification. Click the question title on your account page, and then use the Request Answer Clarification button.

- **Rate the answer:** Usually, the final step in the conversation between you and the researcher is to rate the answer. For some reason, most people don't feel motivated to assign a rating other than five stars. If you're unsatisfied with the answer, the best approach is to request clarification. But no matter how you feel at the end, you're free to rate the experience you paid for. Click the question title on your account page, and then click the Rate Answer button.

- **Tip your expert:** Exceptional answers deserve, perhaps, more than you originally agreed to pay. A tipping system is built into Google Answers. Tip amounts can be between $1.00 and $100.00. The money is charged to the same credit card you have on file in your Answers account. Click the question title on your account page, click the Rate Answer button, and then fill in the amount of your optional tip. Click the Submit Rating button to post your rating and authorize your tip. Both the rating and the tip amount are publicly viewable.

✔ **Request reposting or refund:** For the truly disgruntled user, requesting a refund is the last resort. You may issue the complaint and be finished with it, or you may ask for a price credit and also for your question to be reposted as a new, open question.

The tip is optional. Even though it is bundled onto the rating page, do not feel pressured to issue a tip with your rating — they are different, independent options. Perhaps the implied linkage between the two is why Google Answers experts don't get more ratings.

## Adding a comment

When cruising through Google Answers as an interested observer, with no open questions of your own, you may participate by posting comments to the queries of others. You can join the conversation on both open and closed questions, whether they have been answered by a researcher or not. Everyone in Google Answers is of equal status when it comes to posting comments. Simply click the title of any question, and then click the Add a Comment button.

---

# Refunds and repostings

In the rare event that a Google Answers expert lets you down completely, your recourse is to apply for a price refund. You have two options, actually:

✔ Apply for a refund. Getting a refund closes the question to all further activity, including comments.

✔ Apply for a credit for the amount of your expert payment, plus a reposting of the question. Getting the credit reposts the question for research by a different expert. The second 50-cent listing fee is waived.

Both options are included in one online form. You must go to this page:

```
http://answers.google.
    com/answers/main?cmd=
    refundrequest
```

If you don't want to copy that rather long URL, find the link by clicking the <u>Answers FAQ</u> link, which is listed at the bottom of every Answers page.

Choose Repost My Question or Request a Refund radio button, and explain why you think either option should happen. You need to include the question ID, which is located on the question's page, not your account page. (Figure 7-8 shows a question ID.)

It might sound obvious, but don't add a comment unless you have something worthwhile — and germane to the query — to say. This isn't a message board in the Net-culture sense, so don't indulge in "Me too!" posts, or merely express your interest in the question at hand. Contribute information that helps answer the question, clarifies the subject, or somehow increases knowledge for everyone reading, especially the person who posted the question.

# Good Questions at the Right Prices

The best way to maximize your Google Answers experience is to ask the right question, at the right price. Asking a difficult, multi-part question and offering $2.00 for its answer might not attract the best — or any — researchers. Offering $30.00 for the answer to a simple question will create a researcher feeding frenzy, but leave you feeling ripped off. Additionally, posting an unclear question (even though it can be corrected with the Clarify feature) is liable to generate time-wasting clarifying conversations, perhaps leading to the researcher feeling ripped off or you feeling obligated to tip heavily.

## Good questions = good answers

First off, certain types of question head straight into a dead end because of Google's legal restrictions. In some cases Google will even delete the question from public view. So don't do the following:

- **Don't place any personal contact information in your question:** Don't ask researchers to phone you or e-mail you privately. Google Answers is decidedly an open forum. While you're at it, avoid putting up anyone else's contact information, too. I have seen researchers answer questions in part by providing phone numbers or addresses. But for regular users, the only contact information permissible is the Google Answers user ID name.

- **Don't ask for help doing something questionably legal or outright illegal:** For example, requesting assistance in making unauthorized music downloads would probably get your question removed or at least incite warning comments from researchers.

- **Don't spam:** If you try to use the Google Answers space to promote your Internet business or sell products, you'll get bumped off for sure.

- **Don't get X-rated:** References to porn, and especially links to it, are over the line.

✔ **Don't cheat on your tests:** Google Answers encourages student use while doing homework, but getting a researcher to answer a test question is against the rules. The two uses are separated by a fine line, to be sure, and questions stay or go at Google's discretion.

Questions spawn related questions all too easily. Asking multipart questions isn't against the rules, but you should know what you're doing. Don't ramble on with every query that enters your head. Be aware, too, that you're essentially bidding for a researcher's time, and the more complex your question(s), the more money you should offer. Researchers are generous, and chances are good that you'll get a bit more than you asked for in a simple query.

If you want to hit several points of a query subject, try breaking the subject apart and posting a few low-priced queries. This clarifies your needs to the researchers, and gives them a chance to focus on specific questions rather than grapple with a bundle of them. It doesn't hurt, too, to spell out explicitly the parameters of the answer you need. Include what you already know, and explain what you need to know.

The Google Answers directory is a virtual laboratory of questions, comments, and answers, in which you can discover what works and what doesn't. Surf the directory by following these steps:

1. **Go to the Google Answers home page by clicking the Google Answers Home link on any Answers page or by using the Google Toolbar (see Chapter 9).**

2. **Scroll down the page to see the Answers directory topics.**

   You can drill into the directory from two angles. Either click a subject area in the Browse previously asked questions section, or click a question from the Recently answered questions column. To follow along with this example, enter the directory through a subject heading, as shown in Figure 7-10.

3. **Click any subject category.**

4. **On the category page (see Figure 7-11), click a question, click a subcategory, or scroll down the page to view a summary of comments, answers, and prices in that category.**

You can discover a lot just by glancing down a main category page. Many question titles are fairly explanatory; the price is right there in the far-right column, and you can see the Comment and Answer traffic each question has attracted. Click a few questions, too, to see how researchers handle various types of questioning. You might be amazed at the detail and depth of the answers. Pay particular attention to the star-rated answers — most ratings are five stars, signifying an extremely successful transaction between seeker and expert. Asking a good question is half that equation.

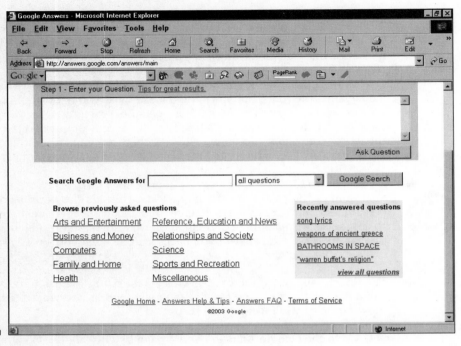

Figure 7-10:
Get into the
Answers
directory
from the
Answers
home page.

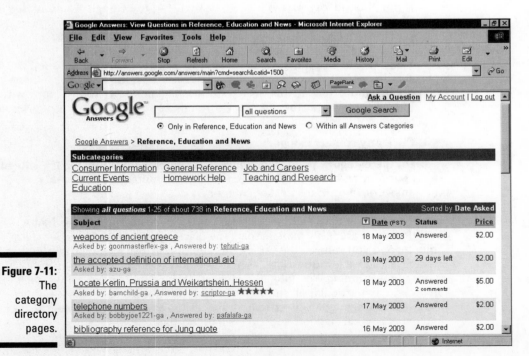

Figure 7-11:
The
category
directory
pages.

Creating a descriptive heading for your question and placing the query in an appropriate category are both as important as good phrasing of the question itself. As I write this, an open query requests information about activity in Saudi Arabia immediately following the 9/11 terrorist attacks and is vaguely titled "current events." After a day, no answers or comments were attached to the question. When creating the query title, don't worry about crafting a good sentence. You can even word the title as if it were a Google search string. (While you're at it, you might want to try Googling your query before posting to Google Answers.) Do whatever it takes to convey the subject of your query precisely.

## *Putting your money where your query is*

Setting your own price for the Google Answers service might seem awkward, and it's best to avoid the temptation to bottom-line your every query. Likewise, don't pay too much for simple questions because you're reluctant to appear cheap. Google recommends estimating how long it will take to research your question and then pricing it accordingly. This advice, although relevant to the researchers, is nearly pointless to regular users who aren't information experts and can't anticipate the type of research needed. A better bet is to gauge, roughly, how demanding your question is based on two factors:

- ✓ **Speed:** Do you have a deadline or are you just impatient? Then attracting a quick answer has more value to you.

- ✓ **Complexity:** If your query contains more than one part or more than three sentences, chances are you're requesting more than $2.00 of expertise.

If you have plenty of time, one pricing strategy is to start at the bottom and work your way up. Post a $2.00 question and see what it brings in. Interested users post comments regardless of price, because they're not getting paid. If your $2.00 post doesn't get the attention you want, raise the stakes to $5.00, and so on.

The overwhelming majority of questions are priced at $20.00 or less. Browse through the directory (see the preceding section, "Good questions = good answers") to get a feel for the type of questions being answered at certain price points.

# Chapter 8

# Experimenting in Google Labs

*In This Chapter*

▶ Lending your computer to science with Google Compute

▶ Watching the Google Viewer

▶ Reading WebQuotes

▶ Finding definitions in Google Glossary

▶ Testing the quirky Google Sets

▶ Calling up Voice Search

▶ Using keyboard shortcuts in your search results

*G*oogle is a brainy company, and its many PhD employees are always conceiving new ideas. Google itself — the main Web index and search algorithms — was a college experiment turned corporate, in the finest tradition of Internet entrepreneurism. Many of Google's now-standard features began as tentative experiments that survived testing and arrived on the home page. At this writing, Google News — one of Google's anchor services — is still a *beta* product, meaning that it's still officially in the testing phase. (Seems to work pretty darn well to me. See Chapter 3.)

Some of Google's newest brainstorms get piled into Google Labs, an open testing area that anyone can play with. You enter this area at your own risk, but honestly, the risk is minimal. In most cases, all that can really go wrong is that something you try won't work as advertised, and even that is rare. All the Google variants described in this chapter except one operate on Google's computers, not yours. You interface with them through your browser, just like regular Googling. The exception, Google Compute, is described in the first section.

The Google variants such as Google Viewer (cooler and more useful than it first seems), Google WebQuotes (fun and revealing), and Keyboard Shortcuts (bound to hurt your mouse's feelings) operate as distinct and autonomous search engines. They hook into the same Google index as the traditional Web search. But you access them from a separate Web page, and their features can't be integrated into the main Google interfaces on the home page. So, when you want to search the Web using Google Viewer, you go to the Viewer page and conduct your search from there.

This chapter covers everything in Google Labs as of this writing. Some of them have been there for more than a year. Be sure to check the Google Labs page at the following URL from time to time to see if anything's new:

```
labs.google.com
```

# Sharing Your Computer with Science

Distributed computing is an Internet-age mantra that can mean a few things. Any scenario in which multiple computers share the work required to accomplish a task is *distributed computing*. In a sense, the Internet itself is a distributed computing environment, though it isn't dedicated to a single task. A relatively new Google Labs experiment invites users to become part of a distributed computing project in the name of science.

Google Compute is a program that embeds into your computer, is controlled by the Google Toolbar, and crunches numbers for a university project when you're not using the computer. Perhaps that combination sounds sinister, but it's neither diabolical nor unprecedented; Internet users have been donating spare computer power for years. SETI, the Search for Extra-Terrestrial Intelligence project, is perhaps the best-known distributed computing project that regular folks can join.

Google, at this writing, is marshaling computer power on behalf of Stanford University's nonprofit protein research, which is called Folding@home. (That's the project name, not an e-mail address.) Google Computing might switch to another project sometime, or give users a choice of project. Google Computing is under development independently of Folding@home. Most of the features of Google Compute operate the same way regardless of which distributed computing project benefits.

## Understanding how Google Compute operates

Your computer's processing chip is a workhorse, and largely underused. I paused for several seconds after writing the preceding sentence, during which my computer was bored to tears. A few idle seconds of computer time represents thousands of idle *cycles* — binary increments that could be used to work on a computation but usually aren't.

# Spyware, adware, and other third-party issues

Anybody who does a lot of downloading from the Internet has developed a healthy apprehension about invasive software that changes computer settings, displays ads, reports your files and mouse clicks back to its source, or otherwise violates your privacy. And it's natural enough to wonder whether Google Compute, which borrows your computer's resources for use by a third party, has an invasive, marketing purpose. It does not.

Google Compute uses idle processing power in your computer, and taps into your Internet connection to transmit its results to Stanford University (the current beneficiary). In the course of this work, the program never displays an ad, alters a computer setting, installs attached software, or tracks your movements on the screen. The reporting process is anonymous and doesn't include anything about you or your computer use. Your computer is logged into the distributed computing groups with a user name. Think of your computer as a dumb processor working on a scientific problem in a network — you are out of the picture entirely. Neither Google Compute nor Stanford University have any interest in you or your Internet activities.

Google Compute and other distributed computing projects use those spare cycles, multitasking superbly to avoid getting in the way of what *you* want to do. Google Compute instantly relinquishes your computer's processor when you move the mouse or press a key, or even when your browser transmits content by itself, as with an automatically reloading Web page. Receiving e-mail has a higher priority than Google Compute. No matter what your personal computing task, it takes precedence over Google Compute.

Even operating with such modesty, Google Compute accomplishes a lot, making significant contributions to the Folding@home project. As to your experience with this instance of distributed computing, you probably won't be aware of it. I never have been, and I've run Google Compute on relatively old computers with fairly weak processing power. In the unlikely event that the program does get in your way or slow your computer's performance, you can adjust its settings as I describe later in this chapter. Or even just turn it off.

While running Google Compute, you are part of "team Google," comprised of all individuals who have installed this enhancement to Google Toolbar. You can fashion a more individual user name to distinguish and track your (or, more properly, your computer's) work.

Surprisingly, Google Compute works even when your browser is shut down. The program is attached to a browser toolbar but does not rely on the browser running. Its toolbar icon is there only to let you adjust settings. If you close the browser with Google Compute running, it will continue to run at the current settings until you open the browser and change settings or turn the computer off.

If you'd like more information about the Stanford project, which involves understanding protein folding, go to this page:

```
www.stanford.edu/group/pandegroup/folding/
```

Google Compute does seem like an anomaly, coming from a search engine. Even in Google Labs, Google Compute is the only experiment not related to searching or viewing search results. The restless minds at Google express the situation like this: "In addition to providing leading search technology, we are also interested in solving other important computationally intense problems."

## Installing Google Compute

Google Compute is distributed as an option on some Google toolbars (see Chapter 9). When it's present on a downloaded toolbar, the default setting is off. Don't feel left out if you don't get the luck of the draw. Anybody who wants to try Google Compute may download a toolbar add-on through Google Labs. Just follow these steps:

1. **Go to the Google Labs home page at the following URL:**

   ```
   labs.google.com
   ```

2. **Click the <u>Google Compute</u> link.**

3. **Scroll down to the bottom of the page, and click the Install Google Compute button.**

   You don't need to be running Google Toolbar at this point, but you do need the Toolbar to run Google Compute. If you don't have the Toolbar bolted to your browser (see Chapter 9), Google Compute will install it now. Windows might pop up a request asking that you confirm your desire to accept a download from Google. Click the Yes button.

4. **When the Thank You page appears, look for the double-helix icon representing Google Compute (see Figure 8-1).**

   If you don't see the icon, close your browser window (and all other open browser windows), and then restart your browser.

## Tweaking Google Compute

Google Compute is what job recruiters call a self-starter. It has lots of initiative. It doesn't need much hand-holding, and it is definitely a team player. After downloading it, you need do nothing more to set it in action. Google Compute jumps in when your computer processor isn't doing anything else. It asks nothing of you and takes nothing from you.

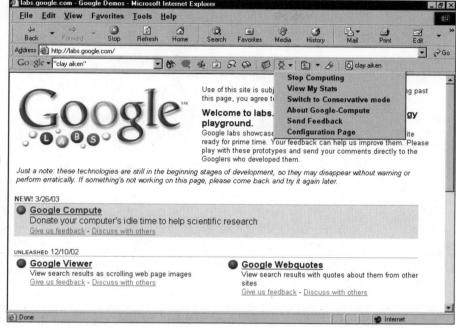

**Figure 8-1:**
Google
Compute is
installed on
the Google
Toolbar.
Access its
settings in
the drop-
down menu.

However, a few settings are available to modify how Google Compute operates. They all pertain to two areas:

✔ How Google Compute uses your computer

✔ How you're identified in team Google

# Further distributed computing

Running Google Compute puts you on a global
team of people donating computer power to a
vast research effort. You can further distribute
your efforts by running Google Compute on
more than one computer, if you have more than
one. Simply do everything this section describes
on the second computer.

To see the results of your expanded contribution,
it's best to consolidate all your computers under
the same user name. Take this step near the
start of your Google Compute work, because
when you switch user names the work performed under the first name is lost to you. (It's
not lost to the project, but it doesn't get added
to your work under the new user name.) When
you bring another computer into the mix, just
change its user name to correspond with the
other computers.

Figure 8-1 shows the drop-down menu under the Google Compute double helix. Four of the six selections are about performance issues; the other two are informational:

- ✔ **Stop Computing:** That says it all. Click this selection to turn off Google Compute. Doing so doesn't disable it permanently; you can turn it on again at any time. I find the program so invisible that I never have a reason to stop it.

- ✔ **View My Stats:** This one gives you a sense of accomplishment, but not immediately. You have to build up some statistics first. Google Compute doesn't list or send to Stanford University what it has accomplished until your computer has finished one work unit. A *work unit* is based on a certain number of processing cycles as measured against a constant — fortunately, none of that matters. Just wait two or three days (without shutting off your computer) and you'll start seeing results.

TIP

Another way (besides View My Stats) is available to get a sense of progress in your Folding@home participation. Simply place the mouse cursor over the double helix icon (don't click) and wait a second or two. Google Compute shows how much your computer has accomplished in its current protein project. (See Figure 8-2.)

- ✔ **Switch to Conservative Mode:** Google Compute operates in one of two modes: Standard and Conservative. When first installed, it starts chewing away at its task in Standard mode, and uses your computer whenever it's idle, even if only for a few seconds at a time. Conservative mode makes Google Compute less ambitious, starting work only after a lengthy idle period. Generally, Conservative mode lets Google Compute work when you're away from the computer, and Standard mode shares the computer with you. When in Conservative mode, this selection reads Switch to Standard Mode.

- ✔ **About Google Compute:** This selection simply displays an information page, which contains the Google Compute FAQ (see Figure 8-2).

- ✔ **Send Feedback:** Use this selection to find an e-mail link for writing to Google about Google Compute

- ✔ **Configuration Page:** This page gives you another way to switch between Standard and Conservative modes. The Max Processor Usage setting (see Figure 8-3) allows you to determine how much processing time Google Compute is allowed to take. This adjustment is not the same as determining processor *priority* — that never changes. Your processor's first priority is always to handle your personal tasks and push Google Compute to the background. In that context, you can further determine how much *idle* processing time Google Compute will take. Finally, this page lets you set a personalized user name.

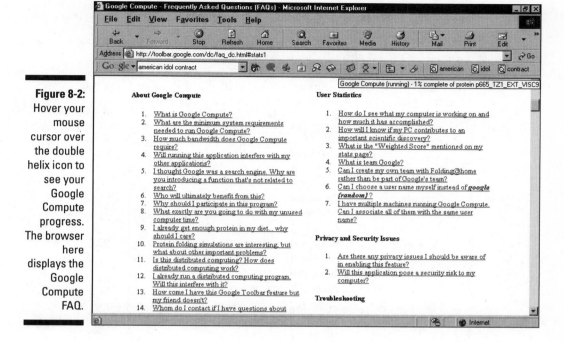

**Figure 8-2:**
Hover your mouse cursor over the double helix icon to see your Google Compute progress. The browser here displays the Google Compute FAQ.

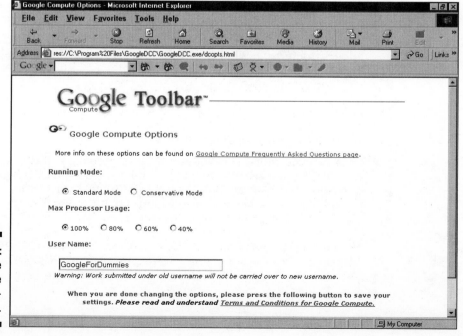

**Figure 8-3:**
The Google Compute configuration page.

# Uninstalling Google Compute

Turning off Google Compute is a two-click option, as described in the preceding section. But what if you want to uninstall it completely?

Problems with Google Compute are unusual, but not unheard of. A few users have complained of sudden bandwidth hogging that they attribute to Google Compute sending large amounts of data in a short period of time. One user complained that Google Compute displayed error messages when the user tried to put his computer in Standby mode. For whatever reason, you might encounter a glitch with this Google Labs experiment, and decide it's not worth trying to correct.

Google Compute can be disabled on four different levels, two of which are not divulged by Google:

✔ **Turn it off:** As described in the preceding section, simply pull down the double helix menu on the Google Toolbar and choose Stop Computing. Google Compute remains on your Toolbar, asleep.

✔ **Disable it:** This option is on the Toolbar Options page (see Chapter 9). Click the Google button on the Toolbar, and then choose Toolbar Options. Scroll down the page until you see Google Compute Is Enabled. Uncheck the box labeled <u>Google Compute Client</u>. Google Compute remains on your Toolbar, in a coma. You must revisit the Toolbar Options page and enable Google Compute again to use it.

✔ **Delete its files:** This is the riskiest way to get Google Compute out of your computer. Do not attempt this unless you're familiar with deleting folder structures in Windows Explorer. If you're comfortable doing so, look for this folder:

```
C:\Program Files\GoogleDCC
```

Delete that folder and all of the embedded folders in it. The double helix icon remains on your Toolbar, but it's thoroughly disabled. None of the selections in the drop-down menu work.

✔ **Uninstall and reinstall Google Toolbar:** The cleanest way to eliminate Google Compute also involves the most hassle. See Chapter 9 for instructions on uninstalling and installing Google Toolbar. (Start your uninstall by clicking the Google button and choosing the Uninstall option.) After the reinstall is in place, Google Compute is off your Toolbar.

You may resume Google Compute work at any time by reinstalling the Toolbar option as described in this chapter. After installing it again, you might want to reset your user name to the same name you used before.

# Watching Google Viewer

In two of its experiments — Google Viewer and Keyboard Shortcuts — Google attempts to make browsing results even easier. Google Viewer builds a slide show into the results page. I was dubious of this trick when I first tried it, but I've found myself returning to Google Viewer more frequently. Whereas my usual position at the computer is hunched forward with a trigger-finger on the mouse, the Viewer persuades me to relax my predatory pose and let Google take control of the search results.

Google Viewer is one feature that works best with a high-speed Internet connection. Google flashes entire pages at you in the style of a slide show, so if your modem displays those pages sluggishly, Google might whisk them away before they are fully loaded. Now, don't misunderstand me: Google Viewer is, by itself, not a good enough reason to invest in a high-speed Internet connection. If your modem struggles to keep up with the Viewer, slow down the rate at which new pages display, as I describe shortly.

Google Viewer is an autonomous search engine that works with the main Google Web index. Give it a try at this URL:

```
labs.google.com/gviewer.html
```

Figure 8-4 shows the Google Viewer search page, which contains a big, explanatory picture of the Viewer control bar that appears on each search results page. Figure 8-5 shows a Google Viewer results page.

When you search through Google Viewer, the search engine doesn't deliver the traditional list of results. Instead, it takes the initiative to display the top result below its single result listing, which in turn is positioned beneath the Viewer control bar (see Figure 8-5). After a few seconds (depending on the control bar's time setting), the Viewer wipes off that page and moves on to the next, loading the single results listing and its page. You control the viewing pace and can launch a new search directly from the control bar.

Following is a brief rundown of the control bar's functions:

- ✔ **First result:** Click the far-left button to return to a display of the top search result.

- ✔ **Previous and next results:** Use these two arrow buttons to move ahead before the time control starts loading the next page or to move backward by one search result.

- ✔ **Start and stop:** Stop the show to examine a page. Click the same button to resume. Note that when the slide show is proceeding, the start/stop button is red (awaiting your instruction to stop), and looks very much like a Record button in music-playing programs. There is no record function in Google Viewer.

✔ **Search:** Use the keyword box and Search button to start a new search.

✔ **Delay:** Use the turtle and rabbit buttons to speed or slow the pace of displayed pages. These controls could use improvement; a slider or type-in box would work better. As it is, I have tediously clicked up to 61 seconds, so I know a one-minute delay is possible.

✔ **Return:** The Google logo on the far right of the control bar returns you to the Google Viewer home page.

The only risk in Google Viewer is forgetting that it's running and clogging your bandwidth with continuously loading pages. Because many Google search results number tens of thousands of hits, you could go on vacation for a week and Google Viewer would obediently grind through page after page after page. Most people have unlimited-use Internet plans, but if you have a usage ceiling based on the amount of data transfer going through your computer, you don't want to walk away from your desk while Google Viewer merrily performs its show for your empty chair. Besides rare cost issues, a forgotten Google Viewer show could affect your computer's performance of other tasks.

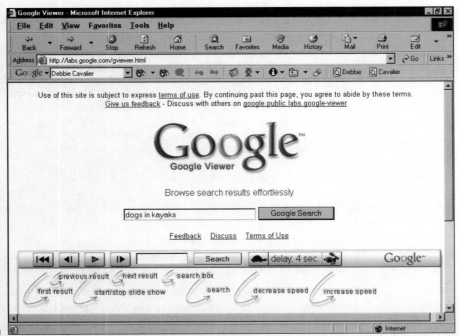

**Figure 8-4:**
The Google Viewer home page. Launch a Viewer search from here.

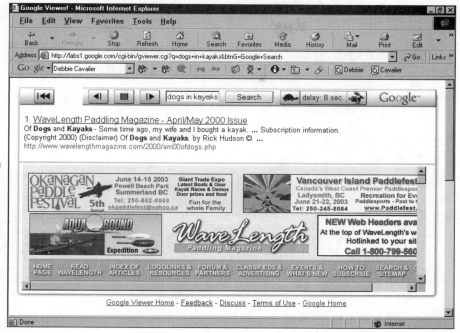

**Figure 8-5:** A search results page in Google Viewer. Use the control bar to adjust the pace of Viewer's slide show.

Google Viewer keeps your time setting when you launch new searches from the Viewer control bar at the top of a results page. But if you return to the Google Viewer home page to start a new search, the control bar resets to its default pace, which puts eight seconds between search result displays.

You can click the standard search result link at any time — it displays above the page in Google Viewer. Google remembers your Preference settings, too (see Chapter 2). This means that if you have Google set to open a new window when you click a search result, with a quick mouse movement you can grab a displaying page and pull it into its own browser window without interrupting the Viewer slide show. (Yet another reason to make that Preferences setting — it's the most important one.)

Google Viewer affects your browser's Back button in a way that might be unexpected. While watching the slide show, you probably feel that you're sitting on one page — the Google Viewer search results page. But your browser thinks you're visiting many pages, because Google Viewer is throwing them into the browser window, one by one. So when you click the Back button, you are returned to the previously displayed page. Clicking the Back button's history list (see Figure 8-6) shows you a list of previous sites in the display. You can take advantage of this quirk to jump backwards several pages.

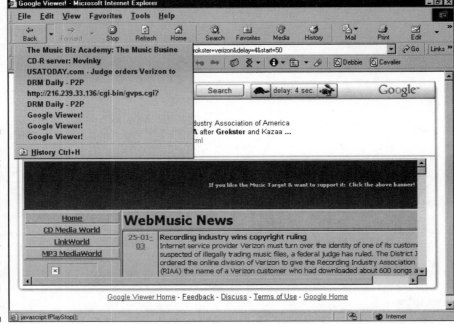

**Figure 8-6:**
Internet
Explorer's
Back button
considers
each
Google
Viewer
search
result to be
a visited
destination.

But wait! None of the preceding paragraph holds true if you activate another window (another browser window or another program) and then return to Google Viewer's window. Likewise, if you stop the Viewer and start it again, your Back-button history list starts over. Good luck!

# Breezing Through WebQuotes

WebQuotes (quotations, not stock quotes) is one Labs experiment that might not be worth the effort. A failure? No, saying that would be unfair and untrue. This specialized search engine, which finds and displays text quotations *about* the sites on your search results list, is an original, ambitious, and even brilliant idea. The problem is that, as a practical application, WebQuotes isn't very useful.

As I see it, the main problem with WebQuotes is that most search results don't yield any quotes at all. This is partly because even when quotes exist for an influential site such as the New York Times (*www.nytimes.com*), quotes are not likely to exist for a certain page within the Times site that appears as a search result.

Finding examples of this insufficiency is easy. In a search for *riaa grokster*, an article from the Boycott RIAA site (www.boycott-riaa.com) appeared as the top search result, with no quotes. But a search for *www.boycott-riaa.com* delivered the main site as the first result, with two quotes from other sites.

Go to the WebQuotes home page (see Figure 8-7) to try it:

```
labs.google.com/cgi-bin/webquotes
```

Start a search just as you would from the Google home page. Adjust the maximum number of WebQuotes you want to see for each search result, but don't count on reaching the maximum (or getting any) for most results.

Figure 8-8 shows a WebQuotes search results page. Two settings are adjustable:

- ✔ The maximum number of WebQuotes displayed
- ✔ A minimum number of WebQuotes, fewer than which Google resorts to displaying an excerpt from the search result site

Mixing quotes (from other sites) with excerpts (from the target site) is mixing apples and oranges, and confuses the WebQuotes experience. I keep the second setting at zero to eliminate site excerpts.

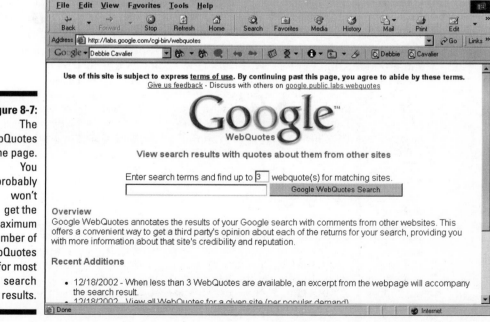

**Figure 8-7:**
The WebQuotes home page. You probably won't get the maximum number of WebQuotes for most search results.

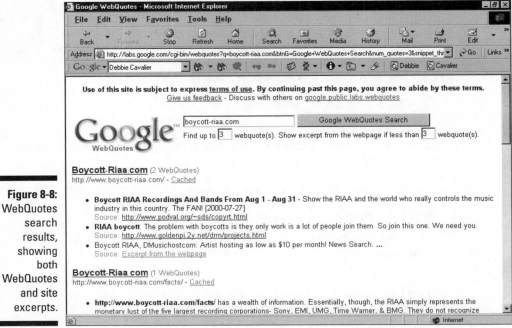

**Figure 8-8:**
WebQuotes
search
results,
showing
both
WebQuotes
and site
excerpts.

# Getting It Defined in Google Glossary

WebQuotes is capricious and lighthearted, but Google Glossary is productive and grounded. In Chapter 2 I describe how to find your way to quick definitions using the main Web search engine. Here, Google takes the guesswork and trial-and-error out of finding word definitions, building a dedicated glossary search engine. I know people who keep Google Glossary bookmarked for regular use. If and when it moves out of Google Labs and becomes an official feature, my hope and expectation is that it will be added to the Toolbar (see Chapter 9) as a primary Google destination.

Try Google Glossary here:

```
labs.google.com/glossary
```

The home page works just like the main Google home page. Type a keyword and press Enter. The keyword(s) should be a term or phrase you want defined. Figure 8-9 shows a Google Glossary results page. Google uses an undivulged collection of Web sources for its definitions. Each definition reveals its source (and links to it), but Google does not divulge what it takes to be a source and keeps the list of sources secret.

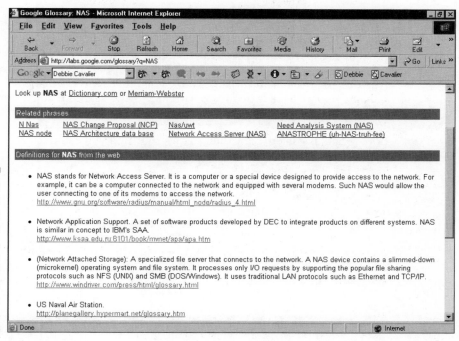

**Figure 8-9:**
Search
results in
Google
Glossary,
showing a
range of
definitions
for an
acronym.

Google Glossary results are erratic. This service is definitely a work in progress, but useful nonetheless. Remember that you can always resort to trolling for word definitions in the main Web search index, as I describe in Chapter 2, if you get poor results here.

Poor results appear rampantly, in unexpected places. Within a couple of minutes I was able to stump Google Glossary with fairly common terms, including *blade server*, *hypothyroid*, and *hyperthyroid*. Amazingly, it was baffled by *mp3*, which is one of the most in-demand search terms on the Internet, and has been for years. Google Glossary did not cope well with "*network attached storage*" but suggested "Network Attached Storage (NAS)" in its stead, and provided excellent definitions when I clicked that suggestion link.

The search results page always offers links to Dictionary.com and the Merriam-Webster site, whether or not it finds definitions for you.

One value of Google Glossary is its lack of bias when defining terms or acronyms with multiple meanings. Figure 8-9 shows this equanimity in action, as Google Glossary offers multiple interpretations of the acronym NAS.

# *Building Google Sets*

A peculiar experiment in creating related keywords, Google Sets is marginally fun and occasionally useful. I can imagine the appeal of this idea to Google researchers, because it turns the tables on most search enhancements. Usually, Google Labs is occupied with improving search results. Google Sets concentrates on using the Google index to enhance keyword selection.

Google Sets is easier to try than to describe, and you can try it here:

```
http://labs.google.com/sets
```

Figure 8-10 shows the Google Sets page, which contains five keyword boxes. Type a word or a phrase into at least one box and press Enter, or choose between the Large Set and Small Set buttons. Results are not guaranteed. In fact, in the test search shown in Figure 8-10, Google Sets could not build a set on the three keywords I provided. Removing one of the keywords, mp3, resulted in the set shown in Figure 8-11. As you can see, supposedly related keywords don't necessarily add to your knowledge.

**Figure 8-10:**
Google Sets attempts to find related keywords.

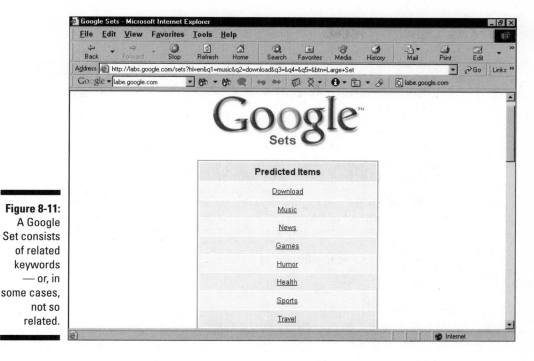

Frankly, Google Sets has limited appeal to most daily Google addicts. I know a
few writers and journalists who use Sets as a sort of research tool to increase
their awareness of key concepts related to an assignment topic. In that way,
Sets could be a homework helper, too. But honestly, it's a stretch to imagine
Google Sets fitting into most people's lives. As one bewildered user posted to
the Google Sets bulletin board, "Who is using Google Sets?"

Actually, there are uses for Google Sets. For one, you can use Sets as a rough
sort of thesaurus: Type a word, select Large Set, and see what synonyms pop
up. Anyone who has a limited English vocabulary might find this use especially rewarding. Google Sets also works well with brand names — type one
car manufacturer, for example, and get a list of others.

You might also try Google Sets as a sort of esoteric recommendation engine
with a mind of its own. Because Sets accepts phrases, try typing one or two
movie titles and see whether it recommends others. The results lead to exer-
cises in "Six Degrees of Separation," as you try to figure out how Google connected the disparate titles in the resulting set. A request for a set built on
"Remains of the Day" and "Silence of the Lambs," two Anthony Hopkins films,
returned *Fargo*, *Reservoir Dogs*, *Pulp Fiction*, *Goodfellas*, and *The Shawshank
Redemption*. (By the way, if you haven't seen *Shawshank*, rent it soon.) It
might be difficult to connect the dots between all those movies, but what's
not fun about lists of movies? Try the same thing with books and music.

# Voice Searching

Voice Search is insanely quirky and irresistible, offering a combined telephone and Web experience. You use the phone to deliver your search query, and Google returns the results on a Web page. Practical? Absolutely not! Fun? Yes! You must try it.

Google is leading up to something here. As it stands, Voice Search is a raw experiment with no logistic value. But voice recognition technology promises immense benefits to the future of computing, in all areas. With the imminent convergence of the Web and cell phones, it's not hard to imagine that Google is positioning itself for the day when it becomes a fully mobile, voice-activated search engine. It's impractical to split your attention between phone and screen for a single task when sitting at a desk, but on a cell phone it would be a relief not to type the query and simple to glance at the screen for results.

Try Voice Search at the following page:

```
http://labs.google.com/gvs.html
```

This page gives you the number to call — it's a California number, and toll charges apply. Call at your own expense. Keep this page in front of you as you call.

Many people are confused when they try Voice Search, so I'm spelling out the exact steps here:

1. **Go to the Google Voice Search home page at the following URL:**

   ```
   http://labs.google.com/gvs.html
   ```

2. **Call the Voice Search phone number seen on that page.**

   The first thing you hear is a recorded voice saying, "Say your search keywords."

3. **Say your keywords.**

   Multiple keywords are fine. It's best to speak naturally but not sloppily. Don't make an extreme effort to enunciate. Voice Search senses (sometimes prematurely) when you're finished and says, "OK, searching." After a pause, the recorded voice declaims, "Your results are ready. Say your search keywords." Don't feel rushed! If you want to conduct a second search after you've finished this one, Voice Search will wait for you as long as you don't hang up the phone.

4. **On the Voice Search page, use the <u>Click this link</u> link to see your search results.**

   A new browser window opens to display results. Voice Search results are identical to normal Web search results, except that, very disappointingly, your spoken keywords are not displayed in the keyword search box atop the page.

5. **Speak new keywords and repeat the process.**

   Handily, the results page reloads automatically when your new results are ready.

You might well wonder how Voice Search communicates with your browser. It doesn't really. There is only one search results window, and only one person can use Voice Search at a time. (If you get a busy signal, wait a bit and try again. And don't hog Voice Search for too long.) The browser window displaying your results can be seen by anybody who goes into Voice Search and clicks the <u>Click this link</u> link. In fact, one fun feature is to keep watching that autoreloading browser window after you've hung up to see search results generated by other users.

The big question is how well Voice Search works, and the answer depends on the effectiveness of its voice recognition technology. The page reloading and results display are fine. The voice recognition can be flaky. I've seen Voice Search translate *Iraq* as *iMac*, and my name (*Brad*) as *brass*. In one spectacular demonstration of obscurity, Voice Search rendered *American Idol* as *of-the-dragon heinkel*. Results improve if you speak naturally, but remember: As of now, Voice Search is not meant to replace regular on-screen searching.

# Fingering Through Results: Keyboard Shortcuts

Unlike Voice Search (see the preceding section), Keyboard Shortcuts might replace the normal Google interface in your habitual searching. The goal of this Labs experiment is to get your hand off the mouse when viewing search results and put full browsing control in the keyboard. In this interface you can scroll up and down the search results list — even launching target sites — using keypresses.

Start your Keyboard Shortcuts search here:

```
labs.google.com/keys/
```

Type your keywords, press Enter, and get to the results page (see Figure 8-12). Keyboard Shortcuts uses a special cursor for indicating your progress through search results: a little cluster of three colored balls. When the search results page first displays, that cursor is positioned next to the first result. Use the K and I keys to move the cursor down and up the results list. This works best when your hands are positioned like a touch-typists, with the middle finger of your right hand resting on the K key, and the middle finger of your left hand resting on the D key.

**Figure 8-12:**
Keyboard
Shortcuts
in action.

Here are some other shortcut functions:

- ✔ Press Enter to open a search results link.

- ✔ Press C to view the cached (stored) page of the indicated result.

- ✔ Press S to see the Similar Pages list.

- ✔ Use the L and J keys to toggle between the AdWords advertisements on the left side of the page (if any are there for your search results) and the main results list.

- ✔ Press N to see the next page of search results, and press P to see the previous page.

- ✔ Press the number keys 1 through 9 to jump to search results down or up the page. (Keyboard Shortcuts ignores the Preferences setting requesting more than 10 results per page.) Beware of using the number keys unless you want to surf directly to the site represented by that numbered result. Google assumes that you want to see the site, not the search result listing, and shoots your browser right to it.

- ✔ Press A to highlight the keyword box for typing new keywords.

✔ Press the question-mark key (it's not necessary to use the Shift key, as you would when typing a question mark) to drop down a cue sheet to the keyboard shortcuts (see Figure 8-12). Press it again to make the list disappear.

Keyboard Shortcuts takes a little practice to master — and is worth it.

# The Labs Upshot

All the experiments in Google Labs are fun. But only three — Google Viewer, Google Glossary, and Keyboard Shortcuts — make practical enhancements to your searching experience.

I don't want to end this chapter without pointing out the <u>Discuss with others</u> link, which appears next to each experiment on the Google Labs page. These links lead to newsgroup message boards dedicated to each service, on which you can share your experience, give feedback to Google, ask for help, and read what others have to say.

Disappointingly, Google doesn't distribute the messages in these newsgroups beyond its own server, so you can't read the boards in your newsgroup program. The groups might appear in your newsgroup program, and you might be able to subscribe to them, but no messages are displayed. Likewise, messages you post using your newsgroup program, through your ISP's Usenet server, do not appear on the boards on Google's end. The point of all this is that to read and participate in these groups, use the links Google provides and stick to Google's server. See Chapter 4 for information about Usenet newsgroups and Google Groups.

# Part III
# Putting Google to Work for You

The 5th Wave    By Rich Tennant

"This is amazing. You can stop looking for Derek. According to a Google search I did, he's hiding behind the dryer in the basement."

# In this part . . .

You might think of Google as the ultimate search engine. You go to it, you humbly feed it your keywords, you heed its magisterial declamations, you surf where it bids us. You live online lives guided, influenced, even determined by Google. All this is true and good. Yet Google stands ready to serve no less than it commands. The Google Toolbar is a loyal information butler that never strays from our side. And Google begs to be a universalist sensibility in our nationalistic culture, translating almost every non-native tongue it is possible to encounter. Then, as a business partner, Google is blindingly innovative and powerful on our behalf almost beyond conception. As a great populist force, Google has singly brought targeted, high-powered Internet advertising to amateur and semi-pro Webmasters the world over.

The chapters in this part encourage you to build a deeper relationship with Google. It is almost a marriage, really: constant companionship, cooperative prosperity, and a partnered relationship with the larger community. Chapter 9 might be the most important in the book, for if you do nothing else in response to these pages, it is my hope that you install and use the Google Toolbar. Likewise, the AdWords program could change your life as it has the lives of countless others. And if paying for traffic is not your way, Chapter 12 provides valuable, subtler methods of broadening your visitor base.

Ramp up your readiness. You've come this far; in your soul's core you know you must not turn back. You cannot: The transformation of online life is in process, and its momentum grips us all with the gleaming vision of new possibilities, new realities, new virtual selves. [Editors' note: Brad Hill has become clinically caffeinated. An intervention has been scheduled. We hope for a return to normalcy by Part IV.]

# Chapter 9

# Google on Your Browser

*In This Chapter*

▶ Installing and using the Google Toolbar

▶ Upgrading to Toolbar 2.0 (beta)

▶ Putting Google's buttons on your browser's toolbar

▶ Making Google your browser's default search engine

*E*ven if you think Google is God, visiting the home page for every little search is an undeniable inconvenience. Shouldn't Google worship transpire in the user's home, wherever that might be? On the Internet, "home" is your browser. Google understands. Google loves you. Google is everywhere — or can be, if you install one (or all) of the three browser enhancements described in this chapter.

Every browser has built-in toolbars near the top of the browser window. They contain navigation buttons, a Web address bar, and other perks that help you move around online with a minimum of hassle. In addition, you can attach third-party toolbars to some browsers. (You are the first party, the company that created your browser is the second party, and the company that created the toolbar is the third party. And not one of them has an open bar.) Google's add-on Toolbar absolutely rocks. If you're using it already, you'll breeze through the first two sections of this chapter.

The Google Toolbar is the star of this chapter, but the other two browser enhancements are also important:

▶ **Google browser buttons:** This feature attaches one, two, or three buttons (your choice) to an existing browser toolbar. They invite you to search Google using any highlighted word on any Web page as a keyword; instantly call up pages similar to the page currently displayed; and go directly to Google's home page through a button that acts as a dedicated bookmark.

## Browsers are not all equal

Most people use some version of the Microsoft Internet Explorer (IE) browser. And only a minority of those folks use a version preceding version 5, much less version 4. That big majority of IE4+ users can proceed to install Google browser buttons and the default browser search engine with no trouble. IE5+ users can do all that plus install the Google Toolbar smoothly. It's clear sailing for AOL7+ users, too, if they use the default Web browser.

For the rest, here's a rundown of the browser requirements for each Google browser enhancement.

✔ **Google Toolbar:** The Toolbar is available *only* for IE versions 5 and 6, running on Windows 95 or later (98, 98SE, ME, 2000, XP). No Mac, no Netscape.

✔ **Google browser buttons:** Windows computers must be running Windows 95 or later, and version 4 or later of Internet Explorer or Netscape. On the Macintosh, IE 4.5 or

Netscape 4.5 (or later in both cases) must be the browser of choice. The browser buttons are the most forgiving browser enhancement of Google's three choices.

✔ **Google as the browser's default search engine.** Internet Explorer versions 4 through 6 can download and install a Google-provided file that changes IE's default search engine. On a Mac, you can change IE5 (but not if you're running Apple's OS X operating system) with help from the visakopu site, endorsed by Google. Go to this link for more information:

`www.visakopu.net/ie5google/`

To make Google the default search engine for Netscape versions 4.0 through 4.7, you must edit the prefs file. Google warns about the danger of doing this but provides instructions at this page:

`www.google.com/options/`
`defaults.html`

✔ **Google as your browser's default search engine:** Every modern browser has a built-in search engine — actually, a licensing agreement with an online engine that forces the browser to run keywords through that engine. Internet Explorer opens a vertical pane in the left portion of the browser, containing a keyword box and other search tools. You can change the default engine to Google.

This chapter steps you through installing each of the three browser enhancements and choosing among the many Toolbar options.

# *Installing the Google Toolbar*

If you're not (yet) using Google Toolbar, you must begin immediately. I mean it. I'm not cutting any slack on this point. It will change your life. It will consolidate awesome information power a click away at all times. It will both deepen and streamline your relationship to Google. You will be free to worship the oracular power of the Googlebeast at all times, in all (virtual) places.

Figure 9-1 shows the Google Toolbar installed, ready for action. The keyword box is evident, over to the left. There's much more to the Toolbar than a portable keyword box, though. The following section describes installing the Toolbar; the section after that explains its many options.

The Toolbar installation process is almost completely automated. You just click your way through a few buttons before Google takes over. Follow these steps:

1. **Go to this page:**

   ```
   toolbar.google.com
   ```

2. **From the drop-down menu, scroll down and select a language.**

3. **Click the GET THE GOOGLE TOOLBAR! button.**

   (The Google folks are just as insistent as I am.)

4. **On the next page, click the <u>Terms of Service</u> link.**

   The TOS specify that Google owns the Toolbar, that Google is not responsible if it blows up your computer (it won't), and that you can't try to make money from the Toolbar (for example, by charging admission to watch you Google with it, which sounds a little bit disgusting).

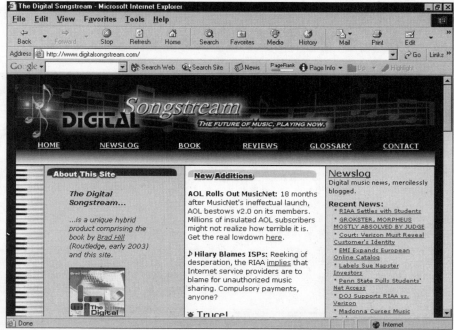

**Figure 9-1:**
The Google Toolbar clamps onto the browser, encouraging Googling from anywhere on the Web.

5. **Click the Back button to return to the previous page.**

6. **Click the I AGREE TO THE TERMS OF USE — INSTALL THE GOOGLE TOOLBAR button.**

(Must they shout?) Now comes yet another notice involving Google's privacy policy. This one you must read. It explains that installing Google Toolbar with advanced features, including the PageRank indicator, allows Google to collect anonymous information about your Web surfing. Google uses this information to calculate accurate PageRanks, thereby improving the performance of the entire service. However, you may opt out of the advanced features on this page, if the thought of surfing feedback clashes with your sense of privacy. Furthermore, after installation, you can visit the Toolbar Options page to activate certain advanced features while still disabling PageRank feedback.

7. **At the bottom of the page, click the INSTALL WITH ADVANCED FEATURES button or INSTALL WITHOUT ADVANCED FEATURES button.**

Google Toolbar downloads and bolts onto your browser at this point. A security window might appear in Windows, requesting permission to proceed. (Click the Yes button.) Installation takes five to ten seconds over a high-speed connection; phone modems might require a minute or two. When the process is finished, you see the Toolbar attached to your browser. Figure 9-1 shows the Toolbar with the advanced features. These advanced features refer to the PageRank display and its corresponding tracking of the browser's movements on the Web. All browsers using this feature of the Google Toolbar contribute to PageRank by telling Google what sites are visited. Many people don't like having their virtual movements tracked, considering it a privacy violation, and decline the advanced features.

## Using the Google Toolbar on other computers

One of the traditional advantages of add-on browser toolbars, such as Yahoo! Companion (which, in *Yahoo! For Dummies*, I recommend with the same verve that I recommend Google's Toolbar here), is that you can transfer your settings to any computer when traveling. This convenience holds in the case of the Yahoo! Companion, which stores the user's Internet bookmarks and other settings on Yahoo!'s computers. The happy result is that you can load all your destinations to the browser of any computer with Web access.

The Google Toolbar doesn't work that way. It is meant to assist you in searching, not in storing your links or other personal information. You certainly can configure the Toolbar to your preferences (see the "Choosing Toolbar Options" section), but those settings are stored in your computer, not Google's. So if you uninstall the Toolbar and then reinstall it, you must reset your preferences. Likewise, when traveling, you may install the Toolbar onto a strange computer's browser, but it doesn't remember your or your home preferences.

You're ready to go. Try a search immediately by typing a keyword in the keyword box and pressing Enter. It's that easy. At first, search results appear in the current browser window, even if your Google Preferences are set to open a new window, as I recommend in Chapter 2. The following section shows you how to make that same setting for the Toolbar.

The appearance of your Google Toolbar might not correspond to Figure 9-1, depending on your settings, browser, and screen resolution. The next section reviews your configurable options.

# Choosing Toolbar Options

Google's Toolbar comes with a host of options that fine-tune the Toolbar's appearance and functionality. You set your preferences on a Web page that's easy to get to from the Toolbar. In fact, most main search areas in Google are a click away from the Toolbar.

Click the Google button on the far left of the Toolbar. The menu that drops down contains links to Google's home page, each of the main search areas (Images, Groups, Directory, and News), the Advanced Search Page, the Preferences page, and a few others. Click the Toolbar Options selection. Figure 9-2 shows the Toolbar Options page.

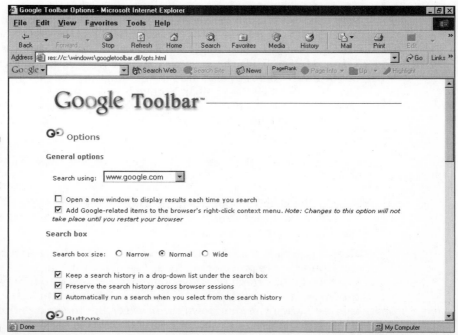

**Figure 9-2:** Use this page to set your Toolbar options. A link to experimental features is located further down the page.

When you adjust your Google Toolbar options, remember that they don't affect — nor are they affected by — your Google Preferences (see Chapter 2). The Google Preferences influence your search experience at the Google site. Toolbar options affect Toolbar searching only.

The next sections provide a rundown of all Toolbar options in three categories: general options, button options, and experimental options.

## General Toolbar options

The first and only drop-down menu in the Toolbar Options page asks you to select a national Google through which your searches will occur. (See Figure 9-3.) The default is the American home page: www.google.com. This menu is basically a language selector, and you need to know your country's top-level domain extension to identify your language. (A list is viewable at www.domainworldwide.com.)

Below the drop-down menu are two important check boxes:

- ✔ **Open a new window to display results each time you search:** I always keep this option checked. It leaves my original browser window anchored at its current site, while Google search results are displayed in a fresh window.

- ✔ **Add Google-related items to the browser's right-click context menu:** This right-click menu pops up whenever you right-click any portion of a Web page. The Google-related items make up the four information items yielded with the *info* operator (see Chapter 2 and the cheat sheet). They are Cached Snapshot of Page, Similar Pages, Backward Links, and Translate Page. These choices are handy to have in the right-click menu, but be aware that they also drop down from the Page Info button if you have it enabled on the Toolbar. Nothing's wrong with repeating the choices in each place. Or keep them in the right-click menu and remove them from the Page Info button (see the "Button options" section) to save space on the Toolbar.

A few options relate to the search box (or keyword box, as I call it elsewhere in this book):

- ✔ **Search box size:** You can select the width of the search box. If you like to see long keyword strings, widen it. If saving space on the Toolbar is a priority, make the box slimmer.

- ✔ **Keep a search history in a drop-down list under the search box:** Select this option to see previous searches beginning with the same letters you type in the search box. Clicking the triangle next to the search box drops down a list of all previous searches. Normally, this search history is erased when you shut down the browser. But the next option saves your searches even if the browser is shut down or crashes.

**Figure 9-3:**
Choose your
country's
Google to
get native-
language
searches
through the
Toolbar.

✔ **Preserve the search history across browser sessions:** Click this option to make your search history permanent. (You can always clear your search history manually by clicking Clear Search History under the Google button on the Toolbar.)

✔ **Automatically run a search when you select from the search history:** This option is great for recurring searches. Selecting this option forces Google into action when you select a previous search, without needing to press Enter or click the Search Web button.

## Button options

The first button option reduces or expands the amount of explanatory text next to the Toolbar buttons. It's not as if each button has a novel associated with it, but one word of text takes a lot of space on a toolbar. This option offers the most dramatic way to save space and squeeze lots of features into a toolbar. The only downside to eliminating all text is the slight learning curve required to remember each button's icon. Presumably, you'll be using the Google Toolbar so often that you'll quickly lose the need for text. Use the radio buttons to choose how much text you want on the Toolbar. Figure 9-4 shows a packed Toolbar with no text.

Figure 9-4:
You can
fit a lot of
features on
the Google
Toolbar by
eliminating
button text.

Below the button text options are a series of six check boxes that determine which search buttons will reside on your Toolbar:

- **Search Web button:** The most obvious and seemingly indispensable button, this is the one you need least. You'll probably find it easier to press Enter on the keyboard to launch a Web search.

- **Search Site button:** Applies your keywords to the page you're viewing.

- **I'm Feeling Lucky search button:** This one corresponds to the big I'm Feeling Lucky button on Google's home page. It takes you directly to the first search results page, bypassing the list of search results.

- **Search Images button:** This button throws your search into Google's image index.

- **Search Groups button:** Put this button on the Toolbar if you want to apply keywords to Google's massive, archived index of Usenet newsgroups.

- **Search Directory button:** This button launches a search in Google's hand-picked Web directory.

The two advanced features buttons, when enabled on the Toolbar, send your surfing information anonymously back to Google:

- **PageRank display:** This is a more valuable option to Google than it is to the user, in most cases. Google wants that feedback information to continue refining its page rankings. You, on the other hand, get nothing out of it except for a display of a page's rank (see Figure 9-5). Knowing a page's rank is, to be honest about it, marginally valuable at best. I leave it on most of the time, because . . . well, why not? And I enjoy glancing at the page rank from time to time.

- **Category button:** I like this button. Resting the mouse cursor on the Category button reveals the Google category in which the current site resides — if it's in the Google Directory at all. If not, the Category button appears dimmed. To visit the Directory page on which the site is listed, click the Category button.

**Figure 9-5:**
The
PageRank
display is
marginally
informa-
tional.

Two page information buttons follow, neither of which I use very often:

✔ **Page Info menu button:** If you enable the right-click Google-specific menu items mentioned previously, you don't need the Page Info menu button. It offers the cached (stored) version of the current page, similar pages, backward links to the current page, and a translation of the current page into your default language. These are the same options that are in the right-click menu.

✔ **Voting buttons:** These buttons are experimental in nature, but they aren't part of the experimental features described in the next section. Click the smiling or frowning faces to vote for or against a page — even a Google search results page. Google compiles these votes and . . . does something with them. At this writing, nobody outside the company knows what. Call me cynical, but I'm waiting to see what votes get me before exercising my Googly democratic right.

The next two navigation features always reside on my Toolbar:

✔ **News button:** Simple and indispensable — the News button surfs you directly to Google News, the essential current events portal of today's Internet.

✔ **Up button:** Cryptically named, this button keeps track of the layers you travel through a Web site and stands ready to jettison you back up to the home page or to an intermediary page. Click the small triangle next to the Up button to display a list of higher levels in the site (see Figure 9-6). Click one of them to begin moving toward the surface.

Next come my favorite buttons of all, two buttons that help locate keywords in found Web pages:

✔ **Highlight button:** This dynamic and extremely helpful button highlights your keywords, each in a different color, on any Web page displayed since your last Toolbar search. Figure 9-7 shows a highlighted Web page that was searched with three matched keywords.

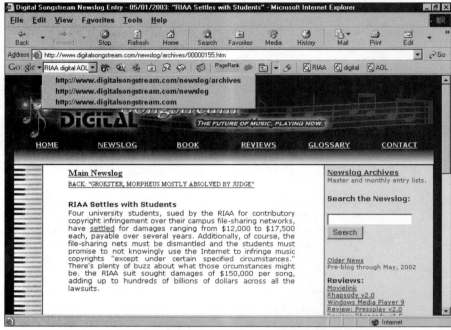

**Figure 9-6:**
The Up button shows the upper levels of a site you've drilled into and resurfaces you with a single click.

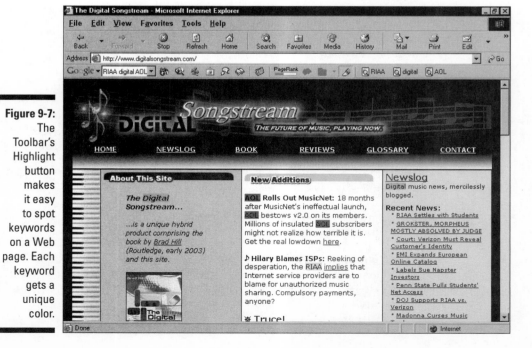

**Figure 9-7:**
The Toolbar's Highlight button makes it easy to spot keywords on a Web page. Each keyword gets a unique color.

✔ **Word-find buttons:** This feature places a button on the Toolbar for each of your keywords. (They appear after you launch the search, not as you type the words.) If you have your options set to deliver search results in a new window, the word-find buttons follow you to the new window. Furthermore, they stay with you when you click search results, *even* if your Google Preferences cause yet another window to be opened. It's when you're at a search results site (not the search results page) that the word-find buttons become useful. Click any one of them to make a highlight bar jump from one instance of that keyword on the page to the next. These buttons should be used with the Highlight button, which accents all instances of all keywords at once. (Honestly, the Highlight button is the more useful of the two. But word-find buttons are great, too, if only to remind you what your keywords are.)

At the very bottom of the Toolbar Options page (see Figure 9-8) are two buttons that reset your options to their default state — as they were before you started playing with them. The first button reestablishes the Toolbar layout with advanced features (the PageRank display and category button), and the second button reverts the Toolbar to its original state without those features. The OK button is for keeping the changes you've made on the Toolbar Options page.

**Figure 9-8:**
One click resets the Toolbar to its original configu- ration, with or without advanced features.

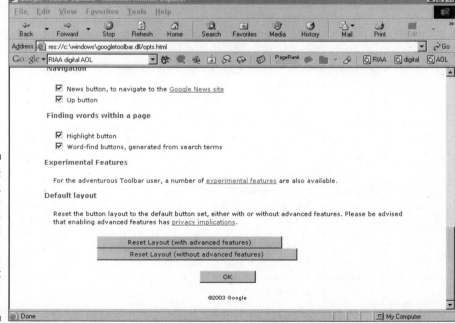

## Experimental features

Near the bottom of the Toolbar Options page is an <u>experimental features</u> link that displays what I'm sure you're dying to see — yet another options page. This one has just three features, and they are definitely worth considering:

- ✔ **Combined Search button:** This single button is meant to replace all other buttons on the Toolbar. Indeed, if you select this option, you might also want to click the <u>turn off all other search buttons</u> link, because the functions of all those buttons are now incorporated under the Combined Search button. Figure 9-9 illustrates what you get for taking this drastic action.

  Clicking the little triangle next to the Combined Search button (which is the Search Web button when this feature is turned off) drops down a menu containing all the search choices. Notice the secondary option under the Combined Search button check box: Keep the last search done with the Combined Search button as the default. Checking this option gives you a consistent search experience without having to pull down the Combined Search menu as often. If you launch a Google Groups search, for example, your next search automatically goes to Google Groups if you launch it by pressing the Enter key instead of dropping down the Combined Search menu. Not bad. This way you can hit Google Groups repeatedly, avoiding pulling down that menu until you want to switch to another Google index. Try it. If you find, over time, that you are inadvertently sending your searches to the wrong place all the time, you can take out that feature.

- ✔ **Suppress the onUnload JavaScript event:** How obscure is this? The onUnload JavaScript event in question is a bit of code embedded in some Web pages that unleashes a pop-up browser window when you leave that page. You know how annoying that can be. Checking this feature forces your browser to check for that little piece of JavaScript and thwart it. Fewer pop-ups, as Martha Stewart might say if she were in a better mood, is a Good Thing. Nothing appears on the Toolbar when this option is activated.

- ✔ **Next and previous buttons:** These arrow-shaped buttons swing into action when you leave the search results page to visit one of its Web sites. After poking around a bit, you can click the next button to surf directly to the next hit on the search results list, without backtracking to the search results page. Of course, if your Google Preferences are set to open a new window when clicking a search result, you always leave one browser window anchored on the search results page, making the next and previous buttons superfluous.

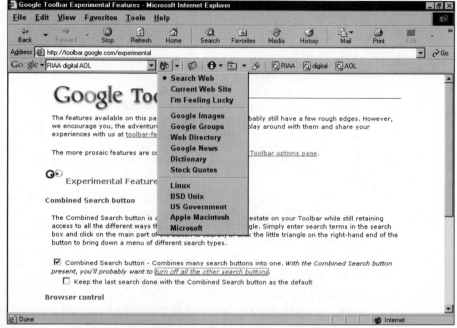

**Figure 9-9:**
The
Combined
Search
button
compresses
the Toolbar
by putting
all search
choices
under one
button.

# *Google Toolbar 2.0 (Beta)*

Shortly before this book went to print, Google released a new version of the Toolbar. At the time of this writing, the new Toolbar was still in *beta*, meaning that it was an unofficial release, available to everyone. Users were welcome to submit feedback, praising or damning, to Google. No schedule was published for its graduation to an official product, and the older version 1.xx was still the default download from the Toolbar page in Google. Google generally keeps new products in beta for a very long time — Google News, for example, was still in beta when this book was completed, despite its long-won acceptance as the preeminent online newsstand.

Accordingly, this chapter covers both the older version and the 2.0 version of the Toolbar, side by side. Version 2.0 might still be experimental when this book is published, and you might still have a choice of the two. I immediately switched over to Toolbar 2.0, and in the short time in which I used it before this manuscript was yanked away from me, I had not the slightest reason to switch back. To the contrary, the new Toolbar is a fantastic product — much improved over the older one, which also is terrific.

Toolbar 2.0 is a mature, stable product, despite its beta status. The upgrade to an entire new product series (1.xx to 2.0) indicates the substantial change in the feature set of the new Toolbar, yet most of the traditional features still exist. Toolbar 2.0 is enhanced and streamlined. Most of its new features have nothing to do with searching, oddly, yet have everything to do with your online lifestyle and management of the Toolbar.

Toolbar 2.0 exhibits five major additions:

✔ **Options panel:** Toolbar options, in both the old and new Toolbars, are stored on your computer. In the 1.xx Toolbar, those option pages open up in the browser window, making it appear that you're using an interactive page stored on Google's computer. In the 2.0 Toolbar, the situation is clarified in the new Toolbar Options panel, which opens on top of the browser window. This panel is more concise and easier to manage than the previous version.

✔ **Blog This!:** This button is for users of Blogger.com, Google's recently acquired Weblog service. Clicking the Blog This! button enables users to post an entry to their Weblog that automatically refers to the Web page currently displayed.

✔ **AutoFill:** This feature fills in online forms with one click — a tremendous time-saver.

✔ **Pop-up Blocker:** Perhaps the most surprising addition to the Toolbar, the pop-up blocker prevents free-floating ads from sprouting atop and behind your browser. In certain conditions, this blocker doesn't touch the ads streamed directly to the desktop in Windows XP. The feature does block ads associated with Web sites, which spoils the sites in many cases. Pop-up ads previously lurk in the sole provenance of X-rated adult sites and were considered the depth of sleaze when the Web was younger. Now they're commonplace at most mainstream sites.

✔ **Search Country:** This button becomes active when you set the Toolbar's Web searches to a domain other than www.google.com. (To change the domain, use the Search using option, shown in Figure 9-3.) Clicking this button restricts your search to the country of your selected server. When you select an alternative server, every search transpires through that server even when you *don't* click the Search Country button. When you *do* click the Search Country button, the search is repeated (in a new browser window if you have that setting activated) through that server, finding sites that reside in that server's country. In other words, the country server finds sites located everywhere, and the Search Country button finds sites located in certain countries. The truth is, the different servers present the same results for the most part. Using a server in your country delivers *faster* results.

These new features deserve — and will shortly have — a more detailed discussion. First, though, follow these steps to download the new Toolbar:

**1. Go to the special download page for the beta version of Toolbar 2.0:**

toolbar.google.com/install-beta

2. **Close all other browser windows.**

3. **Click the I AGREE TO THE TERMS OF USE — INSTALL THE GOOGLE TOOLBAR button.**

   These terms of use are pretty much the same as those related to previous Toolbars.

4. **In the Choose Your Google Toolbar Configuration window, select a version of the Toolbar with or without advanced features.**

   The advanced feature that many people complain about involves displaying the PageRank of any displayed site on the Toolbar. Google tracks your movements on the Web, and uses that information to fine-tune its page ranks. The information sent from your computer to Google's computer is anonymous in nearly all cases; it would take a court order for Google to divulge the identity of a Toolbar user. I run the Google Toolbar with Advanced Features turned on.

Wait a few seconds for the Toolbar to download and install in your browser. At this writing, the new Toolbar is available only for Windows Internet Explorer versions 5.xx and 6.xx, just like the previous Toolbar. Figure 9-10 shows the 2.0 Toolbar immediately after installation, with one of its drop-down menus unfolded.

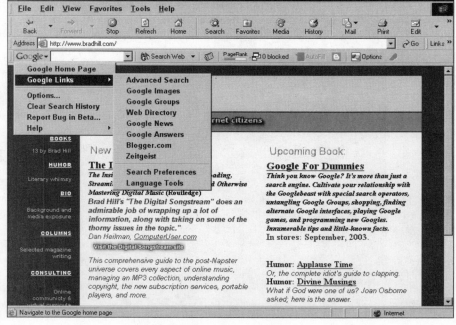

**Figure 9-10:** Google Toolbar 2.0, immediately after installation, before any pop-ups have been blocked and without the Search Country button.

## The Toolbar Options dialog box

Click the Options button to display the Toolbar Options dialog box, shown in Figure 9-11. The first two tabs (Options and More) contain settings for adding and removing Toolbar buttons and controlling how Google and your browser respond to Toolbar searches. Most of these features are identical to those controlling the first version of the Toolbar.

New features and tweaks include these:

✔ You can now make Google the default search engine in Internet Explorer from the Search options section of the More tab. This one-click setting is a big improvement over the complicated procedure necessary before Toolbar 2.0. I describe how to do it the old way, later in this chapter, for those who don't care to use Toolbar 2.0 or who are running Internet Explorer version 4, which can take Google as the default search engine, but can't take either version of the Toolbar.

✔ Also in the More tab, you can tell Google to highlight Web-site form fields that AutoFill can fill in for you. AutoFill can't fill in username field, password fields, and a few other fields. (More on AutoFill a bit later.)

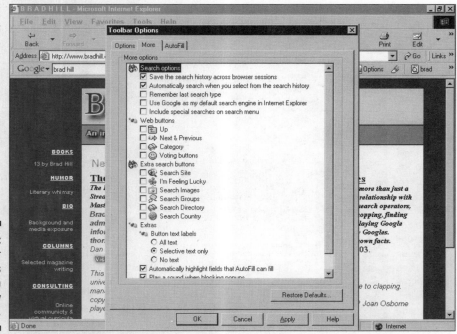

**Figure 9-11:** The Toolbar Options dialog box in the new Toolbar.

✔ Select or unselect the feature that plays a sound when a pop-up ad is blocked. I take satisfaction in knowing when pop-ups have been strangled, but miscellaneous noises drive some people crazy.

✔ The AutoFill tab contains form-field settings used by the 2.0 Toolbar at site registrations and online shopping carts.

Any changes that you make in the More tab are implemented immediately on the Toolbar when you click the Apply button (which leaves the More tab visible) or the OK button (which closes the tab).

## *The Search Country button*

Gratifyingly, the Search Country feature works on news headlines that appear at the top of the search results page. So, if you select Google's server in the United Kingdom (www.google.co.uk) and search for newsy keywords (*george bush*, for example) the resulting headlines are all from U.K. publications. Furthermore, each new browser window that you open by clicking the Search Country button (assuming you have the "Open a new window to display results each time you search" feature activated in the Options panel) remains dedicated to that country's Web sites for as long as you keep searching in that window. This means you can operate parallel browser windows, each searching a different country — the U.S., the U.K., France, and so forth. It's a great way to perform targeted news comparisons in different countries. This feature is so important and so cool that I want to spell out how it works in one possible scenario. Use this set of steps as a template for your own experiments:

1. **Display the Toolbar Options dialog box.**

   To do so, click the Options button on the Google Toolbar.

2. **On the Options tab, select the United Kingdom server from the Search using drop-down menu.**

   It helps to know national domain extensions. A few are: *.uk* (United Kingdom), *.fr* (France), *.jp* (Japan), *.de* (Germany), and *.it* (Italy).

3. **Click to select the option titled "Open a new window to display results each time you search."**

4. **Click the More tab and then click the Search Country option.**

   The option is available only if you selected a different country's index in Step 2. Selecting this option adds the Search Country button to the Toolbar, if it is not there already.

5. **Click the OK button.**

6. **In the Toolbar's search box, type the keywords *george bush* and then click the Search Country button.**

   A new browser window opens to display your search results. The headlines above your search results are all links to U.K. publications.

7. **Open the Options tab, switch to the French server (www.google.fr), and then click the OK button. Click the Search Country button.**

   Your keywords (*george bush*) are already displayed in the keyword box. Clicking the Search Country button launches a new search in a new browser window dedicated to French sites. French-publication headlines appear atop the search results.

8. **Repeat Step 6 if you want, choosing different country servers and opening new windows.**

9. **In any window, type new search terms to look for headlines and sites in that country.**

   Remember to launch new country-specific searches from Google's keyword box, not the Toolbar's keyword box. You have enough windows open without starting new ones.

## The Blog This! button

If you run a Weblog at Blogger.com, the Blog This! button puts one-click blog posting on Toolbar 2.0. The feature is not new to Blogger, which has offered Blog This! as a dedicated browser button for about two years. Putting the button on Toolbar 2.0 is the first sign of Google integrating Blogger, a prize acquisition, into the Google experience.

Chapter 13 covers Blogger.com, including how to set up a free account and begin publishing a blog. After you've got the ball rolling, the Blog This! button capitalizes on the fact that most blog entries are tied to a Web page of some sort — often a news article. If you come across an article about which you'd like to post a comment in your Weblog, here's what you do:

1. **Click the Blog This! button.**

2. **In the pop-up window, sign in to your Blogger account (if you're not already signed in).**

   This is one window the pop-up blocker doesn't block.

3. **Use the drop-down menu to select which blog you're posting to.**

   This step applies if you run more than one Weblog at Blogger.com. Figure 9-12 illustrates the target site, Blogger's pop-up window, and the drop-down menu listing multiple blogs.

4. **Write your blog post around the provided code that will become a Web link to your target page.**

5. **Click the Post button.**

   The blog entry is added to your entry index, ready for editing and publishing, as described in Chapter 13.

**Figure 9-12:**
Blog This!
in action,
ready
to post
an entry
directly
from a
Web page.

# AutoFill

If you register at as many sites as I do and shop online as much as I do, filling out online forms is a tedious hassle. The AutoFill function in Toolbar 2.0 invites you to fill in your crucial information just once, and then let the Toolbar handle any forms you encounter.

Use the AutoFill tab of the Toolbar Options dialog box to enter your information. (See Figure 9-13.) You may add your name, e-mail address, phone number, two mailing addresses, and one credit card. (AutoFill would become much more useful if it accepted multiple credit cards.) Credit card information is protected by a password — and remember, all Toolbar information, including AutoFill, is stored on your computer, not on an Internet computer.

Conveniently, the Toolbar highlights the portions of an online form that it's capable of filling in. You may proceed to fill them in manually if you choose, or just click the AutoFill button on the Toolbar to complete those fields all at once. AutoFill never fills in username and password fields, which can change from site to site. Not so conveniently, AutoFill takes the extra step of telling you what it's about to do, instead of just doing it. That confirmation window (see Figure 9-14) gives you a chance to review your information in a concise format, but also gets annoying after a while.

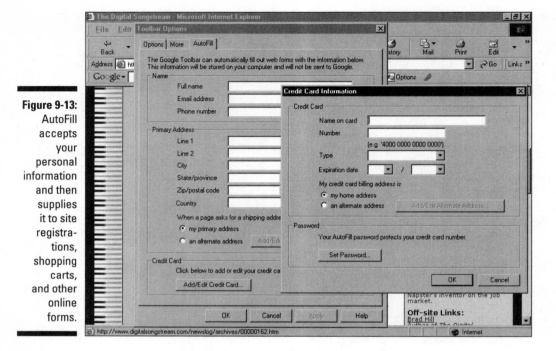

**Figure 9-13:**
AutoFill
accepts
your
personal
information
and then
supplies
it to site
registra-
tions,
shopping
carts,
and other
online
forms.

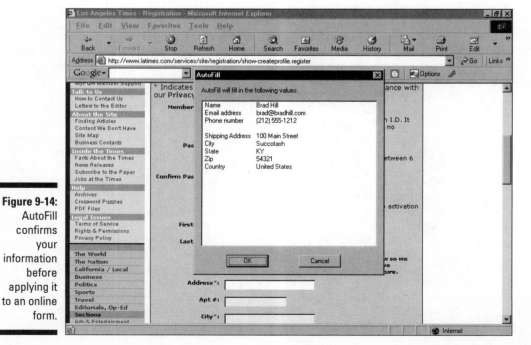

**Figure 9-14:**
AutoFill
confirms
your
information
before
applying it
to an online
form.

## *Pop-up blocker*

Google's new ad-blocker Toolbar add-on is stable, effective, and flexible — an outstanding little utility.

After you add the pop-up blocker to the Toolbar (you can remove and add it at will through the Toolbar Options dialog box), the blocker destroys pop-up browser advertisements before they hit your screen, makes a proud little noise for each blocked ad, and keeps track of the total number of killed pop-ups.

If you want to allow pop-ups from a certain site, simply click the Pop-up Blocker button after you arrive at that site. Google reloads the page, this time allowing the ads to pop up. The button changes appearance (see Figure 9-15) to notify you that pop-ups are enabled for that site and keeps track of your selection. Any time you return to that site, pop-ups are allowed and the button tells you so. The liberation of pop-ups pertains to the entire site. For example, Figure 9-15 shows the changed button on an article page of the New York Times site. The button was changed there, and pop-ups were then allowed through-out the `nytimes.com` site. When you surf away from the liberated site, the button reverts to its original appearance and ads are blocked as normal.

**Figure 9-15:**
Pop-up Blocker allows pop-ups throughout individual sites. The button acts as a toggle, allowing and disallowing ads.

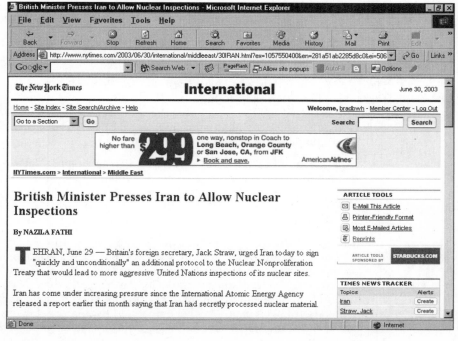

# Pushing Google's (Browser) Buttons

If the Google Toolbar seems a bit complex and overpowering for your needs, the Google browser buttons might be appealing. Three buttons are available, each of which attaches to your browser's toolbar (not the Google Toolbar). One of them performs the simple function of taking you to Google's home page. Another calls up the Similar Pages feature, based on the site currently displayed in your browser. And the last button launches a Google search matching any highlighted word or group of words in the Web page currently displayed.

Follow these steps to get the Google browser buttons:

1. **Go to this page:**

   `www.google.com/options/buttons.html`

2. **Click the <u>Get Your Google Buttons Here</u> link.**

3. **On the next page, follow the instructions to prepare your browser for receiving Google buttons.**

4. **Click and drag the <u>Google Search</u> button link to the Links bar of your browser.**

   A Security Alert window might pop up, warning you that adding the link might not be safe and asking whether you want to continue. Click Yes.

5. **Click and drag the GoogleScout and Google.com buttons to the Links bar, if you want.**

Figure 9-16 shows a browser with both the Google Toolbar and Google buttons. The buttons work as follows:

- **Google Search:** Highlight any single word or group of words on a Web page, then click the Google Search button to run a Web search.

- **GoogleScout:** Click this button to activate the Similar Pages feature, calling up a search results page of sites related to the current page.

- **Google.com:** A simple navigation button, this takes you to Google's home page.

The truth is that the Google buttons don't offer any joy that you can't get through the Google Toolbar. One-click access to Google's home page is available on the Toolbar, as is the Similar Pages feature (under the Page Info button and, if activated, the right-click menu). Google Search is the most interesting browser button, but even that function — instant searching on a text string highlighted in the Web page — is accomplished two different ways in the Toolbar. The first method is highlighting words and clicking the Google Search selection in the right-click menu. The second way is highlighting one or more words and dragging the highlighted excerpt up to the Google Toolbar, which launches a search.

It's important to understand all the methods of highlighting keywords and launching a search to match them, because searching on keywords derived from a Web page is one of Google's most engaging features. First, get comfortable with the three methods of highlighting text in a Web page:

✔ Double-click any single word to highlight it.

✔ In Internet Explorer, triple-click any sentence to highlight the entire sentence.

✔ To highlight a group of neighboring words that don't form a complete sentence, single-click one word and drag the mouse cursor to highlight other words before or after the first word.

You can't highlight words that are displayed as part of a graphics file, such as many advertisements.

After the text is highlighted, you can launch a search on those keywords in one of three ways:

✔ Click and drag the text to any spot on the Google Toolbar and release the mouse button (my favorite method, just because I think it's so cool). The highlighted words appear in the keyword box.

> ✔ Right-click the highlighted text and select Google Search (if the right-click menu selections are activated in Toolbar Options).
>
> ✔ Click the Google Search button if you've put it on your Links toolbar.

# Putting Google Under Your Browser's Hood

Making Google your browser's default search engine casts Google's beneficent shadow over your online life in yet another way. After it's installed, Google springs to action when you click the browser's built-in Search button. This transformation is simple to accomplish in Internet Explorer version 4 or later, and that's the browser used in the following description:

1. **Go to this page:**

   `www.google.com/options/defaults.html`

2. **Click the <u>make Google your default search engine</u> link.**

3. **Scroll down to the Internet Explorer section and click the first <u>this file</u> link.**

   A window appears asking whether you want to Open or Save the file.

4. **Click the Open button.**

   A Registry Editor window most likely appears asking for confirmation to add information to one of your Windows registry folders.

5. **Click the Yes button.**

   A Registry Editor window might appear confirming that information was successfully added to the registry.

6. **Click the OK button.**

7. **Click the Search button on the Internet Explorer toolbar to see Google appear in a left browser pane (see Figure 9-17).**

With Google as IE's default search engine, you can search just by entering keywords into the Address bar (no need to click the Search button and open the left browser pane). Doing so displays Google search results in the browser's main display pane. Figure 9-18 illustrates this method, in a fully appointed IE browser running Google Toolbar, Google buttons, and the default Google search engine in the left pane. Note that the keywords (*wireless home networking*), originally entered into IE's Address bar, are automatically copied to the Google Toolbar's keyword box, but not to the search box in the left pane.

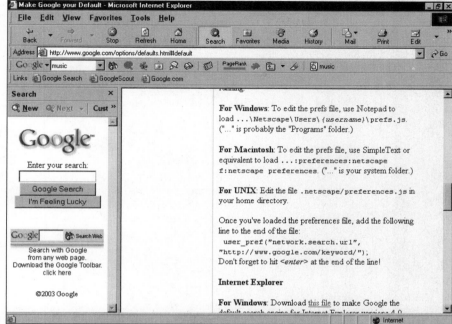

Figure 9-17:
Google as
Internet
Explorer's
default
search
engine: yet
another way
to bolt
Google onto
your
browser.

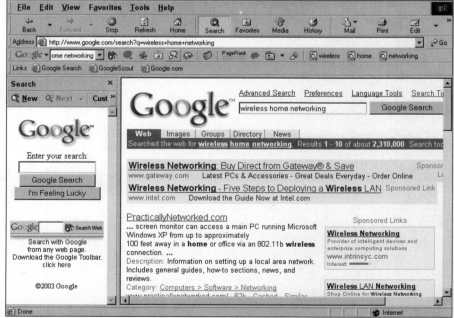

Figure 9-18:
Results of
a search
launched
from IE's
Address
bar, with
Google
as the
default
search
engine. In
this case,
the left pane
is not used.

# Chapter 10

# Googling in Tongues

### In This Chapter

▶ Seeing Google in other languages

▶ Searching for non-English Web sites

▶ Finding Web sites located in other countries

▶ Translating Web sites

▶ Finding a non-English version of Google Toolbar

*T*he global Google has risen. Nobody will be unaffected for long. Google's internationalism is a profound mission that seeks to provide every literate person with a friendly path into the information matrix. This chapter consolidates all Google language initiatives, some of which are also mentioned in other chapters.

More than other U.S.-based Internet portals, Google has extended itself deeper into non-English territory by recruiting the largest workforce in the world: volunteers. Call it distributed computing with brains. Anyone with proper language skills can participate to whatever extent they are able and willing. Even translating a single word gets you into the project. (More on this later in the chapter.)

Besides person power, Google employs machine translation for certain tasks, much as Lycos pioneered. The two-way interface for acquiring a rough machine translation — whereby you may paste text or have Google go get it — takes multilingual ease-of-use to the next level.

Google presents non-English content in three broad areas:

✔ **Interface:** The familiar Google main pages can be displayed in dozens of languages.

✔ **Web pages:** Google can limit a search to Web pages written in any of dozens of languages and even to sites residing in certain countries.

✔ **Ad hoc translating:** Google is always ready to translate text that you enter, either through typing or posting.

This chapter walks you through each of these areas, and adds a section on finding the Google Toolbar in your favorite language.

# Google in Your Native Tongue

Google headquarters for most language tasks is the Language Tools page at this URL:

```
www.google.com/language_tools
```

The Language Tools page (Figure 10-1) is also a menu selection under the Google button of the Toolbar (see Chapter 9), indicating its importance in the buffet of Google services. In the screen shot shown in Figure 10-1, I scrolled down a bit so you could see the main interactive tools on the page. But I want to start lower on the page, where you select an interface language. Oh, heck — I'll show that too. See Figure 10-2.

TIP

Google's interface language can be set on the Preferences page as well as on the Language Tools page. (See Chapter 2 for details about the Preferences page.) This dual placement of the interface language selection is not just duplication. The setting on the Preferences page is more powerful than the setting on the Language Tools page. Use the Language Tools links shown in Figure 10-2 to "audition" Google in different languages, returning to the Language Tools page to try a new one.

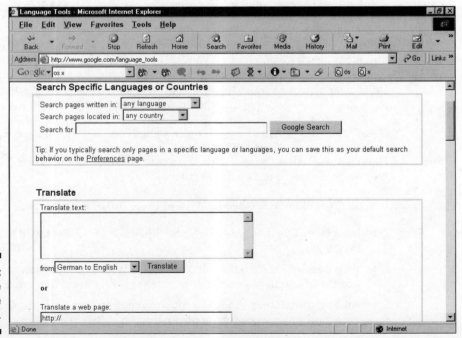

Figure 10-1:
Part of the
Language
Tools page.

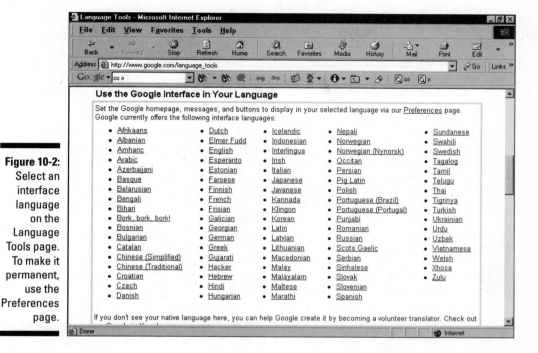

**Figure 10-2:**
Select an
interface
language
on the
Language
Tools page.
To make it
permanent,
use the
Preferences
page.

Trying a new interface language from the Language Tools page doesn't change your language setting on the Preferences page. You remain in your newly chosen language as you surf from page to page in Google (see the following list to find which Google pages are affected by the interface language). But once you leave Google or shut down your browser, subsequent visits to Google return you to the language set on the Preferences page. In fact, simply selecting the Google home page on the Google Toolbar knocks out the language you chose on the Language Tools page and releases Google to your Preferences language.

The *Google interface* is broadly defined as those pages through which you request content, not pages that deliver content. In other words, the Google interface consists of the following:

- ✔ The main home pages for searching the Web, images, groups, and the directory
- ✔ The Google directory
- ✔ All Help pages
- ✔ The Preferences page

✔ All Advanced Search pages

✔ The Language Tools page

✔ The Google Toolbar

(The entire Google directory is, strictly speaking, an interface, and the entire thing is translated into a few major languages — more on this later.) These seven interface areas are all subject to translation. However, language coverage is spotty. Major western languages get the full treatment, including the entire directory. Other major languages (such as Chinese) and many less widely-used languages are works in progress. As you nose around Google in a non-English language, you find that certain pages are still in English. The home pages are always translated — Google doesn't put a link to a language until that basic translation is accomplished. But less essential pages, such as the Language Tools page itself, sometimes await a translator's touch.

The interface language does not affect Web search results. However, Google does translate Google's <u>Cached</u> and <u>Similar pages</u> links on the search results page, as well as other artifacts of the Google interface that appear on results pages. Figure 10-3 shows a results page in the French interface.

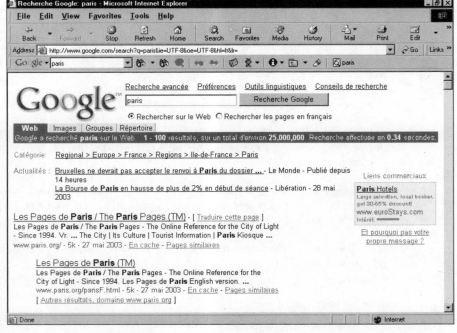

**Figure 10-3:**
A non-English interface delivers normal search results but with supporting links translated.

Who is translating Google into these languages? Maybe you are. If not, you possibly could help. Google puts out an open call for amateur translators. Before you get excited about putting years of high-school Spanish to use, remember that the majors are thoroughly covered. Less in-demand languages still have openings, including Somali, Sanskrit, Samoan, and Cambodian. Others, like Wolof, Lingala, Bhutani, and Burmese, have no translations as of this writing.

To get involved, go to the following page and click the explanatory links:

```
services.google.com/tc/Welcome.html
```

Before enrolling in the language program you must sign off on some legal language (which mostly says that you're not getting paid and Google owns your work) and absorb a translation style guide. Commitment is very light; you may choose to translate a single phrase as your contribution or take over the entire interface for an uncovered language.

If you're interested in following the Google interface translation project, and certainly if you're doing some translating, check out the Google newsgroup devoted to translations. As with other groups originating on Google's newsgroup server, this one is available *only* through Google Groups, and not through a stand-alone newsreader. (See Chapter 4 for details about Google Groups, and Chapter 8 for information about the many Google Labs groups.) Following is the newsgroup address of the message board for translation issues. Type this address in the keyword box at Google Groups to find the message board:

```
google.public.translators
```

# Searching Around the World

No matter what language you choose for the Google interface, you can apply language requests to search results. Not only can you search for Web pages written in certain languages, you can also have Google find pages located in certain countries, regardless of the page's language. These two features are interesting individually — and even more so when combined.

These language controls are near the top of the Language Tools page (Figure 10-1). Operate them using the drop-down menus for language and location. You may use both menus together or either one on its own. Below them is a keyword box for launching the search. Here you may use any applicable search operator (see Chapter 2) in your keyword string.

Your computer's capability to display transliterated languages (those that use a non-Latin alphabet) depends on your browser — Google has nothing to do with it. If you want to read Chinese pages, for example, you might need to download a Chinese plug-in for your browser. Consult your browser's Help menu of Web sites for instructions. If some non-Latin-based pages display part of the text but leave the rest as gibberish symbols, it's because the displayed text is part of a graphic.

I find that a spirit of sheer experimentation overcomes me when searching from the Language Tools page. Fascinating as it is to discover how many pages in Estonian match a certain keyword, it's even more fascinating to discover how many Estonian pages located in Italy match the same word. (Not very many.)

More productively, assuming you're not a linguist, you can get good results by searching in your native language (let's assume it's English) for Web pages in another country. This tactic has the marvelous effect of narrowing the search results while targeting them in some way that relates to your keywords. For example, try searching pages in France for *wine bordeaux.*

More productive still, you can get away from the widespread biases of your home country by searching in other countries. Try this string:

```
alan greenspan filetype:pdf
```

Restrict your search to pages located in Great Britain. Or Japan, for that matter — or any country; just make sure you specify English as the language. Limiting the results to PDF files brings up a lot of academic papers about America's role in macroeconomics and sheds light on the perception of Greenspan outside the U.S.

Figure 10-4 shows the results page for a language-and-location search. Note that you can launch another search in the language you specified on the Language Tools page (using the option under the keyword box), but you can't continue in the location country. If you want to repeat the language-and-location pairing, you must return to the Language Tools page and start over. It would be helpful if Google corrected this limitation.

As with the interface language (see the preceding section), using the Language Tools page to select search languages and countries does not make your choice permanent. In fact, there's no way to make a permanent selection of the country — the Language Tools page is the only interface page that offers a country selection. If you want to permanently select a results language, set that language on your Preferences page (see Chapter 2).

# Translating on the Fly

Google provides machine translation for blocks of text and entire Web pages. Both features are located on the Language Tools page.

You can copy the entire page from a foreign Web page and paste it into the Translate Text: form. But when it comes to Web pages, I find it easier and more satisfying to let Google go get the page and then redisplay it in English. Here's how that works:

1. **Find a Web page in a language you don't understand.**

   You can wait until you encounter one by accident, or you can search for one using the Language Tools page (see the preceding section, "Searching Around the World").

2. **Highlight the page's URL in the Address bar of your browser.**

3. **Press Ctrl+C to copy the URL.**

4. **Go to the Language Tools page.**

   You can also open a new browser window and go to Language Tools there, if you want to remain anchored on the original non-English page.

5. **Press Ctrl+V to paste the URL in the Translate a Web page: box.**

6. **Select a translation from the drop-down menu.**

7. **Click the Translate button.**

The translated page appears with a horizontal frame above it, indicating that it's a Google translation and offering a link to display the original page. (When clicked, that link displays the original page in a new browser window.) Figure 10-5 shows a translated page. Note that English words incorporated in graphics and banners (About This Site, New Additions, and the entire top logo) remain untranslated; only text is recognized by Google as translatable.

Now, here's the great part. Click any link on the translated page, and Google continues translating. You can move through the entire site reading it in the language of your choice. Figure 10-5 illustrates an English-to-French translation so that English-speaking readers can see how the translation works. Normally, though, an English-speaking user would translate a non-English page into English and then click around that site continuing to read in English.

Google doesn't offer many languages in the autotranslate feature. Six, to be exact: English, German, French, Italian, Portuguese, and Spanish. You can't necessarily go from any one of these six to any other.

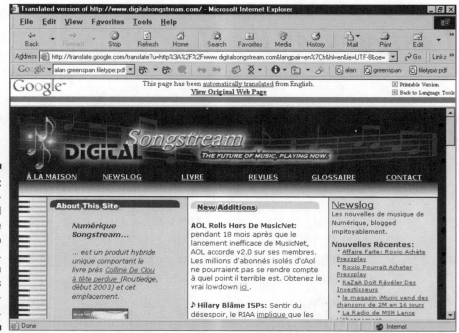

**Figure 10-5:**
A Google-translated Web page (English to French). Words in graphics remain un-translated.

## Making happy of translate by automatic

How good is machine translation? The title of this sidebar gives you an idea of the sort of mangling you can expect. I recently used Google to translate (to English) a long interview from a German Web site. I did the translation as a favor for a friend of mine, who was the interview subject. We laughed ourselves silly over the result, which made my friend sound like a parody of bad English. Nevertheless, the translation conveyed the gist, and that's what you can expect from Google's autotranslate feature. If you don't know the language, Google certainly gets the main points across.

The autotranslate feature described here, and the method of sending Google out to translate pages, enhances the value of the language selection feature described in the preceding section. As long as you stick with a language that Google can translate into English (currently German, French, Italian, Spanish, or Portuguese), searching for pages in those languages is a fantastic way to broaden and internationalize your Internet experience. And you needn't view the foreign page in its original form before sending Google out to translate it. Just use the translation links on search results pages derived from the Language Tools search box.

The following steps describe a streamlined way an English-speaking user can search for foreign sites and read them in English:

1. **On the Language Tools page, use the drop-down menu to select a language to search.**

   For our purposes, the language should be French, German, Italian, Spanish, or Portuguese.

2. **Type one or more keywords.**

   For a true cultural experience, search for something related to the language or its country.

3. **Click the Google Search button.**

4. **On the search results page (see Figure 10-6), click the <u>Translate this page</u> link next to any item you want to read.**

When translating Web pages from search results lists, remember that Google assumes that you want the translation to be in your currently set Google interface language. It doesn't matter whether you've set the language on the Language Tools or Preferences page, that's the language Google translates to. The language Google is aiming for is made obvious by the <u>Translate this page</u> link, which itself is phrased in the target language. (In Figure 10-6, the target language is English.)

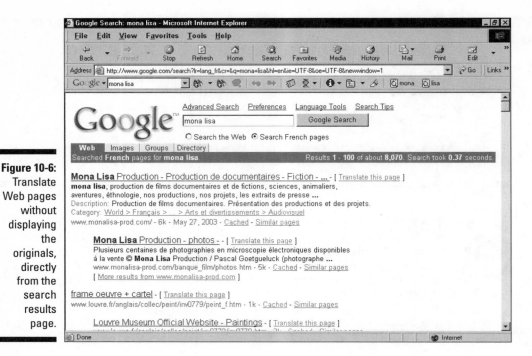

**Figure 10-6:**
Translate
Web pages
without
displaying
the
originals,
directly
from the
search
results
page.

# Non-English Google Toolbars

The Google Toolbar (see Chapter 9) is part of the Google interface, and non-English toolbars are part of the language project. An impressive list of translated toolbars has been assembled, and many target languages remain in the beta test phase at this writing.

Choosing a non-English Google toolbar couldn't be simpler:

1. **Go to the Toolbar page at this URL:**

   ```
   toolbar.google.com
   ```

2. **Scroll down the page and select a language from the drop-down menu, as shown in Figure 10-7.**

3. **Proceed with installing the Google Toolbar, as described in Chapter 9.**

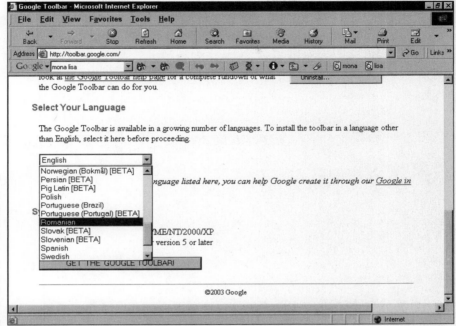

**Figure 10-7:**
Choose a
non-English
Google
toolbar
from an
impressive
list of
languages.

# Chapter 11

# Using Google AdWords

*In This Chapter*

▶ Finding out about AdWords, Google's grass-roots advertising plan

▶ Creating an account and writing your first ad

▶ Activating a created account and running your ad

▶ Managing an ad campaign

▶ Using the Keyword Suggestion tool and the Power Posting tool

*T*hroughout the history of the Web, the game has been to compete for traffic. Perhaps I sound cynical. But anybody who makes the effort to put up a Web page wants somebody else — and preferably many people — to see it. In the Web's earliest days, before companies took a commercial interest, traffic was generated through link lists that were, themselves, popular Web sites. In those giddy and informal days, putting up a great link list, and keeping it fresh, was the ticket to Web fame. At the same time, such a page funneled visitors to the sites it promoted.

Link exchange is still a good way to trade traffic, and the strategy has gained a second wind with the advent of link-intensive Weblogs. But as the Web took hold beyond college campuses (students were its early adopters), surfing traffic began to be valued commercially. That's when paid advertising entered the picture. It was thought, at the beginning, that large banner ads would motivate great interest and drive traffic (clinically called *eyeballs*) through the ad to the sponsoring site. (When an ad works, and somebody clicks it, that event is called a *clickthrough*.) How mistaken that presumption was. Banner advertising never fulfilled the hope surrounding it, though the Web is still clogged with millions of them. Becoming more insistent, perhaps in desperation, the industry has turned to hateful pop-up ads.

Companies still pay good money for banner placement and for the development of new interactive features within banners. But their effectiveness has been devalued, and in the Web's amateur, semi-pro, and small-business space, the supposed effectiveness of banners has largely been debunked. New ways of reaching individuals with targeted, relevant links is what's needed. The natural placement of a highly relevant promotional link is on a search results page, because the person viewing that page is obviously looking for something and is ready to click through to another online destination.

Purchasing placement on search results pages is not new, and the history of this business strategy is rife with disrepute. Many a pre-Google search engine ruined its reputation by polluting its search results with advertisements that were difficult to distinguish from the real listings.

Google aggressively sells space on its search results pages. Several aspects of Google's ad business distinguish it and make it amazingly popular:

- ✔ The ads are clearly separated from search results, keeping Google's integrity untarnished.

- ✔ Google enforces language and style guides that create accurate promotions in the true spirit and tone of the search results page.

- ✔ Anybody can get in on the game, at a price of their own choosing.

- ✔ The ads are distributed across all Google search areas, enhancing their impact and effectiveness. Some ads (the advertiser chooses which) are also eligible to appear on Google search pages run on partner sites.

- ✔ The ads are text-only presentations, which don't slow the display of search results.

- ✔ Ads are not charged upon display. Advertisers pay only when an ad works — that is, upon clickthrough. This policy differs from traditional online advertising, which is billed by *impressions* — in other words, whenever an ad is displayed. (Google sponsorships, which appear across the page above search results, are priced by impression.)

- ✔ The ad-purchase process is almost totally automated and interactive, putting all control of price and frequency in the hands of the advertiser.

Google offers two types of search advertising: AdWords and sponsorships. This chapter concentrates on AdWords, which has quickly dominated the amateur and small-business advertising segments of the Internet. Even large enterprises use Google AdWords as part of their online advertising strategy. With Google's immense traffic flow (more than 200 million searches every day) and superbly targeted search results, reaching eyeballs on the search results page is an essential promotional tactic for Web sites of all shapes and sizes.

# Understanding the AdWords Concept

A business of any size, even an individual just starting out, may purchase AdWords ads. There is no exclusivity based on type of business, amount of revenue, promotional budget, or any other criterion. You do need a Web page. You do not need to be selling something, though there is probably a low limit on the amount of money anybody would spend on advertising a hobby site.

Beginning an AdWords campaign consists of four main steps:

1. Sign up for an AdWords account.

2. Write an ad.

3. Choose keywords with which your ad will be associated.

4. Price your ad and decide on an overall payment budget.

You may create the account and your ads before committing to the campaign; your ads can be activated anytime after creating them.

AdWords ads are nothing more than blurbs. With no graphics and minimal text, they fit concisely along the right side of search results pages. Figure 11-1 shows a results page with several AdWords placements, as well as two sponsorships above the listings. Sponsorships are more expensive, and this section deals only with AdWords.

**Figure 11-1:** AdWords ads appear in a column on the right side of search results pages.

## Google's placement formula

Nothing succeeds like success, the old saying goes — and it holds true for ad placement on Google's search results page. The cost you assign per clickthrough is a big part of the story, but it's not the only part. Google rewards successful ads by placing them higher on the page and reducing their clickthrough costs. Success is measured by clickthrough rate — that is, the number of clickthroughs an ad attracts compared to its display rate. This formula is shown as an *Interest Bar* (looking very much like the PageRank bar for Web sites) at the bottom of each ad. (See Figure 11-1.)

Google rewards high clickthrough rates by lowering the *effective* CPC price assigned to that ad. This means the more popular ad might get top placement even when competing with an advertiser who assigned a higher CPC price. Google does not divulge the exact formula that determines ad placement (just as Google remains silent about its PageRank formula for Web sites). Generally, though, ad placement depends on a combination of CPC price (your bid) and clickthrough rate (your ad's success).

This formula has a flip side. Just as Google rewards success with higher placement, it punishes failure with reduced distribution. That means that if an ad doesn't generate a certain clickthrough level (usually one percent for new advertisers), Google reduces the rate at which it's displayed. This measure might seem harsh, but Google is primarily concerned with the end-user experience on behalf of people using the search engine, and Google wants useful, magnetic ads appearing in the right column of its results pages. If the Interest Bar gets too small, Google doesn't want the ad on its pages.

Google sends a notice to the control center of any advertiser whose ad has been knocked into reduced circulation. You can restore full delivery with a button click, and Google provides tools and tips for improving the clickthrough rate. If Google again pushes aside your ad, and you restore full delivery a third time, Google charges a $5.00 reactivation fee.

The essential item that you create in an AdWords campaign is the ad group. An *ad group* contains one ad, its keywords, and its underlying cost structure. (In truth, an ad group may contain more than one ad, but just one set of keywords targeted by the ads. In the interest of keeping things simple, this section considers an ad group as containing a single ad.)

Following is a breakdown of every element in an ad group:

- ✔ **Headline:** Each ad starts with a headline that links to the target page.

- ✔ **Description lines:** Two very short lines. That's all you get in the way of descriptive content. Concise writing is crucial.

- ✔ **Destination URL:** Each ad spells out the target page address, which is the same as the Headline link address.

- ✔ **Keywords:** Every ad is associated with search keywords that cause its appearance on a results page. Keyword phrases may be used. You can change the keywords at any time.

✔ **Cost-per-click (CPC):** You decide how much the ad is worth to you by deciding the price you will pay whenever somebody clicks it. Google enforces minimums for some keywords. (The total CPC price range for all ads is $.05 to $50.00.) Your ad competes with other ads associated with the same keyword(s), and advertisers willing to pay more get better (higher) positioning on the page.

Google's international sensibility is reflected in AdWords; you may specify a language and a country for your ads. Google determines, more or less successfully, the country from which each user's computer is logged in. The language requirement is more certain: Google shows your ad to users whose Preferences language setting (see Chapter 2) matches your chosen language.

You control the cost of your advertising in two ways: by establishing a CPC (cost-per-click) price for each ad you create, and by creating a daily expenditure budget. If you get many clickthroughs on a certain day and hit the top of your budget, Google pulls your ad for the rest of the day.

Here's how it all works. You create an ad (or ads). You choose one or more keywords (or phrases) to associate with each ad. You decide how much to pay for visitors clicking through each ad. You establish a limit on your daily expenditure on Google advertising. Then, if and when you *activate* your ad, Google automatically places it on search results pages when people search for keywords associated with your ad. Your ad's visibility (placement on the results page) depends on your CPC price compared to that of other advertisers sharing your keyword(s). Most likely, placement varies over time as advertisers come and go, or as they adjust their CPC prices.

The CPC price you set is a *maximum* price. Google charges less if it can, and over time, in most cases, your average CPC price is less than the price you set. In this regard, AdWords is like an eBay auction, in which you're bidding for high placement on a Google search results page. By setting a maximum CPC price, you authorize Google to go up to that price for the top spot. But in reality, you pay only one penny more than required to get that top spot (in other words, one penny more than the top CPC rate set by competing advertisers). If your top bid is less than the top CPC price of two other advertisers, you earn third place in the placement sweepstakes.

You manage your Google advertising activity through a personal *control center* attached to your account. There, you activate and deactivate individual ads, change keywords, and adjust cost settings.

# Creating an Account and Your First Ad

Feel free to check out the AdWords tools before deciding whether you want to advertise. You can open an account and create ads without making a commitment. Your ads don't go into play until you *activate* the account.

Get started by beginning an AdWords account:

1. **Go to the following Welcome to AdWords page:**

   ```
   adwords.google.com
   ```

   After creating your account you can continue to use this page for logging in.

2. **Click the Click to begin button.**

   Google gets you started by creating an ad group. Nothing about this process requires money or payment information.

3. **Under the Step 1 of 4 banner (see Figure 11-2), select languages and countries.**

   This option determines who will see your ads. Users whose Preferences settings match your language selections see your ads. Google uses the computer's IP (Internet Protocol address), which is roughly accurate, to determine a person's location by country (. The default selections here are All Languages and All Countries. If you don't want to waste your ad displays on people who don't speak English (or whatever language your ad uses), select English from the language column. You may select more than one language and country by making selections with the Ctrl key pressed.

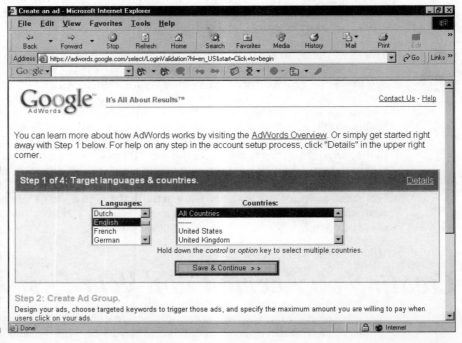

**Figure 11-2:**
Use this page to select the language and country of people who will view your ads.

4. **Click the Save & Continue button.**

5. **Under the Step 2 of 4 banner (see Figure 11-3), create an ad.**

   This is where you write a headline, description, and target page URL. Take some time here. Google has strict editorial guidelines that must be followed; click the AdWords Editorial Guidelines link to understand them. The limited description space requires you to be extremely concise, and I can tell you from personal experience that pithiness is a lot harder than wordiness. Take the time to make every word count.

6. **Click the Create Ad & Continue button.**

7. **On the next page, choose your keywords.**

   People searching on the keywords you place here will see your ad. Type one keyword or phrase per line; press the Enter key to add each subsequent keyword. Later, you'll be able to adjust your keyword selections based on Google's estimate of how much your choices will cost. Assigning keywords is a crucial part of the success and budgeting of an AdWords campaign, but the words you type on this page are not etched in stone. *Note:* See "The Keyword Suggestion tool" section for help with the Keyword Suggestion tool and Power Posting tool, and other keyword tips. For now, throw in some keywords and move on.

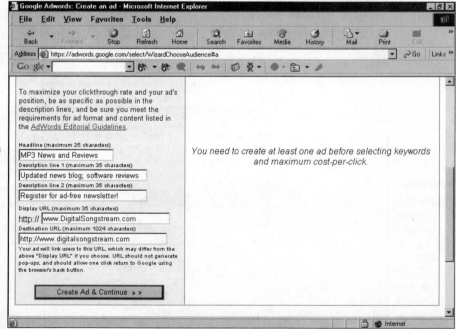

**Figure 11-3:**
Write your heading, description, and URL in these fields. The display URL may be different than your target URL.

8. **Click the Save Keywords button.**

9. **On the next page, choose the monetary currency to use to pay for AdWords and choose the maximum CPC for your keywords.**

   You are not committing any money at this point, nor are you activating your ad. Google opens this page with a suggested CPC price; that number is a competitive price based on other advertisers using your keywords. Feel free to override the suggested price and lower it.

10. **Click the Calculate Estimates button.**

    Google reloads the page with the CPC chart filled in with estimated costs of your ad campaign, broken down by keyword. Google estimates the number of clickthroughs based on current data from advertisers using the same keywords. In the Average Cost-Per-Click column in Figure 11-4, note that the estimates are lower than the assigned maximum cost that you set above the table — quite a bit lower. These numbers are based on competitive prices from other advertisers, and give you an opportunity to adjust you maximum accordingly. (Remember, Google will always charge you the least amount below your maximum to deliver the top spot on the page.) The cost estimates are your first indication of how you should budget your campaign.

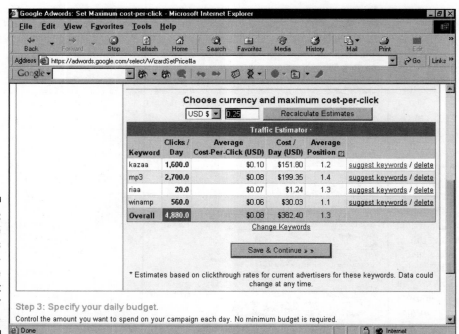

**Figure 11-4:** Google estimates the click-through rate and cost of your campaign.

11. **Click the Save & Continue button.**

    Before continuing, Google gives you a chance to create another ad, starting this process over. Feel free to do so. I'm moving on to the daily budget section.

12. **Click the Continue to Step 3 button.**

13. **Under the Step 3 of 4 banner, enter a daily maximum you want to spend.**

    Creating a daily budget instead of using a longer time frame keeps your ad's exposure fairly even throughout the month (Google's billing period) even if you don't want to spend much. Notice that Google displays this page with a figure already loaded, and that it's higher than your estimated daily expense shown in Step 10 of this list. The higher amount is meant to give you some breathing room and ensure that your ads appear maximally. Feel free to lower the number.

14. **Click the Save & Continue button.**

15. **On the next page, scroll down to the Step 4 of 4 banner and fill in the fields below it.**

    Start by reading the terms and conditions — this is one time when a summary isn't sufficient, so I won't attempt one. (If you activate your ads, you are entering into a business relationship with Google, and you should know the terms and conditions firsthand.) Then fill in an e-mail address and password. Nothing on this page, including clicking the button in the following step, commit you to running your ads. This page creates the account that holds the ads you just created, which may remain inactive for as long as you want.

16. **Click the I agree — Create my AdWords account button.**

    Google send a verification letter to your e-mail address. It should arrive within seconds.

17. **In the e-mail you receive from Google, click the provided link.**

    The next page appears either in the browser window you were using or a new one, depending on your browser and e-mail settings.

You're set. From this point on, log in to your control center by going to the AdWords login page:

```
adwords.google.com
```

There, type your e-mail address and password. Figure 11-5 illustrates the control center before the account has been activated.

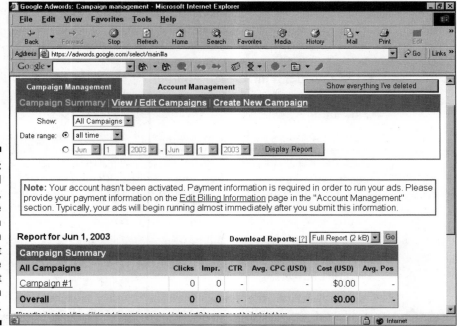

# *Activating Your Account*

The AdWords account is activated by providing credit card information for payment. There is no additional activation procedure after providing your billing information. When your credit card is verified (which takes mere seconds), your ads immediately begin running, as shown in Figure 11-6.

Given Google's continual tidal wave of search traffic, chances are good that your ads and their potential clickthroughs will start appearing before you make any adjustments to your campaign. **Therefore, you should make those adjustments before giving Google your billing information.** If you're confident of your campaign expenses, go ahead and activate the account. But if you created an ad as an experiment and are unsure whether to proceed, *do not* fill in your billing information.

Activate your account with these steps:

1. **Go to your control center.**

   To do so, go to adwords.google.com. Then type your e-mail address and password.

2. **Click the <u>Edit Billing Information</u> link.**

**Figure 11-6:**
This ad
appeared
on this
results page
within ten
seconds of
activating it.

3. **On the Edit Billing Information page, fill in your credit card and address information.**

4. **Using the drop-down menus, choose a primary business type.**

5. **Click the Record my new billing information button.**

Google charges $5 to activate the AdWords account.

# Managing Your Campaigns

The AdWords control center lets you control five main areas of the AdWords experience:

- ✔ View the details of your ads and campaigns
- ✔ Display activity reports showing your ad impressions and clickthroughs
- ✔ Change keywords and prices
- ✔ Create new ads and campaigns
- ✔ Track expenses and manage your billing arrangements

This section gives you a brief tour of the control center. Figure 11-7 shows the main page of the control center.

## Viewing your campaign reports

Google provides two levels of campaign reporting: summary and report. The summary view displays whenever you first enter the control center (see Figure 11-7). The following elements go into the summary report:

- **Campaign selector:** Use the top drop-down menu (Show) to select which campaign you'd like summarized. The default selection shows summaries of all current campaigns. Clicking a single campaign automatically reloads the page with a full report of the selected campaign.

- **Date range:** Use these drop-down menus to select a date range for which Google will summarize your report. Click the lower radio button to choose your own date range.

- **Display Report button:** Click this button to see a summarized report, limited by the campaign selector and date range.

- **Campaign Summary table:** In this green-highlighted table are vital statistics of your campaign's performance, detailed in the following items.

- **Clicks:** The numbers in this column represent clickthroughs on your ad. See the full report for a breakdown of clickthroughs per keyword. The full report appears when you click the <u>View/Edit Campaigns</u> link.

- **Impr.:** This abbreviation stands for impressions, and is a measure of the number of times your ad has been displayed on search results pages.

- **CTR:** This all-important figure represents your clickthrough rate. If it falls too low, Google restricts the distribution of your ad.

- **Avg. CPC:** This dollar (or other currency) figure tells you the average cost-per-click accounted to your ad.

- **Cost:** This column displays the total cost of your clickthroughs to date.

- **Avg. Pos:** Here, you can track how your ads are positioned on the page. One way to increase a low clickthrough rate is to bid higher for better placement.

Google's reporting is reasonably quick but hardly instantaneous. Take into account a time lag that could be as long as three hours.

To see the unsummarized report, click the <u>View/Edit Campaigns</u> link, directly below the Campaign Management tab. A full report is shown in Figure 11-8.

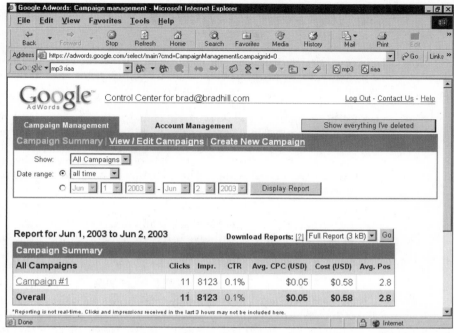

**Figure 11-7:**
The
AdWords
control
center
displays and
edits all
aspects of
your ad
campaign.

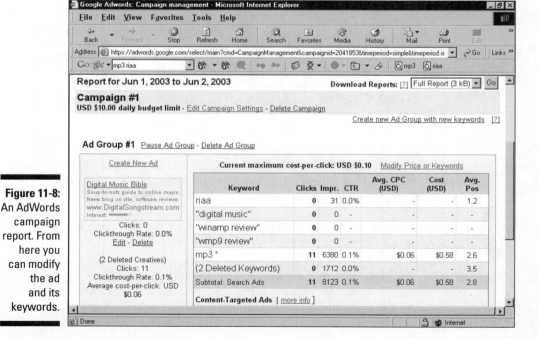

**Figure 11-8:**
An AdWords
campaign
report. From
here you
can modify
the ad
and its
keywords.

## *Editing your campaign*

The full report contains all the information in the summaries, but itemized by keyword. Further, from the report page you can make changes to the campaign's ad text, keywords, costs, and timing. Following is a rundown of editing features you can launch from the report page:

- ✔ **Edit Campaign Settings:** Click this link to alter crucial basic information about the campaign, including its name, daily budget, start and end dates, language and country settings, and network distribution settings. These are the settings you established before activating the account; you always have the opportunity to adjust them. Figure 11-9 shows the options of the Edit Campaign Settings page.

- ✔ **Delete Campaign:** This self-explanatory link not only halts the campaign from running (see the Delete Ad Group item in this list), but erases your ad and all campaign settings. Although Google allows you to view deleted content in AdWords, it does not allow you to restore deletions. So be careful. If you want to stop advertising but preserve the campaign for later reactivation, use the Pause Ad Group option.

- ✔ **Pause Ad Group:** Clicking this link instantly removes the ads associated with the currently displayed keywords from distribution. Big red letters indicate that the ad group is paused, wherever the ad group is listed or referred to in the control center. Click the <u>Resume Ad Group</u> link to get it going again.

- ✔ **Delete Ad Group:** Another dangerous link, this one eradicates an ad group in the currently displayed campaign.

- ✔ **Create New Ad:** This link takes you to the same ad-creation page you went through before setting up the account. There, you can write a new ad (headline, description, and URLs) to associate with the same set of keywords. Google places both ads in distribution. Every ad group may contain multiple ads but just one set of keywords. You may have multiple ad groups in a campaign and multiple campaigns in your account.

- ✔ **Edit and Delete (ads):** Below each ad on the report page for your ad group are <u>Edit</u> and <u>Delete</u> links. Use <u>Edit</u> to reach the ad-creation page, where you can adjust your wording and URLs. The changes take effect immediately, as long as your ad group is not paused. Deleting the ad deletes it instantly.

    After you delete the ad, you can't restore it. You can, however, view the ad — and it's not hard work to write it again.

- ✔ **Modify Price or Keywords:** Click this link to reach a complicated page (see Figure 11-10) for assessing and changing keywords and for altering your price bid for clickthroughs. Change your cost-per-click, and then use the Calculate estimates button to see the same estimation graph as when you set up the account (described earlier in this chapter). Scroll down the page and use the <u>Change Keywords</u> link to adjust your ad group's keywords. See the "More about Keywords" section for a detailed look at choosing keywords for your ads.

✔ **Create new Ad Group:** Use the Create new Ad Group with new key-words link to establish a new leg of your ad campaign. A new group enables you to branch out with new keywords and a new cost structure.

Keywords and cost-per-click remain constant across an ad group, regardless of how many ads are in the group. You may use the same ads in different groups, associated with different keywords and costs. In fact, doing so is a good way to test the performance of certain ads when displayed against different keyword sets.

## Starting a new campaign

In the control center (refer to Figure 11-7), click the Create New Campaign link to start a new set of ad groups. Remember the hierarchy in AdWords: one or more ads in an ad group (all associated with the same keywords and cost-per-click); one or more ad groups in a campaign.

Creating a new campaign takes you through the same process (assigning languages and countries, writing the ad, and establishing costs) described earlier in this chapter.

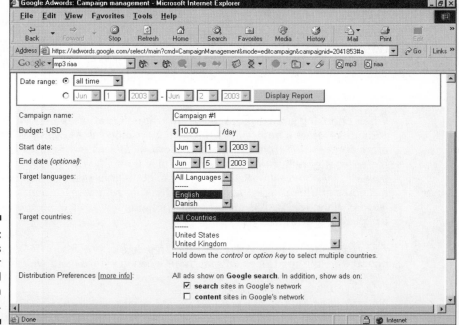

**Figure 11-9:**
Use this page to alter your general campaign settings.

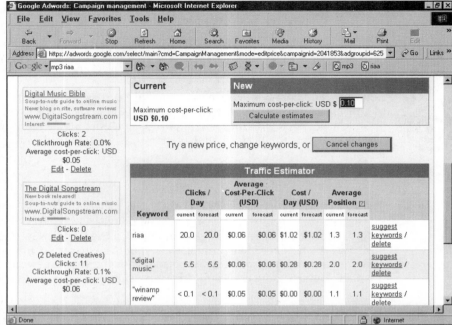

**Figure 11-10:**
You can change your cost-per-click and keywords at any time. Google helps by estimating keyword performance.

# *More About Keywords*

AdWords places a huge emphasis on choosing effective keywords. Getting your ad on the right results pages, where it can be noticed by the right people, is the free method of increasing your clickthrough rate. (The only other method is to raise your placement level, which usually costs more money.)

When choosing keywords, an inherent tradeoff is at work between traffic and placement. Here's how it works. If you choose popular keywords, you have more competition from other advertisers. That means you must bid with a higher cost-per-click price to get good placement. If you choose more obscure keywords with less competition, you can get higher placement more cheaply, but you sacrifice the raging river of traffic that searches for high-profile keywords. Of course, with Google's overwhelming level of traffic, even a relative trickle might be sufficient.

The answer to this tradeoff is to think in terms of precision, not popularity. Spend time finding the exact match between keywords and what you're offering. To this end, Google provides a few tools.

# *Keyword modifiers in AdWords*

Just as Google understands certain search operators when trolling the Web, Google AdWords understands certain keyword modifiers when applied to your ad groups. Of course, you may list single keywords and multiple-word strings. In addition, remember these conventions:

- ✔ **Quotes:** Exact phrase quotes work in AdWords as they do in the search area. Put quotation marks around any set of two or more keywords to denote an exact phrase. Google places your ad on results pages that searched for that exact phrase *plus* any other words the user might have included in his or her search string. For example, *"leather belts"* would force the ad to display on results pages for *leather belts* and also *leather belts handbags*.

- ✔ **Brackets:** Use square brackets around any phrase to keep it exact *and* to exclude any other words in a search string. This tactic limits the appearance of your ad to results pages for your phrase standing alone as the entire search string. For example, *[leather belts]* forces the ad to appear only on results pages for *leather belts*.

- ✔ **Negative keywords:** Exclude keywords by placing a minus sign directly before them. This modifier is identical to the *NOT* search operator (see Chapter 2). When the excluded keyword is used by someone searching Google, your ad does not appear on the results page. For example, *"leather belts" -handbags* means the ad won't appear on results pages for *leather belts handbags*.

# *The Keyword Suggestion tool*

Google has accumulated a great deal of intelligence about search trends and keyboard use. That research is at your disposal when creating an ad group. The Keyword Suggestion tool is how you access Google's ideas for related keywords.

Links to the Keyword Suggestion tool are prolific in the AdWords section; you encounter them when setting up your account and using the control center. But you know how it is — when you really want something, it's nowhere to be found. Follow these steps when you're ready to edit your keywords with Google's help:

1. **In the control center, click the <u>View/Edit Campaigns</u> link.**

2. **On the View/Edit Campaigns page, click the <u>Modify Price or Keywords</u> link.**

3. **On the next page, scroll down to the bottom and click the <u>Change Keywords</u> link.**

If you pause on this page, try the <u>suggested keywords</u> link, which I describe a few paragraphs down from here. This link provides a quicker way to get keyword phrase ideas than proceeding onward to the Keyword Suggestion tool.

4. **On the next page, scroll down to the bottom and click the <u>Open the Keyword Suggestion Tool</u> link.**

Finally! A new window pops open with the Keyword Suggestion tool, as shown in Figure 11-11.

This page reaches into Google's repository of keyword groupings and displays common, short keyword strings related to your keywords. The left column, which is usually very long (much longer than shown in Figure 11-11), shows keyword strings that Google automatically matches with your ad's keywords. Look through this list to approve these extra associations. Exclude any keywords strings you *don't* want by adding them as negative keyword phrases to your list, like this:

```
-"leather furniture"
```

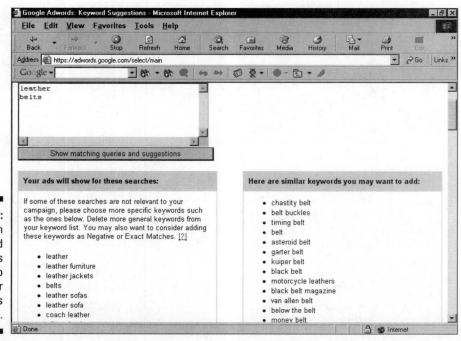

**Figure 11-11:**
Common keyword strings related to your keywords are listed.

Also, consider adding any of these suggested keyword strings as exact phrases with either the quote or bracket modifiers (see the preceding section).

The right list, which is usually much shorter, contains related keyword phrases that don't share a keyword with your list. These provide more general ideas for you to add, exclude, or ignore. Google *does not* automatically match your ad to these keyword strings.

Look back to the previous instruction list, and read Step 3 again. It mentions a quicker way to get keyword ideas. Proceed through those three steps, and then follow these extra steps:

1. **Click any <u>suggest keywords</u> link next to a keyword in the Traffic Estimator table.**

   Doing so breaks out a new section within that table, containing suggested keyword phrases associated with that keyword, as shown in Figure 11-12.

2. **Click the check boxes next to any suggestions that you want included in your keyword list.**

3. **Click the Add these keywords button.**

4. **After the page reloads, click the Save changes button.**

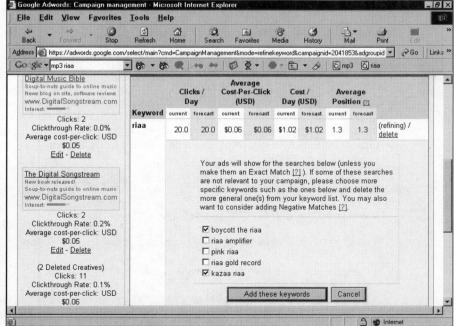

**Figure 11-12:**
Use the Traffic Estimator for quick keyword phrase ideas.

I find the Traffic Estimator suggestions to be just as valuable (perhaps more so) than the ideas generated by the Keyword Suggestion tool. And the Estimator is much faster.

## The Power Posting tool

Advanced AdWords users can assign a different cost-per-click price to each keyword in an ad group and even assign a different target URL to ads that appear for certain keywords. To do so, you use the Power Posting tool.

The Power Posting tool is not a hands-on tool in the same sense as the Keyword Suggestion tool, which is an on-screen form residing on a distinct page. Instead, it's an advanced format for entering keywords, and might better be called a tutorial.

Until now, this chapter has promoted the idea of each ad group containing one cost-per-click (CPC) price for all keywords in the group and one destination URL applying to them all. In fact, Google can assign a different CPC for each keyword and can change the target URL of the ad that appears on results pages for certain keywords. It's all in how you list your keywords — and, best of all, this power trick is easy.

Here's the Power Posting format:

```
keyword ** CPC price ** target URL
```

Honestly, that's all there is to it — those dopey asterisks separate the three elements of keyword, price, and target page. Make sure you put a space before and after each double asterisk.

Suppose that you value some keywords more than others and want some keyword matches to lead to a certain page of your Web site. Following are some sample power-posted keywords. The first one assigns a new price and keeps the default URL:

```
mp3 ** 0.50
```

Next, I keep the default CPC but set a new target page:

```
riaa ** www.digitalsongstream.com/newslog
```

And in the last one, I set a new price and a new target page:

```
winamp ** 0.25 ** www.digitalsongstream.com/reviews/winamp3.htm
```

Enter your power-posted keywords at any time, whether initiating an ad group or revising keywords that have been running in a campaign.

# Chapter 12

# Bringing Google and Its Users to Your Site

*In This Chapter*

▶ Understanding the Google crawl

▶ Preparing your site for the Google spider

▶ Avoiding Google's wrath

▶ Keeping Google (and other search engines) out

From the inception of the Web, it has been the goal of every person with even the most modest Web page to attract visitors. Advertising, reciprocal linking, word of mouth, getting listed in directories — all have been tools in the mad scramble for traffic. In the Google era, getting into the index has become the single most important task of Webmasters large and small.

Search engine listing has always been crucial. Page owners have spent hours submitting requests to innumerable directories and engines. Coding a page in a way that attracts a search engine crawler and puts the page high on the search results list became a crafty art form in the late 1990s. Google has become so dominant in the search field that if your page can't be Googled, it might as well not exist — that's today's presumption.

Getting your site into the Google index requires patience and networking skill, but it's not hard. Improving your *position* in the index — how high your site places on search result lists — is another matter. Old coding tricks don't work in Google, which means bad news and good news. The bad news is that there are no shortcuts to prominence in Google. The good news is that the index is utterly democratic, affording any Web site, large or small, a chance to gain good positioning based on merit. In this way Google is different than, and superior to, other search engines.

This chapter covers how Google crawls the Web, how a new page can get into the index, and how a new or established site can improve its position in Google's search results.

# The Google Crawl

As with most search engines, Google's work has two parts: searching the Web and building an index. When you enter a search request, Google doesn't really go onto the Web to find matching sites. Instead, it searches its index for matches. Google is special at both ends of its work spectrum: first in the scope of its Web searching (and therefore the size of its index), and second in the method by which it matches keywords to Web pages stored in the index.

Most search engine indexes start with an automatic, wide-flung search of the Web, conducted by automated software fancifully called a *spider* or *crawler*. Google's crawl is farther-flung than most, resulting in an index that includes between three and four billion Web pages, as of this writing.

Google performs two levels of Web crawl. The main survey, often referred to as Google's *deep crawl*, is conducted once a month. Google's spider takes slightly more than a week to accomplish its profound examination of the Web. Then, as a bonus, Google launches a so-called *fresh crawl* much more frequently. The fresh crawl is an experimental update to Google's index that began in mid-2002 and runs almost every day, at the company's discretion. Naturally, the fresh crawl is shallower than the deep crawl and is designed to pick up new material from sites that change often. Material gleaned from the fresh crawl is added to the main Google index, though the schedule for the incorporation of new pages is a company secret.

Webmasters can see the fresh crawl in action by searching for their new content in the main Google index. The continual index shifting (sometimes called the *Everflux*) is all part of the Google dance described in Chapter 14. Eager Webmasters should never forget that the Everflux is unpredictable, and one should never pin one's hopes on the Google dance. There are no guarantees in the Google index, including one saying that any particular site must be included in the daily crawl. Hold fast to persistence and patience. The daily crawl is by no means designed to provide the Google index with a daily comprehensive update of the Web. Its purpose is to freshen the index with targeted updates.

# Getting into Google

You can get your site into the Google index in two ways:

- Submit the site manually
- Let the crawl find it

## Checking your status

How do you know whether your site is in the Google index? Don't try searching for it with general keywords — that method is hit-and-miss. You could search for an exact phrase located in your site's text, but if it's not a unique phrase you could get tons of other matches.

The best bet is to simply search for the URL. Make it exact, and include the *www* prefix. If you're searching for an inner page of the site, precision is likewise necessary, and remember to include the *htm* or *html* file extension if it exists.

The *link* operator (see Chapter 2) is invaluable for checking the status of your incoming links, and by extension the health of your PageRank. Use the operator followed immediately by the URL, like this: `link:www.bradhill.com`. The search results show every page containing a link to your URL. When you try this operator with an inner page of your site, remember that you most likely link to your own pages with menus or navigation bars, and Google regards those links as incoming links, artificially inflating your incoming link count. Incoming links within a domain do not contribute to PageRank. You need to get other sites linking to you.

Both these methods lead to unpredictable results. Google offers no assurance that submitted sites will be added to the index. Google does not respond to submissions, and it does not promise to add or discard the site within a certain time frame. You may submit and wait, or you may just wait for the crawl. You may submit *and* wait for the crawl. Submitting does not direct the crawl toward you, and it does not deflect it. Google is impassive and promises nothing. But Google *does* sometimes add sites that are not linked on other pages, and would probably not be found by the crawl.

If you have added a new page to a site already in the Google index, you do not need to submit the new page. Under most circumstances, Google will find it the next time your site is crawled. But you might as well submit an entirely new site, even if it consists of a single page. Do so at this URL:

```
www.google.com/addurl.html
```

The submission form could hardly be simpler. Enter your URL address, and make whatever descriptive comments you feel might help your cause. Then click the Add URL button — which is a bit misleading. Submitting a site is not the same as adding it to the index! Only the Google crawler or a human Google staffer can make additions to the index.

## *Luring the spider*

The key to attracting Google's spider is getting linked on other sites. Google finds your content by following links to your pages. With no incoming links, you're an unreachable island as far as the Google crawl is concerned. Of course, anybody can reach you directly by entering the URL, but you won't pluck the spider's web until you get other sites to link to you.

In theory, any single page currently crawled by Google (that is, in the index) that links to your page or site is enough to send Google's spider crawling toward you. In practice, you want as many incoming links as possible, both to increase your chance of being crawled (sounds a little uncomfortable, doesn't it?) and to improve your PageRank after your site is in the index.

Keep your pipes clean. That is to say, don't make life difficult for Google's spider. In other words (how many different ways can I say this before I finally make myself clear?), host your site with a reliable Web host, and keep your pages in good working order. The Google crawl attempts to break through connection problems, but it doesn't keep trying forever. If it can't get through in the monthly deep crawl and your site isn't included in the fresh crawl, you could suffer a longish, unnecessary delay before getting into the index.

Don't expect instant recognition in Google when you add a page to your site. If your site is part of the fresh crawl, new page(s) show up fairly quickly in search results, but there's no firm formula for the frequency of the fresh crawl or the implementation of its results. If the spider hits your site during the deep crawl, the wait for fresh pages to appear in the index is considerably longer. The same factors apply if you move your site from one URL address to another. (Although not if you merely change hosts, keeping the same URL.) Complicating that situation is that your site at the old address might remain cached (stored) in Google's index, even while search results are matching keywords to your site at the new address. This confusion is one reason some Webmasters don't like the Google cache — when they make a change to a site or its address, they don't want the old information living on in the world's most popular search index.

## Index or directory?

Most of this chapter is devoted to getting a foothold in Google's Web search index, which should not be confused with the Google Directory. Although the search index is largely automated, the Directory consists of hand-picked sites selected by a volunteer staff numbering in the hundreds. Chapter 3 describes the Open Directory Project, which Google uses and upon which Google imposes its PageRank formula.

Getting into the Directory is more direct than getting into the search index, but you must go to the Open Directory Project, not to Google. Go to this URL

    www.dmoz.org/add.html

and follow the instructions there. See also the section called "Submitting a Web Page to the Directory" section in Chapter 3.

## On your own

Creating the Google index is an automated procedure. The Google spider crawls through more than three billion pages in its surveys of the Web. Some sites (small ones in particular) might be tossed around by the Google dance, even to the extent of dropping out of the index for a month at a time and then reappearing. PageRank can fluctuate, influencing a site's position in search results. Some sites have trouble breaking into the index in the first place.

Although Google receives and attends to URL submissions, as described in this chapter, the company does not provide customer service in the traditional sense. There is no customer contact for indexing issues. The positive aspect of this corporate distance is that the index is pure — nobody, regardless of corporate size or online clout, can obtain favorable tweaking in the index. The downside is that you're on your own when navigating the surging tides of this massive index. Patience and diligent networking are your best allies.

## Spider-friendly tips

Getting into the Google index is largely a waiting game, in which preparation, persistence, and patience are the tools of success. However, a number of techniques incline Google's spider to look on you more favorably:

✔ **Place important content outside dynamically generated pages:** A dynamic page is one created on-the-fly based on choices made by the site visitor. This method of page generation works fine when the visitor is a thinking human. (Or even a relatively thoughtless human.) But when an index robot hits such a site, it can generate huge numbers of pages unintentionally (assuming robots ever have intentions), sometimes crashing the site or its server. The Google spider picks up some dynamically generated pages, but generally backs off when it encounters dynamic content. Weblog pages do not fall into this category — they are dynamically generated by *you*, the Webmaster, but not by your visitors.

✔ **Don't use splash pages:** Splash pages, (which Google calls doorway pages) are content-empty entry pages to Web sites. You've probably seen them. Some splash pages employ cool multimedia introductions to the content within. Others are mere static welcome mats that force users to click again before getting into the site. Google does not like pointing its searchers to splash pages. In fact, these tedious welcome mats are bad site design by any standard, even if you don't care about Google indexing, and I recommend getting rid of them. Give your visitors, and Google, meaningful content from the first click, and you'll be rewarded with happier visitors and better placement in Google's index.

✔ **Use frames sparingly:** Frames have been generally loathed since their introduction into the HTML specification early in the Web's history. They wreak havoc with the Back button, and they confuse the fundamental format of Web addresses (one page per address) by including independent page functions within one Web page. However, frames do have legitimate uses. Google itself uses frames to display threads in Google Groups (see Chapter 4). But the Google crawler turns up its nose when it encounters frames. That's not to say that framed pages necessarily remain out of the Web index. But errors can ensue, hurting both the index and your visitors — either your framed pages won't be included, or searchers are sent to the wrong page because of addressing confusion. If you do use frames, make your site Google friendly (and human friendly) by providing links to unframed versions of the same content. These links give Google's diligent spider another route to your valuable content, and give us (Google's users) better addresses with which to find your stuff. And your visitors get a choice of viewing modes — everybody wins.

✔ **Divide content topically:** How long should a Web page be? The answer differs depending on the nature of the page, the type of visitor it attracts, how heavy (with graphics and other modem-choking material) it is, and how on-topic the entire page is. Long pages are sometimes the result of lazy site building, because it takes effort to spin off a new page, address it, link to it, and integrate into the overall site design. From Google's perspective, and in the context of securing better representation in the index, breaking up content is good, as long as it makes topical sense. If you operate a fan page for a local music group, and the site contains bios, music clips, concert schedules, and lyrics, Google could make more sense of it all if you devote a separate page to each of those content groups. Google also likes to see page titles relating closely to page content. Keeping your information bites mouth-sized helps Google index your stuff better.

✔ **Keep your link structure tidy:** Google's spider is efficient, but it's not a mind-reader. Nor does it make up URL variations, hoping to find hidden content. The Google crawler is a slave to the link. If you want all your pages represented in the index, make sure each one has a link leading to it from within your site. Many site-building programs contain link-checking routines and administrative checks to diagnose linkage problems. Simple sites might not warrant such firepower; in that case, check your navigation sidebars and section headers to make sure you're not leaving out anything.

# The Folly of Fooling Google

For as long as search engines have crawled the Web, site owners have engineered tricks to get the best possible position on search results pages. Traditionally, these tricks include the following:

✔ Cloaking, in which important, crawl-attracting keywords are hidden from the view of site visitors but remain visible to spiders

✔ Keyword loading, related to cloaking, in which topical words are loaded into the page's code, especially in page titles and text headers

✔ Link loading, through which large numbers of incoming links are fabricated

Spider manipulating tricks have worked to some extent in the past thanks to the automated nature of search crawling. Google is highly automated, too, but more sophisticated than most other spiders. And as a company policy, Webmaster chicanery is dealt with harshly. Obviously, you're not breaking any laws by coding your pages in a certain way, even if your motive is to fool Google. But Google doesn't hesitate to banish a site from the index entirely if it determines that its PageRank is being artificially jiggered. No published policy states when or if a banished site is reinstated. Google is serious about the integrity of PageRank.

The best rule of thumb is this: Create a site for people, not for spiders. Generally, the interests of people and Google's spider coincide. A coherent, organized site that's a pleasure to surf is also a site that's easy to crawl. Keeping your priorities aligned with your visitors is the best way to keep your PageRank as high as it can get.

# Keeping Google Out

Your priority might run contrary to this chapter, in that you want to *prevent* Google from crawling your site and putting it in the Web search index. It does seem pushy, when you think about it, for any search engine to invade your Web space, suck up all your text, and make it available to anyone with a matching keyword. Some people feel that Google's cache is more than just pushy, and infringes copyright regulations by caching an unauthorized copy of a site.

If you want to keep the Google crawl out of your site, get familiar with the robots.txt file, also known as the Robots Exclusion Protocol. Google's spider understands and obeys this protocol.

The robots.txt file is a short, simple text file that you place in the top-level directory (root directory) of your domain server. (If you use server space provided by a utility ISP, such as AOL, you probably need administrative help in placing the robots.txt file.) The file contains two instructions:

✔ **User-agent:** This instruction specifies which search engine crawler must follow the robots.txt instructions.

✔ **Disallow:** This line specifies which directories (Web page folders) or specific pages at your site are off-limits to the search engine. You must include a separate Disallow line for each excluded directory.

A sample robots.txt file looks like this:

```
User-agent: *
Disallow: /
```

This example is the most common and simplest robots.txt file. The asterisk after `User-agent` means *all* spiders are excluded. The forward slash after `Disallow` means that *all* site directories are off-limits.

The name of Google's spider is Googlebot. ("Here, Googlebot! Come to Daddy! Sit. Good Googlebot! Who's a good boy?") If you want to exclude only Google and no other search engines, use this robots.txt file:

```
User-agent: Googlebot
Disallow: /
```

You may identify certain directories as impervious to the crawl, either from Google or all spiders:

```
User-agent: *
Disallow: /cgi-bin/
Disallow: /family/
Disallow: /photos/
```

Notice the forward slash at each end of the directory string in the preceding examples. Google understands that the first slash implies your domain address before it. So, if the first `Disallow` line were found at the `bradhill.com` site, the line would be shorthand for `http://www.bradhill.com/cgi-bin/`, and Google would know to exclude that directory from the crawl. The second forward slash is the indicator that you are excluding an entire directory.

To exclude individual pages, type the page address following the first forward slash, and leave off the ending forward slash, like this:

```
User-agent: *
Disallow: /family/reunion-notes.htm
Disallow: /blog/archive00082.htm
```

Each excluded directory and page must be listed on its own `Disallow` line. Do not group multiple items on one line.

You may adjust the robots.txt file as often as you like. It's a good tool when building out fresh pages that you don't want indexed while still under construction. When they're finished, take them out of the robots.txt file.

# Part IV
# Tricks, Games, and Alternatives to Google

The 5th Wave                    By Rich Tennant

"Look, I've already launched a search for `reanimated babe cadavers' three times and nothing came up!"

# In this part . . .

*L*ike a supportive parent, Google is there when
you need it but wants you to soar on your own.
Blogging is one way Google helps you become an independent force on the Web, and Google's Weblog service,
Blogger.com, is the topic of this part's first chapter.

Then come two chapters that will open your eyes to new
ways of Googling. Google freely gives away its most valuable asset: access to its index. The result is a host of alternate Google sites that deliver the same search results as
Google.com but through a variety of different interfaces.
The TouchGraph browser described in Chapter 14 will
twist your mind into a new perspective on the living network surrounding every Web site. Chapter 15 lightens the
intensely determined mood in which most of us search by
presenting online games based on poking the Google index
in new ways. You would never think the Googlebeast was
so playful.

Prepare to have your horizons widened and your world-
view expanded. You're going far afield in this part, to
Googlish dives most people don't know exist. The atmosphere is heady with experimentation. The sites covered in
Chapters 14 and 15 are relatively new, and some are a
little rough around the edges. No matter — you're on an
adventure in this part of the book. Third-party Google
development will get better and more interesting. In the
meantime, take satisfaction knowing that you're a pioneer
in the Googlesphere. [Editors' note: The good news is that
Brad's caffeine saturation is wearing off. The bad news is
that he's headed to the espresso maker for another jolt.]

# Chapter 13

# Hosting a Weblog with Google's Blogger

## In This Chapter

▶ Starting a free Blogger account

▶ Creating a Weblog and selecting a template

▶ Posting, writing, and publishing to your blog

▶ Formatting your blog

▶ Changing templates

*W*eblogs (blogs) have been steadily growing in popularity for years, and now represent a massive, unstoppable online trend. Many people have heard of blogs, but not many can quite describe what they are, and even fewer people know how to get their own blog started. A company called Pyra operates a service called Blogger.com that makes it almost ridiculously easy. Google snapped up Blogger.com in February, 2003, and Blogger.com is now a Google service.

Blogs make it easy to operate a Web site that's updated frequently. Most bloggers update their sites at least once a day and sometimes several times during the day. And night. (Bloggers instinctively shy away from sleep.)

Blogs are popularly regarded as online journals, and rightly (if incompletely) so. Blogging tools are perfect for divulging the minutiae of your daily existence for the world to read. Well, part of the world. A small part. A few friends. Your mother. But who knows? Many an amateur blogger has attained virtual fame in online society by hitting a unique blogging angle, or by designing the blog cleverly, or through excellent research and linking, or simply by having something worthwhile to say.

Blogs are also used for less personal projects than diary publishing. Any site that updates its content frequently uses something similar to a blog or a blogging program. For example, anyone interested in MP3 and digital music can get the latest industry news at the Digital Songstream site:

www.digitalsongstream.com/newslog

That was a shameless plug — the site is mine. It illustrates how a relatively impersonal, newsy site can deliver fast-changing content through blogging.

It's a fine line between journaling and journalism, and professional journalists have joined the blogging ranks with differing degrees of enthusiasm. In some cases, they have felt forced into blogging by the amateur journalists who use blogs to link to news articles on the Web, commenting on them — with quite a bit of vitriol in some cases. The authors of those articles take to blogging to defend themselves in some cases and to provide their readers with a less formal, less edited, more personal interpretation of the news. During the 2003 war in Iraq, some journalists traveling with the troops used blogs to fill in the gaps of their official reporting. At least one news organization (CNN) forced one of its reporters to discontinue his unofficial blogging.

So Weblogs are controversial, influential, increasingly popular, and definitely fun. Google, with its Blogger service, makes it easy to get started.

# Starting Your Blogger Account

Basic Blogger accounts are free, though you can upgrade to a Pro account with more features. I cover Blogger Pro later in this chapter, but many casual bloggers find no need to upgrade. You can maintain a slick and satisfying Weblog with the basic free tools.

Follow these steps to get started with a basic account.

1. **Go to the Blogger.com home page, which is shown in Figure 13-1:**

   ```
   www.blogger.com
   ```

2. **Scroll down to SIGN UP, enter a username and password, and then click the sign up button.**

3. **On the next page, fill in your real name and e-mail address.**

4. **Check the box agreeing to the terms of service.**

   Blogger's terms of service are benign, even friendly, asserting that you retain ownership to all blogged content and that you won't post anything illegal. Click the terms of service link to read the exact wording of typical TOS stipulations. By the way, if you're using Google Toolbar 2.0 (described in Chapter 9), you can use AutoFill to complete the name and e-mail address forms.

5. **Click the Enter button.**

That's all there is to it. You now have a free Blogger account and can begin designing and publishing your blog.

**Figure 13-1:**
Blogger, the
Google
Weblog
service that
offers free
Internet
publishing.

# Creating a Blog at BlogSpot

The following steps describe the simple process of naming, describing, and addressing a new Weblog, and choosing a page-design template. These steps are for hosting the Weblog at BlogSpot, Blogger's free Weblog host. Like any site, a Weblog must be hosted on an Internet server. BlogSpot provides that server, making it easy to get started even if you've never made a Web page or created a Web hosting account.

If you have a Web site already or want to open a new Web host account (not at BlogSpot) for housing your Weblog, Blogger gives you that option. I describe how to proceed with this option in the next section.

The quickest path to blogging for beginners is to host at BlogSpot. Follow these steps to get started:

1. **After signing in to Blogger, click the <u>Create a new blog</u> link.**

2. **On the Step 1 of 4 page, create a title and description for your Weblog, select whether it's a public blog, and then click the Next button.**

   Making a private blog keeps it out of Blogger's directory and off the Fresh Blogs and Blogs of Note lists on Blogger's home page. However, making a private blog does not hide it from the Internet at large — you can do that only on your Web host's server. The Google spider (see Chapter 12) can find private blogs on Blogger just as easily as public ones.

3. **On the Step 2 of 4 page, choose to host the Weblog at BlogSpot.**

4. **On the Step 3 of 4 page, choose a URL, read and accept the BlogSpot Terms of Service, and then click the Next button.**

   You are choosing the portion of the URL preceding `.blogspot.com`. For example, if I were to choose `bradhill`, the entire URL would be `http://bradhill.blogspot.com`. As you can see in Figure 13-2, all you need to focus on is the portion of the URL that you have control over.

5. **On the Step 4 of 4 page, select a blog template, and then click the Next button.**

   The template is your blog's page design. Click any thumbnail sample you see on this page for a full-size version. You may change from one template to another at any time, even after you've started posting entries to your blog.

After Step 5, Blogger has everything it needs to set up your Weblog. A page appears asking you to wait a few seconds. The next window to appear is Blogger's main editing screen, as shown in Figure 13-3.

**Figure 13-2:** Choose the identifying portion of the URL that will be your blog's Web address.

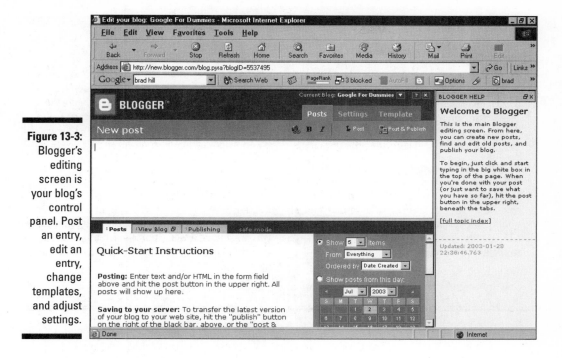

**Figure 13-3:**
Blogger's
editing
screen is
your blog's
control
panel. Post
an entry,
edit an
entry,
change
templates,
and adjust
settings.

At this point, even before making your first blog post, your Weblog appears on Blogger's home page whenever you sign in.

# Creating a Blog at Your Own FTP Server

Hosting a Blogger Weblog on your own server is more complicated, but the Blogger service remains the same. Blogger provides the template, manages your posts, and performs the necessary uploading. The difference is that it uploads to a Web host elsewhere, not BlogSpot.

Starting your blog at your own FTP site follows almost the same steps as starting it at BlogSpot. The only variation is on the Step 3 of 4 page. In the instructions in the preceding section, you choose a URL for your BlogSpot address. When creating the blog elsewhere, that step asks you to fill in the address and routing details of your Web host. Three required pieces of information, and one optional piece of information, are inserted on this page:

✔ **FTP server (required):** This is the IP address of your Web host server. If you are unsure of the FTP address, contact your Web host administrator or look at the control panel of your Web site.

## Untangling Pro and Plus

Blogger's basic account, which enables you to create a Weblog, is free. Likewise, the basic BlogSpot agreement enables you to host the blog at Blogger without cost. (Advertisements are displayed on your blog when hosted for free at BlogSpot.) Both basic services offer upgrades.

Blogger Pro upgrades the basic blogging features and also claims to be more reliable than basic Blogger. (I never found the basic version to be unreliable.) The upgrade is charged an annual subscription fee that, at this writing, is $35. Blogger has been promising (threatening?) to raise it for a long time.

BlogSpot Plus costs $15 a year at this writing, and its major upgrade is the elimination of advertisements. BlogSpot Plus also allows multiple blogs in one account and provides traffic statistics. The cost is much less expensive than full-featured Web hosting plans. So if the blog is your entire site (you don't need e-mail and shopping carts and a multitude of other features), BlogSpot offers an attractive deal.

It's important to remember that some Blogger Pro features don't work with a basic BlogSpot-hosted Weblog — in particular, uploading images. So to get full mileage from Blogger Pro, you must have a BlogSpot Plus account, or you must host the blog at a different Web host (your own FTP server).

✔ **FTP Path (optional):** Fill this in if you want your Weblog located somewhere other than the root directory of your server. If your blog is the entire site or will share the root directory with other pages, you can leave this field blank.

✔ **Blog filename (required):** Common filenames include *blogger.html*, *blog.html*, *weblog.html*. In most cases, either the *.htm* or the *.html* extension works. If you use server-side scripting, you know to use the extension required by your scripts.

✔ **Blog URL (required):** Here, fill in the entire URL of your blog, which consists of your domain plus the blog filename, like this: *http://www.bradhill.com/blogger.html*. In this example, the domain is *www.bradhill.com* and the blog filename is *blogger.html*.

After filling in this information and clicking the Next button, you choose a template. Then you're in business, just as you would be at BlogSpot.

## *Running Your Blog*

After you create a blog, the creative part begins when you start writing, posting, and publishing yourself. The edit screen (look back at Figure 13-3) is your blog's main control panel. On that screen you can write a blog entry, edit previous entries, delete previous entries, search for an entry, and publish newly written entries. You can also change settings (including quite a few you didn't encounter when creating the blog) and choose a new template at the edit screen.

The following sections provide a rundown of the operations of the edit screen. Examples and illustrations are all from the perspective of a BlogSpot blog, but the basic functions of operating a Blogger blog work identically when hosting it at another FTP server.

## Writing, posting, and publishing

Blogs are all about writing. So get started! If it makes it easier to overcome that first blush of self-consciousness, remember that you can delete any posted entry, at any time.

Figure 13-4 shows a blog's first post in progress, just before posting. It probably won't win a Pulitzer, but it does show off the formatting features of the edit screen, which follow:

- **Bold typeface:** Highlight any word of groups of words, and click the B button on the toolbar. If you click before typing, you must position the cursor between the <strong> bracket and the </strong> bracket, and then type.

- **Italics:** Highlight any word or group of words, and click the I button on the toolbar. Again, if you click it before typing, you must position the cursor between the <em> and </em> brackets.

- **Hyperlinks:** Use the button that looks like a globe to insert hyperlink tags, creating a link to another Web page. (The button appears next to the B and I buttons.) You must know the outside page address and type it into the URL dialog box that opens when you click the button. Figure 13-4 shows the hyperlink box floating above the edit screen.

After writing your entry, post it to the blog. Remember that posting and publishing are not the same. Posting an entry lets you see it properly formatted, with tags invisible. At that point your entry is placed in proper order in your blog's data, but is not yet visible to anybody visiting your blog. Publishing makes it visible. You may post without publishing (using the Post button) or post and publish simultaneously (using the Post & Publish button). Figure 13-5 shows a posted entry. If you post an entry without publishing, use the large PUBLISH button in the lower frame when you're ready to let the world see your entry.

You can post an entry to your blog from any Web site, without displaying the Blogger edit screen, by using the Blog This! button on Google Toolbar 2.0. See Chapter 9 for details about this.

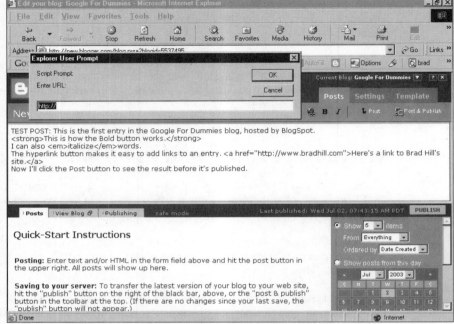

**Figure 13-4:**
Creating a
test post is a
good idea,
and it can
be deleted
later. This
entry has
not yet been
posted.

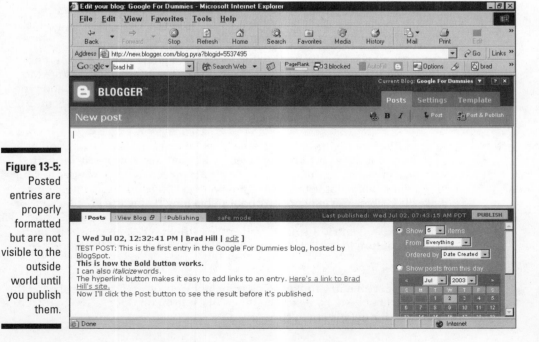

**Figure 13-5:**
Posted
entries are
properly
formatted
but are not
visible to the
outside
world until
you publish
them.

When you want to see how your blog looks to visitors, you have two choices. The quicker of the two is simple: Just click the View Blog tab in the lower frame of the edit screen. Your blog appears in that lower frame. You might want to adjust the relative sizes of the lower and upper frames by dragging the center divider upward. Even so, as you see in Figure 13-6, the space is cramped, especially on small screens. The alternative is to open a new browser window and type in your blog's URL, viewing it in a full browser window.

Any post, even a published post, can be edited. When you edit a published post and then republish it, the entry resumes its previous place (that is, its previous date and time) in the Weblog. Editing a post does not push it out of order. Follow these steps to edit any entry:

1. **In the lower frame of the edit screen, display the entry you want to edit.**

   Early in your blogging process, you don't have many entries to choose from. When your blog grows, though, use the search tool in the right-hand portion of the lower frame.

2. **Click the <u>edit</u> link next to whichever entry you want to edit.**

   The entry moves up to the edit frame, displayed in raw form with formatting tags. Only one entry at a time can appear in the editing frame. Figure 13-7 shows an entry waiting to be edited. Note that it still appears in the lower frame. The two frames are not interactive — that is, changes you make in the upper frame are not immediately reflected in the lower frame. When you post (or post and publish) your edited entry, the new version appears in the lower frame.

3. **Make whatever changes you want in the editing frame.**

   You may also delete the entry (using the Delete button) or cancel the edit (with the Cancel button).

4. **Click the Post button or the Post & Publish button.**

   Your edited entry appears in the lower frame.

## Adjusting your blog settings

Blogger lets you change the settings you created when first setting up your Weblog, including the blog name, the description, and even the URL. In addition, you can move the blog from BlogSpot to another FTP server. You also have choices to make about how your blog is formatted within the template you've already chosen. These choices have default settings that are in place, but you may change those settings at any time.

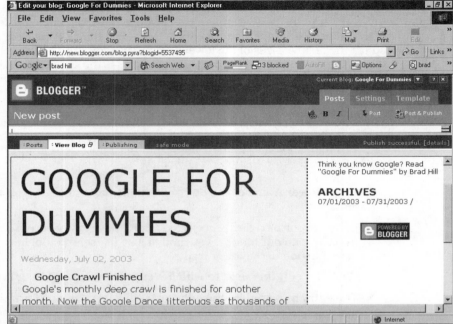

**Figure 13-6:**
Viewing a
blog in the
edit screen
is quick
and easy
but also
cramped for
space.

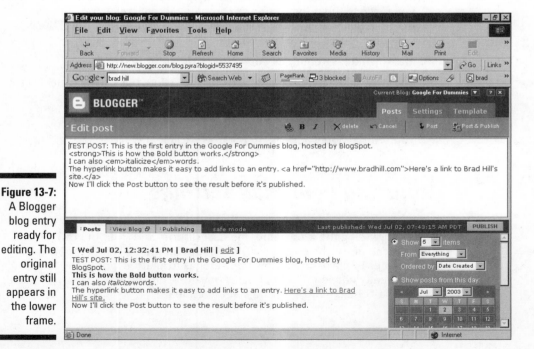

**Figure 13-7:**
A Blogger
blog entry
ready for
editing. The
original
entry still
appears in
the lower
frame.

Click the Settings tab in the top frame of the edit screen. There, you see five new tabs that represent folders holding the available settings. They are

✔ **Basics:** This is where you change your blog's name and description. Also, you may change it from a private to a public blog, or vice versa.

✔ **Publishing:** Use this tab to move out of BlogSpot to another FTP server, or to change your URL.

Change the URL with caution! If you've spent any effort promoting your blog, you might have incoming links from other sites. If you change your URL, all those links to your pages stop working and your promotions start again from scratch. My advice: Choose your URL carefully at the beginning, and then leave it alone. (Moving from BlogSpot to another FTP server necessarily changes the URL.)

✔ **Formatting:** Several options lurk under this tab, as shown in Figure 13-8. I describe them in the next section, "Formatting your blog."

✔ **Archiving:** Use these settings to choose weekly or monthly archives of your past entries. If you are prolific, making several entries each day, the weekly archive is better. Otherwise, a monthly organization is easier for visitors to navigate. The Archive Index File setting defaults to No, and you should probably keep it that way for at least several months. Then, when your blog has grown, you can consider spinning off the archive as a separate file, with its own template and settings.

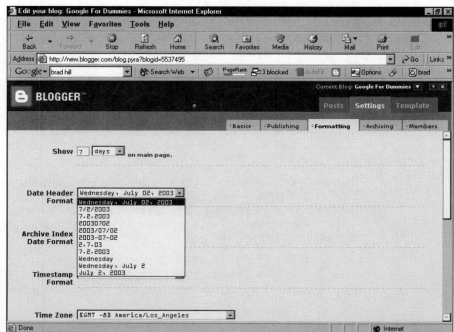

**Figure 13-8:**
The formatting settings of a Blogger blog.

- **Members:** When you set up your blog, only you can post an entry to the blog. Some people blog in teams, and the Members tab is where you add new blog members.

## Formatting your blog

In this section, I describe the formatting settings, as promised. Click the Settings tab on the edit screen and then click the Formatting tab to see the following choices:

- **Show:** Use the number setting and drop-down menu to select how many days or posts that you want to appear on your blog's front page. Seven days is the most common setting and the default. If you post several entries per day, consider shortening the allowable time span or setting the number of allowable posts to keep your front page at a reasonable size.

- **Date Header Format:** Use the drop-down menu to select how you want the date displayed above each of your entries. (Refer again to Figure 13-8.)

- **Archive Index Date Format:** This setting determines how your archive groups (monthly or weekly) are identified.

- **Timestamp Format:** Entries are posted by both date and time. Use this drop-down menu to select how the posted time is displayed.

- **Time Zone:** Click your time zone or city in this extensive drop-down menu, and hope that Blogger simplifies its choices soon. (Getting rid of the cities choice and sticking with time zones would help.)

- **Language:** This one is self-explanatory. Use the drop-down menu.

- **Encoding:** If you are posting in English, leave this setting on its default, Universal (Unicode UTF-8).

- **Convert line breaks:** You probably want to keep this set on the default, Yes. Blogger understands that when you press the Enter key, the HTML code for a line break should be inserted. Basically, the result is that your posts look the way you expect them to.

- **Show title field:** The default here is No, but I keep it on Yes so that I can type a title for each entry. Figure 13-9 shows the edit screen with the title field turned on. The upper frame contains an entry with a typed title, and the lower frame shows what that entry looks like after posting, typo and all.

**Figure 13-9:**
Posting with
the title field
turned on
provides an
easy way to
generate
a clear
heading for
each entry.

You can change your blog's template at any time, overhauling the look-and-feel of your site. No need to do your own design work; a few clicks do the job and transform your entire Weblog. Just follow these steps:

1. **Click the Template tab of the edit screen.**

2. **Click the Choose New Template tab.**

3. **Click any template thumbnail to see a larger version.**

   The sample does not display your blog.

4. **Click the Use [template name] button below your selection.**

Another point to remember: If you know HTML, you can fiddle with your template's code to your heart's content. Blogger encourages tweaking and whole-sale template revision, in fact, by providing the template's code in an edit window under the Main Template tab (under the Template tab on the edit screen). Cut and paste the entire thing to an HTML editor for a more spacious environment if you want to seriously edit.

# Chapter 14

# Alternatives to Google

• • • • • • • • • • • • • • • • • • • • • • • • • • • • • • • • • • • • • • • • • •

## In This Chapter

▶ Getting compact, bare-bones results

▶ Finding newly added sites with GooFresh

▶ Experiencing the astounding and addictive TouchGraph

▶ Google via e-mail

▶ Understanding and tracking the Google dance

▶ Using the amazing Google Ultimate Interface

▶ Proximity, relational, and host searching from Staggernation.com

▶ Chatting with Google through IM

▶ Flashing Floogle

▶ Instant recipe searches

▶ The bucolic Boogle

• • • • • • • • • • • • • • • • • • • • • • • • • • • • • • • • • • • • • • • • • •

Most of this chapter strays outside Google, yet remains within. Googles are sprouting up all over the place. These alternative Google interfaces are not endorsed by Google, for the most part, and don't enjoy any official relationship with Google, the company. But every search engine described in this chapter enjoys a close relationship with the Google index, which disgorges its treasures to any developer with the know-how to program into it.

Think of this chapter as a big, unofficial Google Labs, whose experiments are transpiring on the desktops of individuals and small companies. We, the lucky users, get to try them out. And let me tell you something startling: A few of these things are better than the original in certain ways. Google's innovative power resides in the index and the intelligence algorithms that power it. But as an interface design company, Google is more efficient than elegant, more brusque than thorough. If these characteristics can be called weak spots, they represent an opening for resourceful programmers.

For this chapter I selected sites that are free to use, mostly easy, and worth whatever small efforts are required. Some of these alternatives to Google concentrate on delivering a single Google service better (or differently) than

Google does. One of them ropes together almost all of Google's engines into one glorious interface.

---

# Getting the Google license key

Google offers a free license to software developers to access the Google Web index. This license enables alternate Google sites to deliver Google search results through new interfaces. Developers download a software kit that includes the Google Web API (Application Programming Interface). An API is necessary whenever one program or Web site hooks into a necessary underlying system, such as Google or the Windows operating system. If your computer runs Windows, every application program you have uses the Windows API. Similarly, every alternate Google interface uses the Google API.

Developers using the Google API also must obtain a Google license key, which is used every time somebody conducts a search through the alternate site. Without "seeing" the license key (which is just a string of letters and numbers), Google will not perform the search.

All this might seem irrelevant if you're not planning to develop a new Google search site. But anybody can get a license key, even people with no intent to program. The license key is separate from the developer's kit. And it's a good idea — even good manners — to own a free license key. The reason is that each license key allows the owner a certain number of searches per day. That number is currently set at 1000, which might seem like a lot. But in a public site, a daily quota of 1000 searches can be used up quickly, disabling the site for other users until the next day. So many sites in this chapter provide a space for entering your license key. By doing so, you "pay" for your own searches out of your quota. (All this is completely free of charge, of course.)

You don't need to download a developer's kit to get the license key; you merely need to create a Google account in the Web APIs section:

1. **Go to the Google Web APIs page here:**

   www.google.com/apis

2. **Scroll down to Step 2, Create a Google Account, and click the create a Google Account link.**

3. **Create a username and password.**

   If you've already created a Google account for Google Answers (Chapter 7) or Google Groups (Chapter 4), click the Sign in here link and use the username and password you established then. You must sign in (or create a new account) from the Google Web APIs page before Google sends you a license key.

4. **Click to check the box accepting the Terms of Service.**

5. **Click the Create My Google Account button.**

If you create a new account this way, and if you sign into an existing Google account through the Web APIs page, Google sends your license key to your e-mail address. The e-mail includes the Terms of Service for the Web API program, which are distinct from the Terms of Service you agreed to when creating a Google account.

The license key contains more than 30 characters, so obviously you shouldn't try to memorize it. Keep it in a safe place in your computer, ready to copy and paste into alternate Google sites that request it.

If you have a Google license key (see the "Getting the Google license key" sidebar), have it handy as you cruise among the sites in this chapter. Very few alternate Googles insist on a bring-your-own-license policy, but some request that you "pay" your own way, and others surreptitiously position an entry box for the key number with the hope that you'll use it. It is polite to other users to put your searches on your own key's quota, thereby saving the site from burning quickly through its own quota and shutting down until the next day.

Onward, then, into realms of Googleness that you never dreamed of!

# Bare-Bones Results

You wouldn't think Google could be simplified. The home page is spare to the point of being stark, with no ads or miscellaneous graphics whatsoever. But there is room to make it simpler still, by removing the Images, Groups, Directory, and News tabs. Then strip away the links to Advanced Search, Preferences, and Language Tools. And get rid of the miscellaneous corporate links. Finally, clear out everything on the search results page except the target site links — no descriptions, ads, summaries, or anything else.

Do all that, and you'd get Google's bare-bones search interface, at this page:

```
www.google.com/ie
```

This first destination in a mostly non-Google chapter is an official Google page. But it's one that Google doesn't promote, and in that sense it's an alternative search experience.

Figure 14-1 shows what a search looks like through this interface. You don't get much information, but you also don't get a heavy page load. This point is important if you have your Preferences set to deliver 100 hits per results page (see Chapter 2).

This simplified search format supports the search operators described in Chapter 2 and the specialized operators explained in other chapters. Basically, you can conduct any search on this page that you can on the regular Google home page. The phone book and dictionary work here, too.

Run your mouse cursor over the compact results to see a snippet from each target page in a small pop-up blurb. This tip works in compact search results in other sites, too. In the "Dancing the Google Dance" section later in this chapter, I highlight a few sites that also deliver bare-bones results.

**Figure 14-1:**
A bare-
bones
search
result.

# Finding the Freshest Google

Google is not particularly strong at letting you determine the freshness of search results. The vagueness surrounding page freshness is due to several reasons:

- Google uses more than spiders to crawl the Web, and more than one *type* of spider. (See Chapter 12 for more about spiders and Web crawling.) These crawlers operate at different speeds and different depths. It's possible for a newly created Web page to go undetected by one crawl and then turn up in the index two weeks later after a deeper crawl.

- Google uses more than one server (Internet computer) to deliver search results. The servers are not perfectly synchronized. At any moment, one server might give slightly different search results than another server. This fact, plus the multiple spiders, results in what observers call the *Google dance*. Later in this chapter I point you to a few sites that allow you to track the Google dance.

- The freshness of a page is determined by the time it was created, or the time it was added to Google's index, or both.

Google does enable a certain degree of freshness filtering on the Advanced Search page in Web search. (An advanced search in Google Groups lets you specify dates exactly because newsgroup posts are dated more precisely than Web pages. See Chapter 4.) On the Advanced Search page, you can ask for Web pages updated within the past three months, six months, or year. These large time frames are safe for Google, because the three variables just listed cause confusion only within time periods shorter than three months.

An alternate Google engine called GooFresh invites you to fine-tune the freshness setting by drastically narrowing the time frame. GooFresh is located here:

```
www.researchbuzz.com/toolbox/goofresh.shtml
```

GooFresh accomplishes the time-narrowing trick by using the *daterange* operator. I don't discuss this operator much in this book because *daterange* doesn't understand dates formatted in a typical fashion — month, day, and year. Google understands only the Julian date system, which involves long and cryptic strings of numbers. Online Julian date converters are available for use with the *daterange* operator. If you do so, you are still subject to the Google dance depending on when a page is added to the index and when it hits all the servers.

Assuming that your freshness needs aren't too precise or imperative, GooFresh is a fine alternative. Figure 14-2 shows the GooFresh page ready to launch a search. The search results look completely normal and are drastically narrowed compared to an undated search. A recent search for the keyword *internet*, which normally returns hundreds of thousands of results, yielded only three when GooFresh looked for pages added on the current day.

 Widen your search results by enlarging the time frame. Selecting Today from the drop-down menu (see Figure 14-2) delivers the fewest results. Also, because of the restricted time frame, you get better (or, at least, more) results by using fewer keywords. At the same time, limit your use of operators, especially when choosing Today or Yesterday. In other words, give Google some breathing space: Be less demanding in your keywords when you're more demanding about the time frame.

 GooFresh provides results based on when pages were added to the Google index, not when the pages were created. Here's something else to remember: GooFresh (that is to say, the Google engine lurking behind GooFresh) does not understand some of the special search operators described in Chapter 2, such as the *link* operator. Some operators are shut out because they don't work in combination with the *daterange* operator that GooFresh employs behind the scenes of your search.

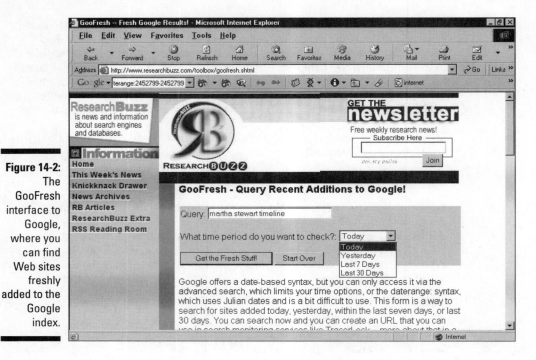

**Figure 14-2:**
The
GooFresh
interface to
Google,
where you
can find
Web sites
freshly
added to the
Google
index.

# The Amazing TouchGraph

For a truly unusual and stunning graphical representation of Google search results, dig into this section and get familiar with TouchGraph GoogleBrowser. TouchGraph uses the Java programming language to create alternative displays for databases. When you type a URL in TouchGraph, it displays sites related to the URL — just as if you had clicked the <u>Similar pages</u> link of a Google search result.

In this section, you first explore TouchGraph GoogleBrowser, devoted to related sites. Then you are introduced to Google-set-vista, created by different individuals but using the TouchGraph browser technology, and displaying Google Sets.

## Visualizing related sites

Be clear about one thing from the start: TouchGraph GoogleBrowser does not perform keyword searching. You do not get a visual representation of a standard Google search here. Somebody might develop something like that, but the TouchGraph system is all about displaying related items (Web pages, in this case). In a keyword search, there is nothing to relate to except the key-words, and all the hits relate in the same way: They match the keywords. TouchGraph reveals constellations of sites surrounding the related sites, and you can extend the model outward again and again. This type of multiple-universe display doesn't lend itself to straight keyword matching, but I hope to be proven wrong very soon.

For now, though, go to TouchGraph to see URL relationships that aren't easily apparent in a long list of text links — and for the sheer delight of playing with one of the coolest Java interfaces around. Here's your starting point:

```
www.touchgraph.com/TGGoogleBrowser.html
```

When typing this URL in your browser, note the uppercase letters in TGGoogleBrowser. Because they are part of a filename (not part of a domain name), they must be typed exactly as they appear here. Otherwise, the page will not load. And your computer will explode. (Sorry, my inner demons made me say that.)

TouchGraph requires a certain Java component, called a plug-in (specifically, Java plug-in 1.3). Fortunately, you don't need to know whether you have that component; the site tells you if you don't, and helps you get it. So, in blessed ignorance, hop over to the TouchGraph GoogleBrowser site, type a URL in the search box, and click the Graph it! button.

A URL consists of three parts separated by periods: the *www* part, the *domain* part (often the name of the site or company), and the *domain extension* part (such as *.com* or *.org*). An example, pulled randomly from the millions of Web URLs, would be:

```
www.bradhill.com
```

TouchGraph GoogleBrowser allows elimination of the *www* part, just like most Web browsers do. But don't leave off the extension.

If you don't have the Java plug-in 1.3 component, a Security Warning window pops open, asking whether you want to install and run Java plug-in 1.3. The required Java plug-in is free of charge and third-party hassles. It's a safe download, and installs easily with the assistance of a few mouse clicks on your part. The Google TouchGraph browser is one very good reason to get the 1.3 plug-in, but not the only reason: If you surf a reasonable amount, you're bound to find other sites that use it.

On some computers, the download proceeds without the Security Warning pop-up, but that is rare. Assuming you do get the Security Warning window, proceed as follows:

1. **In the Security Warning box, click the Yes button.**

   The plug-in is more than 5 megabytes in size, so if you're using a dial-up telephone modem, now is a good time to brew a double mochaccino. After the download, an autoinstallation program runs.

2. **In the Select Java Plugin Installation window, choose a locale and region, and then select Install.**

3. **In the License Agreement page, click the Yes button.**

   It's always a good idea to read the terms before agreeing. In this case, I doubt you'll find anything objectionable.

4. **In the Choose Destination Location window, click the Next button.**

   Use the Browse button if you want to change the default location of the Java plug-in. I don't see much point to changing it, personally — this isn't a stand-alone application that you access outside the browser.

5. **In the Select Browsers window, check one or more boxes and click the Next button.**

   There's no harm in selecting all listed browsers, but at least select the browser you're currently using.

At this point the Java plug-in installs. After a few seconds, the installation program disappears and you're returned to the TouchGraph browser window. This window is a new one, leaving your original window anchored at the TouchGraph Web site.

This rigmarole might seem like a lot of work to experience an alternate Google, but it's worth it. Figure 14-3 shows TouchGraph in action, displaying search results for the `www.msnbc.com` URL.

The TouchGraph display is interactive. As you run the mouse over its screen, two things happen to indicate relationships between sites (called *nodes* in the TouchGraph system):

- The strands connecting nodes light up when touched by the mouse cursor.

- The node labels expand to show full site titles when touched (as long as the node label is in URL or Point mode, as I describe a bit later), and the strands between a touched node and its related nodes all light up when a node is touched. Pink strands indicate outgoing links. Blue strands indicate incoming links. A small info button also appears above any mouse-touched node label. Click that button to see more information about the site.

You may click and drag any node. You must try this, in fact, — it's fun to see the entire web of related sites shift, like a living being, to accommodate the dragged node's movement.

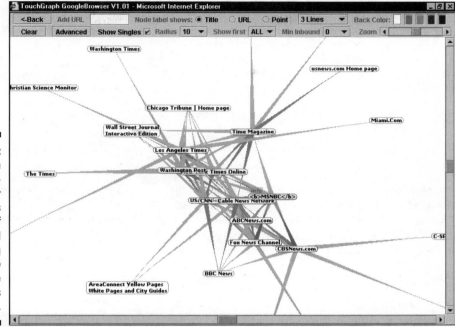

**Figure 14-3:**
TouchGraph
Google-
Browser
displays
clusters of
related
sites. Drag
any site to
shift the
cluster's
shape.

Figure 14-4 shows lighted strands of relatedness, an expanded node label, and the information window that opens when you click the info tab of the expanded label. The information window contains some of what you'd get in a regular Google search result, without the capability to display a cached page. Because the TouchGraph display is all about showing similar pages, there's no link to display similar pages.

You can order up a new constellation of related sites around any node on the graph, simply by double-clicking the node. When you do, a small red tab pops up from the node, titled 0-10. TouchGraph receives the first ten results from Google and displays them. If you double-click that node again, the red pop-up reads 11-20, and so on for every double-click. Keep doing this, or move from node to node opening new clusters of relatedness, and you can end up with a seething mass of nodes and connecting strands (see Figure 14-5).

The display of node clusters might extend beyond the window, especially on small monitors or screens running low resolutions such as 800 x 600. The illustrations in this section were taken on an 800 x 600 screen, and, as you can see, the TouchGraph strands reach out beyond the window's boundaries. My larger screens aren't big enough either, after I start double-clicking nodes. Notice the scroll bars at the bottom and right edges of the TouchGraph browser. Use them to scroll from side to side, and up and down.

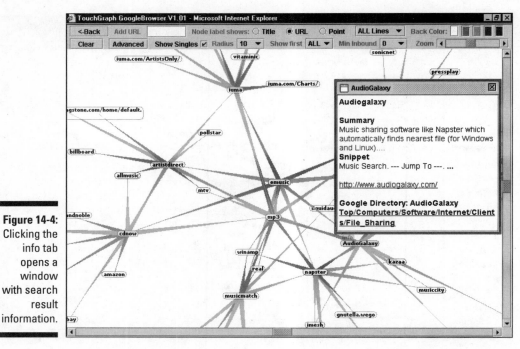

**Figure 14-4:** Clicking the info tab opens a window with search result information.

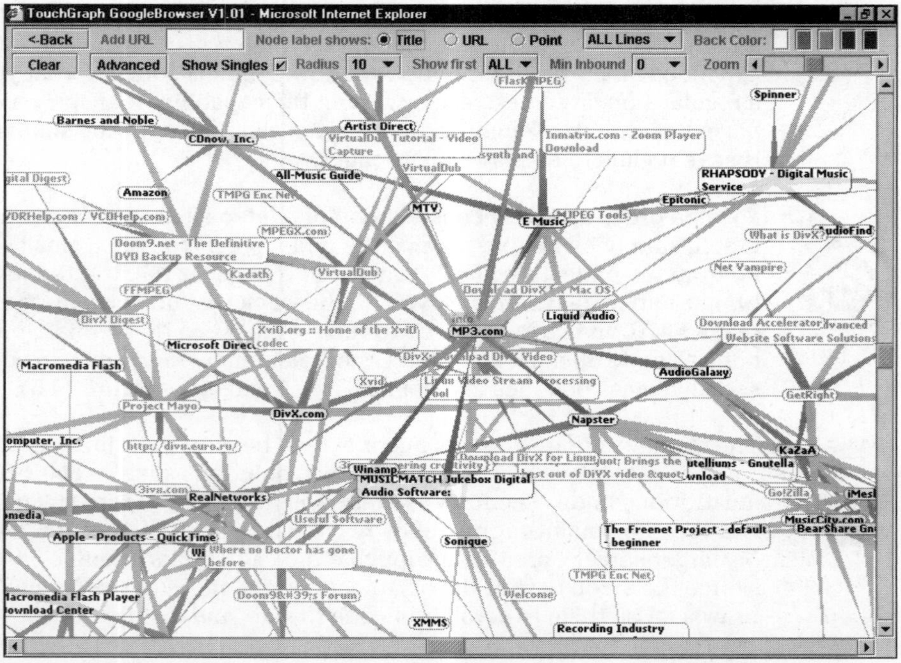

**Figure 14-5:** Add constellations of related sites by double-clicking nodes. In this screen, the Advanced controls are toggled on.

**TIP**

Use the Zoom bar in the TouchGraph toolbar to pull back, getting all your node clusters into view. Figure 14-6 shows a zoomed-out screen with all nodes labeled as points instead of titles or URLs. Notice the radio buttons in the TouchGraph toolbar with those choices. The point labels display the first two letters of the site's title. Run your mouse cursor over any abbreviated node to see its title.

Other control features of the toolbar include these:

- ✔ **Back:** The Back button highlights the previously highlighted node.

- ✔ **Add URL:** Use this search box to launch a new search. If you don't click the Clear button first, TouchGraph puts the new search results right on top of the old graph. There might be no relatedness whatsoever between the two sets of results, in which case the graph holds them both with no connecting strands between the two sets of constellations.

- ✔ **Node label shows:** Use these options to determine how the node labels appear. The Title setting creates the most cluttered display. The URL setting shortens most node labels a bit. The Point setting displays only the first two letters of the site title and is great when the screen gets packed with nodes. Run your mouse cursor over the nodes in URL or Point mode to see their titles.

**Figure 14-6:**
Use the Zoom function and relabel nodes as Points to present a coherent overview.

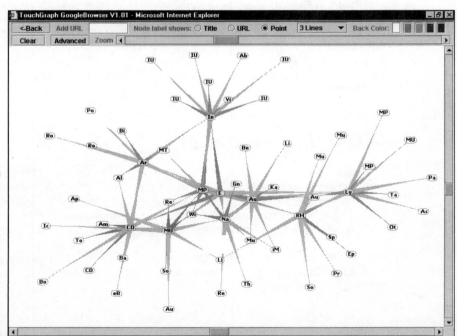

✔ **Clear:** Beware of this button: It clears the entire screen, potentially wiping out a long session of playing around . . . I mean, of productive searching.

✔ **Advanced:** This button toggles the advanced controls on and off.

✔ **Show Singles:** When checked, this feature expands the node clusters by displaying those with only a single link to the central URL. Uncheck this box to reduce screen clutter.

✔ **Radius:** This setting determines the number of edges surrounding the URL you've searched. Reducing the number lowers the number of related constellations around your main cluster.

✔ **Show first:** This option determines how many search results are displayed to start. I usually keep this set to All, greedy searcher that I am.

✔ **Min Inbound:** The lower this number, the more numerous your results. The default setting is 0. The setting determines the minimum number of incoming links a site must offer to register on the graph. When no incoming links exist from one site to another, Google sometimes assigns relatedness based on other factors in the index that connect the two sites.

✔ **Back Color:** Click one to change the graph's background color. If you stare at this thing for as long as I do, the change of hue relieves the eyes.

TouchGraph GoogleBrowser, in addition to being insanely fun, provides a good way to find new Web destinations of interest. When you click an info tab, the pop-up box always displays a link to that Web site, and clicking that link opens a new browser window for that site.

The next section discusses the same TouchGraph technology as applied to Google Sets.

## Visual keyword sets

Keyword sets are discussed in Chapter 8. One of Google's technology experiments open to the public, Google Sets are collections of related keywords. Type one or more words (presumably related in some way), and Google finds many other words related in the same way. (Reminiscent of the standardized tests you took in high school, isn't it? Don't panic. You're not being graded.)

Google Sets provides a perfect application for TouchGraph viewing, which specializes in showing relatedness connections. Start your graphical Google Sets experience at this site:

```
www.langreiter.com/space/google-set-vista
```

Launching the TouchGraph viewer and installing (if necessary) the Java plug-in are identical here as with TouchGraph GoogleBrowser described in the preceding section. If you installed the Java plug-in 1.3 component for the GoogleBrowser, you don't need to install it again here (or ever again at any site).

This Google Sets tool, created by Christian Langreiter, is called google-set-vista. Easy as it is to use, it differs in important ways from TouchGraph GoogleBrowser and from the Google Sets home page at Google. Follow these steps to get started:

1. **On the google-set-vista home page, type a word.**

   Remember that typing not a search keyword, but a word that will generate related words. The results are not Web pages; they're groups of words or names. It is important that you start with just one word. Google lets you enter several related words, but google-set-vista doesn't understand multiple words and thinks they're one big hybrid word.

2. **Click the Set me some! button.**

   The site activates the Java applet (which takes a few seconds) and displays results (see Figure 14-7). Notice that google-set-vista displays the TouchGraph viewer within the browser rather than opening a special window.

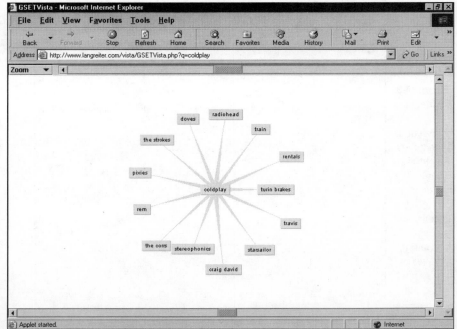

**Figure 14-7:**
Here's google-set-vista in action, displaying a Google Set around the word Coldplay, the name of a music group.

The google-set-vista tool makes substantial changes to the TouchGraph viewer as deployed in the GoogleBrowser. The basic display is the same, in that you can grab a node (a word in this case, not a Web site) and drag it around, pulling the whole set with it. The strands connecting words do not behave with the same color-coded responsiveness as in the GoogleBrowser, naturally, because there are no incoming and outgoing links in a Google Set. The same scroll bars are found along the bottom and right edges, for viewing portions of a large array of sets.

There's no Clear button in google-sets-vista, as there is in the GoogleBrowser. Nor is there an entry box. So, you can neither clear the screen of its current search nor launch a new search within the TouchGraph window. To start a new search, click your browser's Back button, returning to the google-set-vista home page. Unfortunately, this process requires a reload of the Java applet with each new search. (That's not the same as downloading Java plug-in 3.1, which you do only once. Loading the applet takes just a few seconds.)

As in the GoogleBrowser, google-set-vista nodes can be expanded. Simply double-click any node to create a set around that word. It's always interesting to see how the two sets are connected — in other words, which words belong to both sets. Continue expanding nodes repeatedly to get a complex web of Google Set connections (see Figure 14-8).

**Figure 14-8:**
Overlapping and contiguous Google Sets, TouchGraph style. The Zoom bar is set to Locality and is pushed to the right, revealing all node groups.

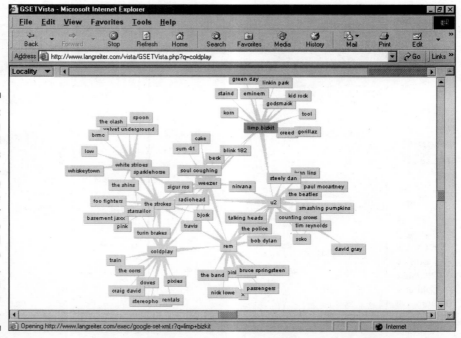

The Zoom bar atop the google-set-vista viewer has three functions, only one of which is displayed and functional at any time. Set the function of the Zoom bar with the drop-down menu to its left. Its three functions are

- ✔ **Zoom:** Set the slider here to zoom in and out of your field of nodes.

- ✔ **Rotate:** Handily, you can use the slider to rotate the entire network of nodes. Doing so can bring a partially hidden field into view without zooming.

- ✔ **Locality:** This is where I normally keep the scroll bar set. Moving the Locality slider to the left folds the node groups into themselves, one by one, simplifying the screen. Moving it to the right expands the node clusters again, revealing all connections.

When I first encountered google-set-vista, I thought it was a poor second cousin to TouchGraph GoogleBrowser. My prejudice was due partly to my disaffection for Google Sets, which seemed like one of the more boring Google Labs experiments, and partly because google-sets-vista didn't have all the toolbar bells and whistles of the GoogleBrowser. I quickly changed my mind, though, and now I turn to the two TouchGraph sites equally. The google-set-vista tool refreshed my attitude about Google Sets, which I now use often as a way of discovering new bands, books, movies, and ideas. But I never use the official Google interface — only google-set-vista. I only wish the right-click menu included a Search option for launching a Google keyword search.

Concerning google-set-vista's inability to directly launch a keyword search, the solution isn't so hard. Right-click any node, and then click the Show in Browser selection. Your browser window (not the TouchGraph window) displays the Google set for that node in normal Google fashion. Using the Show in Browser feature, you can easily launch a keyword search from the official Google display of your word set.

If you're using Google Toolbar 2.0 (see Chapter 9), and have the pop-up Blocker enabled, the Show in Browser feature doesn't work. The Toolbar's blocker prevents the browser from opening a window to display your Google set. Activate the browser window displaying the google-sets-vista home page, and click the Pop-up Blocker button, deactivating the blocker for that site. Then return to the google-sets-vista display and try the Show in Browser feature again. Now your browser swings into action with no trouble.

# Google by E-Mail

This section describes two free services that access Google through e-mail. The first lets you query by e-mail. The second takes your keywords at a Web site, and then sends search alerts to your e-mail box.

## Searching by e-mail

I don't know how useful this one is, but receiving Google search results by e-mail is a nifty demonstration of how ubiquitous Google can be. Later, this chapter introduces how to query Google from an instant messenger.

This Google-by-mail service was developed by Cape Clear and is provided by that company. Cape Clear acts as a bridge between your e-mail and the Google search engine. You need know only this e-mail address:

```
google@capeclear.com
```

Trying out this gimmick could hardly be simpler. Send an e-mail to the preceding address with your search keywords in the Subject line. The response comes shooting back within a minute, at most. Cape Clear delivers 10 results per search. Each result contains a site link, the site's title, and a short snippet. Missing are the links for pulling up a cached version of the page and related pages.

Launch a new e-mail search by replying to the search results e-mail. You don't need to delete the results from the body of your new e-mail, if your e-mail program includes them as an outgoing quote. Just delete the Subject line, which probably reads, "Re: Google results: your keywords" and replace it with new keywords.

If you're extremely fluid with e-mail and don't require more than 10 keyword hits, this service could be handy. It would be more handy if the phone book feature worked — then you could shoot off phone numbers and receive back addresses (see Chapter 2). The good news, though, is that search operators *do* function as expected in this medium.

## Google e-mail alerts

Google Alert operates a free service whereby your search is run daily, and when new results come up in response to your keywords, those results are e-mailed to you. Follow these steps to try it out:

1. **Go to the Google Alert home page:**

   ```
   www.googlealert.com/
   ```

2. **Click the Sign Up link.**

3. **Type a username, password, and e-mail address into the proper boxes.**

   Click the terms of use link for a brief document. It stipulates that Google Alert is a free service, and that your e-mail address will not be shared with any third parties.

4. **Click the Sign Up! button.**

5. **On the Edit Search page, type up to three keyword strings.**

   Remember, you are not entering three keywords for a single search. You are entering three keyword strings for three searches. Feel free to use operators.

6. **Click the More Options link.**

7. **On the Search Settings page (see Figure 14-9), use the drop-down menus to determine the number of results per search and the frequency of your searches.**

   Set a different number of results for each search, if you like, but the frequency is a single setting for all searches. Notice that you get two more search strings on this page, for a total of five.

8. **Click the More button next to any search string to see advanced search settings.**

   You can tweak settings similar to those on Google's Advanced Search page (see Chapter 2). The format of this page, in my opinion, is a little clearer than Google's Advanced Search and is unquestionably more powerful in one respect: You can select multiple file formats instead of the all-or-one option Google offers. Not bad. Figure 14-10 shows an excerpt of this page. Remember that your advanced search settings apply only to the search string whose More button you clicked.

9. **Click the Update button.**

10. **Back on the Search Settings page, click the Run Now button.**

    That does it. Google Alert runs your searches and notifies you of new results added since your previous search. If your searches are on the obscure side, don't expect to get new results every day.

Google Alert has a special relationship with Google, which provided the alternative service a single license key with a much higher usage ceiling than the standard license key. That's why you can select more than 10 results per search, and why Google Alert doesn't ask you to provide your own key.

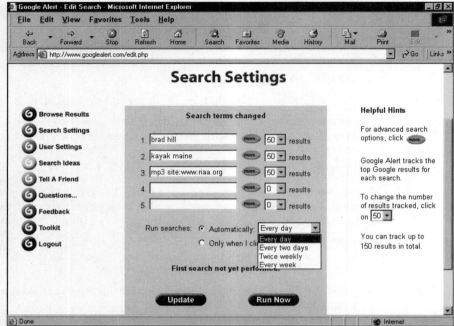

**Figure 14-9:**
The Google Alert Search Settings page. You get two extra searches on this page.

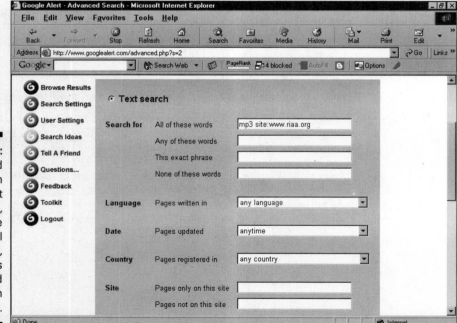

**Figure 14-10:**
Advanced Search in Google Alert is similar to, but more powerful than, Google's Advanced Search page.

# Dancing the Google Dance

Google dances. It's not a hip-hop or jitterbug deal. Google's dance is slow, majestic, elegant, gradual — as overarching and inevitable as the dance of the cosmos. The pace of Google's dance is quickening, as its indexing technology becomes swifter. Even so, its gently heaving shifts escape the notice of most people dashing in and out for quick searches. Only through close examination can the dance be discerned.

The Google dance results from cycles of index building and multiple servers. Google's crawlers sweep through the Web in varying time frames depending on the depth of their crawl. It can take a week or more to deeply assess the World Wide Web, but a more superficial roundup can be accomplished more quickly. Google uses both approaches. In all cases, there is a lag as the spider's results are integrated into the index. Then, Google's globally distributed array of computers sweeps the new index through the entire network. All this activity creates an ever-shifting index that is sometimes not exactly the same on each server.

Normally, you have no choice of Google server to use, and no awareness of which server is used. Several Google dance engines give you that choice and that awareness, and this section introduces you to four of them. For some reason, multiserver searching is a particularly popular Google API application, and the four I've selected for this chapter are not the only ones out there.

Google servers are distinguished in name by the domain prefix and extensions — that is, by the *www* portion and the *com* portion of *www.google.com*. The prefixes include *www2*, *www3*, and so forth. The extensions include domain extensions of other countries, such as *.de* (German) and *.ch* (China). Some servers are identified by IP (Internet Protocol) number. It's not important to memorize server domains. The important thing is to get a sense of the Google dance by comparing results across servers, and possibly get a head start on newly added search results. The alternate Googles in this section should be treated as comparison engines.

## My Google-Dance-Machine

The My Google-Dance-Machine site presents the most configurable of the Google dance trackers. Figure 14-11 shows the Web page from which you launch a multiserver search. As you can see, some of the options are in German. Not a problem. A quick review of this page's high points is in order, because many of its features are universally found on Google dance sites.

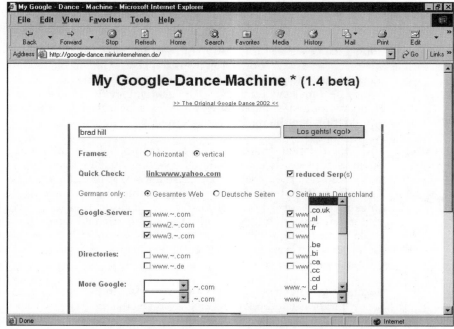

**Figure 14-11:**
The My
Google-
Dance-
Machine
search
engine.

Follow these steps to set up the page for your first search:

1. **Go to the My Google-Dance-Machine home page:**

   ```
   google-dance.miniunternehmen.de/
   ```

2. **For the Frames option, choose vertical.**

   This setting refers to the layout of frames on the search results page. All Google dance engines display results in distinct frames, either stacked or side-by-side. I don't mean to be pushy, but the vertical arrangement makes it easier to scan results and compare servers.

3. **Check the box marked Reduced Serp(s).**

   This feature eliminates the descriptions, ads, and other miscellany from results, leaving just links. In a multiframe display, where screen space is crunched, this setting is crucial.

4. **In the Germans only line, leave the Gesamtes Web choice selected.**

   Anybody, not just Germans, can use these settings, which restrict a search to German language or German location results. I'm assuming for now that you want to search the entire Web.

5. **Next to Google-Server, use the check boxes to select two or more servers.**

   In Figure 14-11, I selected four servers.

6. **Next to Directories, leave all boxes unchecked.**

   There's nothing wrong with mixing directory searches with Web searches. But for simplicity's sake, stick to the Web in this example.

7. **In the search box at the top the page, type a keyword string and then press the Enter key.**

   Your search is launched.

Notice that more options lie in the bottom half of the page. You can select a number of search results (for each server chosen), up to 100. Next to that, the cryptic drop-down menu labeled "ab 1. Treffer (=>Serp.1)" determines whether you will receive the first ten Google results for your keyword, the second ten results, the third ten, and so on. This is handy for leaping deeply into search results, where the Google dance is sometimes more apparent than in the first ten. Below that, another series of drop-down menus lets you choose yet more Google servers.

Figure 14-12 shows a set of search results. Notice the Google dance in the fifth through eighth slots. In most searches, the dance does not appear in the first ten results. Try the same search to retrieve results 51 through 60, using the drop-down menu to select "ab 51. Treffer (=>Serp.6)." I often see significant dancing at that level and the revelation of an important search result appearing in just one server.

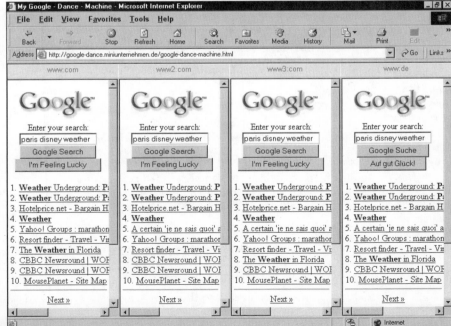

**Figure 14-12:**
Search results at My Google-Dance-Machine. Notice the dance in the fifth through eighth slots.

You can use the <u>Previous</u> and <u>Next</u> links in the search result frames to get the previous and next ten search results — no need to backtrack to the keyword page, unless you want to leap to a deeper result level.

## Google Dance Tool

The Google Dance Tool is a tried-and-true dance site that's one of the easiest to use. Its preset configuration makes it easy to throw in keywords and launch a search quickly. Give it a try here:

```
www.google-dance.com/
```

Figure 14-13 shows the search page with its presets in the default position.

Here's a rundown of your options:

- ✔ **Check:** Use this drop-down menu to switch from the default three servers to nine servers.

- ✔ **Include:** Use these options to include servers in Germany, France, Canada, Britain, and Italy.

**Figure 14-13:** The Google Dance Tool is one of the easiest dance engines to use. Launching a search with default settings delivers good results.

- ✔ **With:** Drop down this menu to select the number of results for each server.

- ✔ **Aligned:** Choose vertical or horizontal frames here; vertical is better.

- ✔ **In:** Compact or standard mode. Standard mode is a mess. Choose Compact.

- ✔ **Store Preferences:** You may tell the Google Dance Tool to remember your option preferences without registering. The site places a cookie in your computer. If you dislike cookies, skip this feature; after all, the limited set of preferences are easy enough to adjust manually whenever you visit.

Figure 14-14 illustrates a Google Dance Tool search of nine servers, results number 31 through 50. Notice the substantial dancing taking place this deep in the results.

## Two more Google dance sites

Two other multiserver engines are worthy of mention, not so much because of their features, but because of their clean interfaces. One is called the Google Dance Tool, like the preceding site, and is located here:

```
www.google-dance-tool.1hut.com/
```

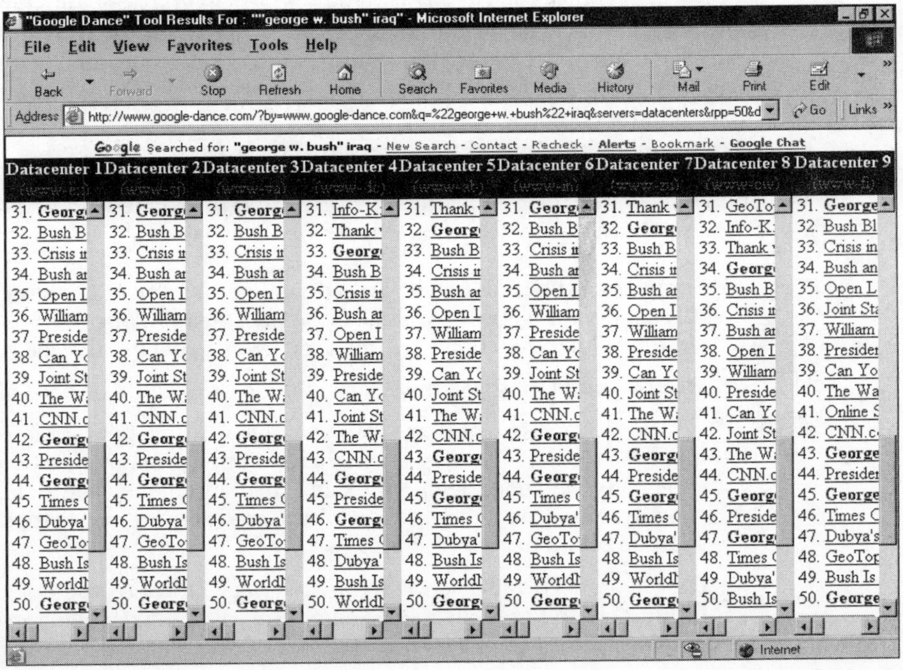

**Figure 14-14:** Google Dance Tool results. The servers are dancing fairly vigorously in results numbered 31 through 50.

The other is called the Google Tool. Go here to try this dance engine:

```
www.void.be/googletool.html
```

# Very Advanced Searching: The Google Ultimate Interface

Google offers Advanced Search pages in most of its engines. But the Web-search advanced page lacks power, as anyone would agree after seeing the monstrous Google Ultimate Interface. In a reasonably concise format, this extraordinary search form reaches into the Google index with exceptional flexibility. If this page was represented on the Google Toolbar, you'd probably use it routinely as your primary Google interface. In fact, you might use this page every day even though it is absent from the Toolbar. For a quick, darting search, it doesn't make sense. But when you want nearly all of Google gathered onto a single page, the Google Ultimate Interface site lives up to its name.

The Google Ultimate Interface is located here:

```
www.faganfinder.com/google.html
```

Figure 14-15 shows the Google Ultimate Interface in its default state. This view is just one of the available forms; you are two clicks away from equally impressive forms for launching searches into Google Groups, Images, Directory, Answers, Glossary, Froogle — nearly every Google engine documented in this book.

The following points discuss the important features of the Web search form shown in Figure 14-15. Advanced features that duplicate Google's Advanced Search page in a Web search are described in Chapter 2:

✔ **Scope:** Use the upper-right drop-down menu (shown in Figure 14-15 with *all* as a default setting) to select compact results, one of the specialty searches introduced in Chapter 6, or even a specific Google server.

✔ **File Format:** Use these menus to include or exclude certain file formats.

✔ **Window:** Choose whether to open a new window for search results or use the original window. I strongly recommend using a new window, especially because the complex and form-intensive search page takes time to reload, so using the Back button to retrace your steps from the search results page is sluggish.

✔ **Date:** This feature seals the deal. This page is where you come for easy, intuitive date-range Web searching. The top menu (labeled *in the last*) duplicates the broad ranges Google provides on its Advanced Search page. For more precision, click the *between* option and use the drop-down menus to determine a date range within which your search results must fall.

- ✔ **Country and Language:** Google's Advanced Search page provides a language setting but not a country setting. (Both settings are included on the Google Ultimate Interface.)

- ✔ **Duplicates Filter:** Use this menu to toggle Google's filter for removing duplicate and near-duplicate search results.

- ✔ **Keyboard:** In a fantastic, even show-offy stunt, the Google Ultimate Interface provides special characters to include in your search string. Click any one of them, and it appears in the keyword box. This feature is great when searching for pages in other languages.

This interface reaches into the Google engine, of course, so search results are identical to a standard Google search.

When searching within a date range, Google can determine only when a Web page was added to its index, not when the page was created. There can be a lag of weeks between the two dates.

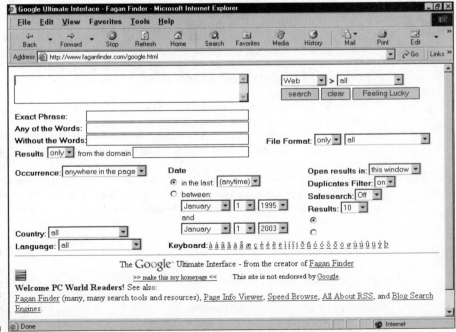

**Figure 14-15:** The amazing Google Ultimate Interface, worthy of being one's primary view of Google.

Now look at that Web menu to the right of the search box. Pull it down to choose one of Google's other search engines. Click a selection, and the Google Ultimate Interface changes its configuration, becoming an advanced search page for that search engine.

For basic, thorough searching, the Google Ultimate Interface is the site in this chapter that should be taken most seriously. I find it indispensable.

# GAPS, GARBO, and GAWSH

That section title should get your attention. The GAPS, GARBO, and GAWSH search engines are presented by the same site and provide three distinct search experiences, each valuable in its own fashion.

If you have a Google license key, this site encourages you to use it in all three areas. Remember, your key enables more searches in a day than you can probably launch. But a public site like this can exhaust its key allowance quickly. The considerate course is to deploy your key number whenever asked.

Unlike too many alternative sites, this one provides detailed explanations of its features. Click the Read Me link on the GAPS, GARBO or GAWSH pages to get some help with that engine. The following sections convey the basics, certainly enough to get you started.

## Proximity searching with GAPS

The Google API Proximity Search (GAPS) invites you to search for two keywords that occur within a certain proximity to each other. This tool strikes a useful middle ground between two extremes: keywords that might be located anywhere on the page, and keywords located directly next to each other, as in the case of an exact phrase. Putting the keywords close to each other but not necessarily next to each other encourages relevance without the restriction of an exact phrase. Putting the keywords close to each other but not necessarily next to each other encourages relevance without the restriction of an exact phrase.

GAPS is located here:

```
www.staggernation.com/cgi-bin/gaps.cgi
```

Figure 14-16 shows the GAPS form.

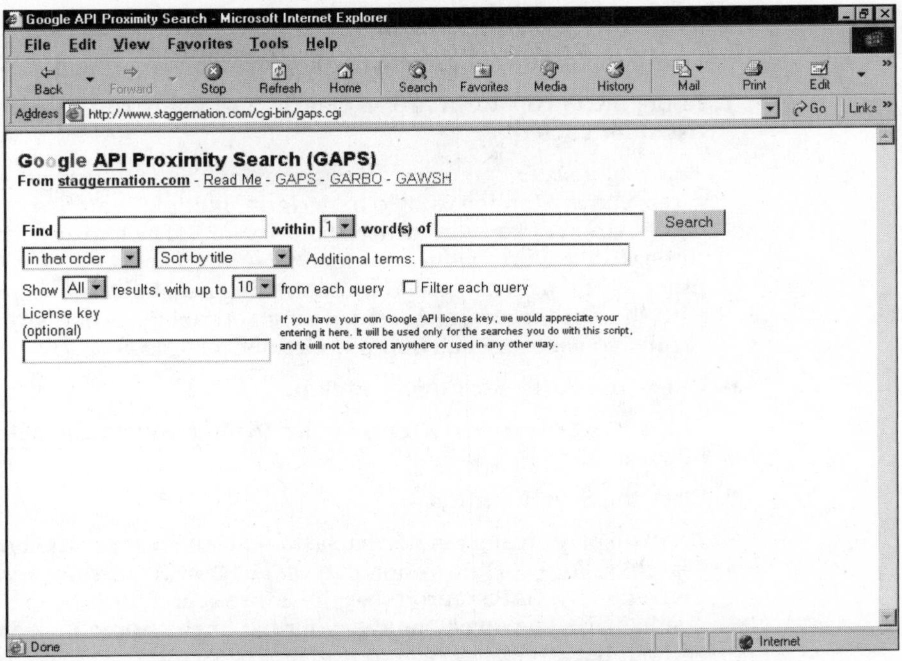

**Figure 14-16:**
Locate Web
pages
with two
keywords
in close
proximity.

Follow these steps to design and launch a GAPS search:

1. **In the Find search boxes, type a single keyword in each box.**

2. **Use the drop-down menu between the keyword boxes to select a proximity range.**

   The GAPS engine is currently limited to finding keyword pairs separated by no more than three intervening words. Google doesn't insist on this limitation, but GAPS enforces it to contain search results.

3. **In the first drop-down menu, choose *in either order*.**

   The alternate, *in that order,* reduces results by forcing Google to match your first and second keywords in that order.

4. **In the next drop-down menu, choose *Sort by ranking*.**

   Ranking is Google's assessment of relevance. You may also sort by URL, page title, and keyword proximity. It's easy to reset the search parameters after you see the results.

5. **In the Additional terms box, type any other keyword that you want as part of the search string.**

   Here you may use operators, exact phrases, and multiple keywords.

**6. In the Show menu, select how many results you would like overall.**

I leave this setting in its default All state.

**7. In the next drop-down menu, choose how many results should be listed for each query.**

This might seem confusing. With a proximity search using these features, you are forcing Google to perform multiple searches, one for each combination of keyword order and proximity. The two keywords can be three words apart, two words apart, one word apart, or next to each other — and furthermore, they could match any of those conditions with their order reversed. This setting determines how many search results you see for each of those distinct searches.

**8. Check the Filter each query option.**

This setting refers to Google's duplicate filter, which eliminates multiple hits from the same site.

**9. Click the Search button.**

GAPS displays results in normal fashion, with no separation of individual searches. Your sorting option determines how the results are ordered. Conveniently, GAPS reproduces the entire search form atop the search results page, so you can modify your parameters or launch a new search without backtracking.

You may use the exact phrase (quotes) operator in either of the two proximity keyword boxes. Google treats the phrase as a single keyword that must exist within a certain proximity to the other keyword. The two keywords can both be phrases, for that matter. I like doing that to search for articles about two closely paired public figures. Try searching this way for "Clay Aiken" and "Ruben Studdard," the two most recent (as of this writing) American Idol winners.

## Relation browsing with GARBO

The GARBO engine performs the same sort of search as TouchGraph GoogleBrowser, described earlier in this chapter — namely, searching for sites related to a certain Web domain. Google API Relation Browsing Outliner (GARBO) adds a twist by also enabling you to search for sites that link to a certain page (Google's *link* operator). Instead of displaying results in an interactive graphical spread, GARBO delivers text results that are unusually customizable. In fact, the intelligence of the results display puts GARBO on the map.

As with TouchGraph GoogleBrowser, you type a URL, not keywords, into GARBO. The search form (see Figure 14-17) is located here:

`www.staggernation.com/garbo/`

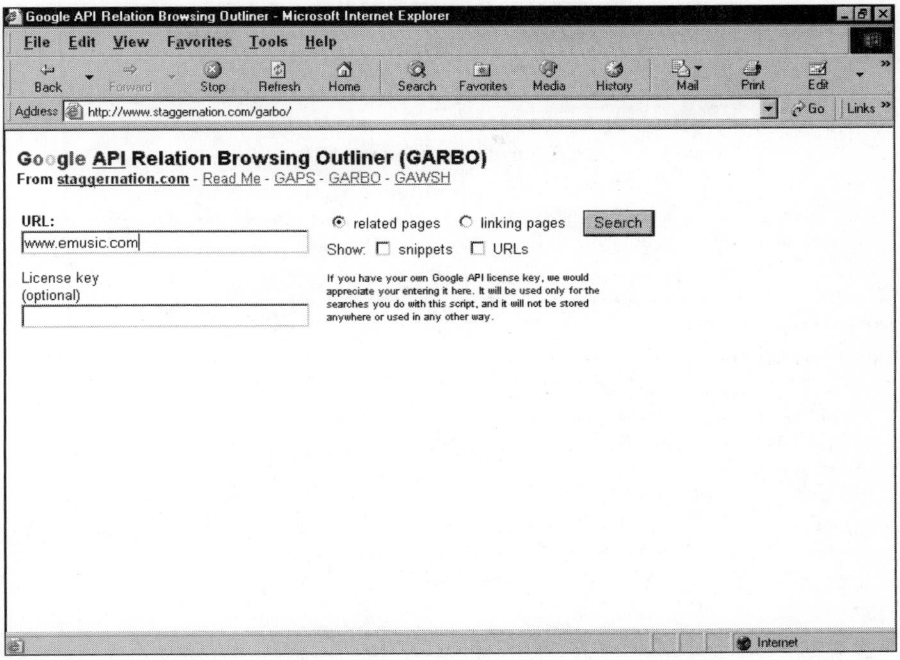

![Screenshot of the Google API Relation Browsing Outliner (GARBO) in Microsoft Internet Explorer showing the address http://www.staggernation.com/garbo/ and a search form titled "Google API Relation Browsing Outliner (GARBO)" with a URL field containing "www.emusic.com", options for related pages or linking pages, Show snippets and URLs checkboxes, a Search button, and a License key (optional) field.]

**Figure 14-17:**
The GARBO
search form.

The form contains three main elements:

- **Search box:** Type a URL here.

- **Related pages or linking pages:** You can select related pages (Google's Similar pages feature) or linking pages (which delivers sites containing links to your search URL). Google allows one of these searches at a time; you can't do both.

- **Snippets and URLs:** I prefer to keep the search results clean in GARBO, so I leave both these options unchecked. GARBO then displays a concise and useful folder-like results page (see Figure 14-18).

The beauty of eliminating snippets and URLs is revealed on the search results page, which comes up with a beautiful economy. The results look and behave like a list of folders. Click a triangle next to any item to open it, revealing more detailed results within.

Engagingly, GARBO encourages secondary searching on the search results with the <u>View in Google</u> link next to each opened folder when you search without snippets and URLs. Doing so conducts a relation search (or a link search, if that's how you started) on the result URL. *That* is cool.

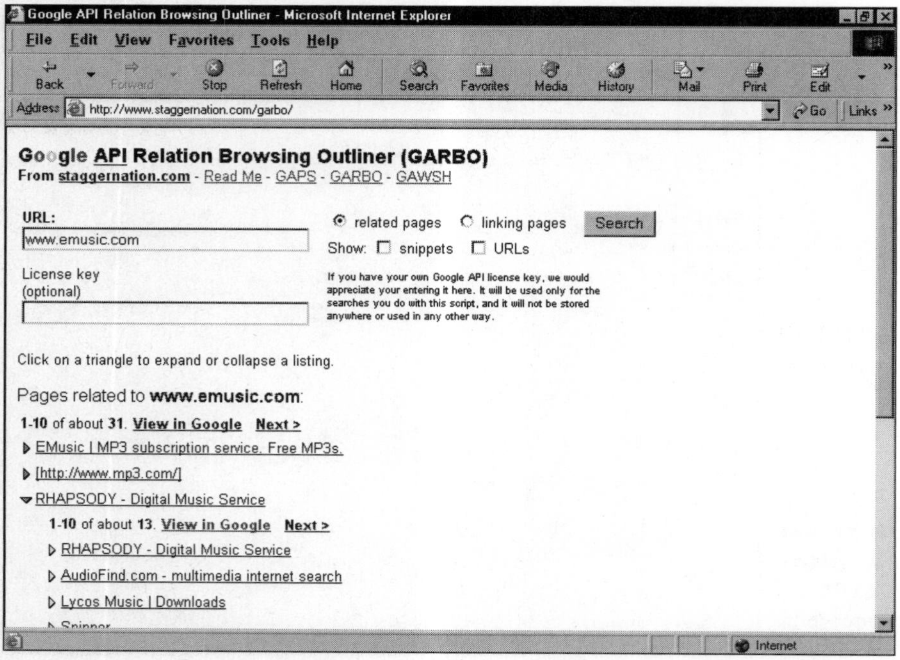

**Figure 14-18:**
GARBO
search
results can
be displayed
in folder
style. Click
the triangles
to expand
the folders.

## *Search by host with GAWSH*

Rounding out this invaluable trio of alternate Googles is Google API Web Search by Host (GAWSH). This engine takes the folder approach to results available in GARBO and makes it the default, irrevocable result format. Here, you search by keyword (with operators) and get results organized by Web domain. Each domain in the search results list can be opened, like a folder, revealing matching pages that come from that site. These revealed inner results are displayed in traditional Google format, within the opened GAWSH folder.

GAWSH is not as trivial as its description might sound — or as it might look when you first visit the search page. That page is located at this URL:

```
www.staggernation.com/gawsh/
```

The search form consists of nothing more than a keyword box and a Search button. The action is in the results page, shown in Figure 14-19. In this screen shot, I expanded one of the folders to illustrate the mixture of GAWSH formatting and Google formatting.

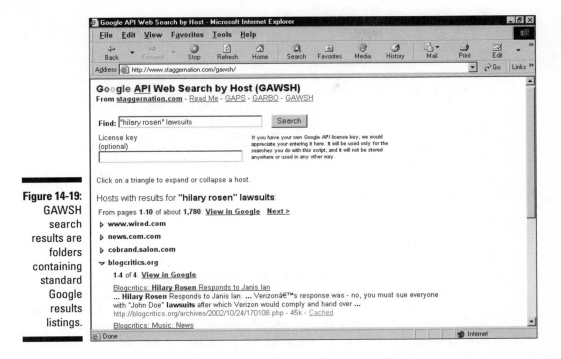

**Figure 14-19:**
GAWSH
search
results are
folders
containing
standard
Google
results
listings.

GAWSH is fantastic for bundling essential search result information into a small space for quick scanning. Most of us prefer getting information from favorite sites but don't want to specify those sites every time we search. GAWSH reveals at a glance which sites have pages matching your keywords, enabling you to zoom into favored domains for exact matches. Every time you click an expanding folder triangle, GAWSH launches the search again, limiting it to the selected domain.

GAWSH provides the perfect environment in which to use the negative *site* operator (see Chapter 2). Eliminating obvious host matches makes the resulting host list even more valuable. Try this search:

```
boycott RIAA -site:www.boycott-riaa.com
```

# Chatting with Google

Is no medium safe from Googling? Well, instant messaging isn't, that's for sure. At least three developers have contrived to let you conduct a basic Web search in Google, through one of the three major IM programs:

✔ AOL Instant Messenger (AIM)

✔ MSN Messenger

✔ Yahoo! Messenger

Each one works the same way. You use your IM program's features to see whether the Google search service is online, and then simply send your keyword string as an instant message. The problem is, these services are very often *not* online. Remember, this isn't Google itself, which is always available. These instant-messaging searches are third-party services, alternate Googles, and the developers are regular folks who go online and offline just like you and I do. (Actually, I never go offline. Nor do I venture outside. I am fed intravenously and hunger for simple human touch that I will never receive. But enough about me.)

Here are the three IM services:

✔ **Googolator:** This one works in AIM. Add Googolator to your Buddy list and send keywords whenever it's online. Five results are returned.

✔ **Googlematic:** This one works identically in AIM and MSN Messenger. Again, five results. In MSN Messenger, you need an entire e-mail address to locate a new Contact. Look for `googlematic@interconnected.org`.

✔ **YIMGoogle:** This one is set for Yahoo! Messenger. The *YIM* stands for Yahoo! Instant Messenger, even though that's not really the name of the program. YIMGoogle is the screen name to look for and add to your Friends list. Query when it comes online to get five results.

# Flash with Floogle

Here's an alternate Google with no added functionality. Floogle is an experiment in programming, and it delivers Google search results in the Flash environment. Flash is a multimedia programming language usually used to display moving images and sound. In this case, it delivers static Google search results. The site does make fun beeping sounds, though, when the mouse cursor touches screen items.

Go to the Floogle page here:

```
www.flash-db.com/Google
```

Searches are launched and results delivered within the same Flash frame residing in the Web page. You need Flash 6 for this to work; the page tells you immediately if you don't have Flash 6, and it downloads it for you if you approve. Downloading and installation are transparent and automatic; just wait a minute or so (depending on connection speed) until the search engine appears in the Web page. Figure 14-20 shows Floogle and its search results.

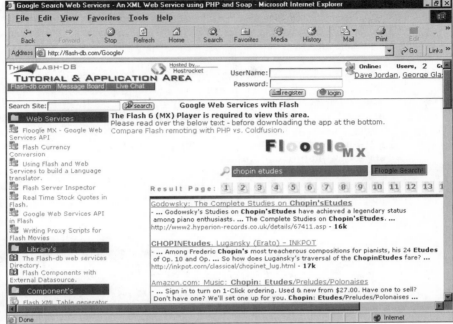

**Figure 14-20:**
Floogle is
fun, but not
particularly
important
as an
alternative
to Google.

Simply enter a keyword string and click the Floogle Search! button. Note that
pressing the Enter key to launch a search doesn't work here; doing so merely
clears the keyword box.

Search results look fairly Googlish, but without the Similar pages and Cached
links. Oh, and without the entire top-page summary that Google provides.
Floogle dishes up pure results and nothing but. Even the AdWords and sponsored links are missing. Click any result link to see the target page, opened in
a new window. See results beyond the first ten by clicking a numbered button
above the results pane — this is where the beeps are located.

# Two Final, Frivolous Alternatives to Google

The final two entries are somewhat fun, undeniably trivial, and appear in this
chapter more for the sake of comprehensiveness than because I particularly
recommend them.

Recipe Search queries Google with food types and ingredients, delivering
Web pages with recipes. This simple task appears to be accomplished by

adding the keyword *recipe* to your keyword string. You could do that yourself. Nonetheless, the site resides at Stanford University, so by using it you're
probably encouraging somebody to start an Internet business. Go here to
check it out:

```
theory.stanford.edu/~amitp/recipe.html
```

Boogle (`www.boogle.com`) is even more trivial, yet more attractive, as shown
in Figure 14-21. Boogle provides a straight, simple Google Web search with no
added functionality and adds a picture and quote to the search page. The
attribution of the quote is searchable — that's a nice touch. Click refresh to
see a new picture and quote.

You might never be tempted to visit Boogle again, but stop into the forum
linked on the front page. You might get hooked on the lively discussions and
quote suggestions posted by fans.

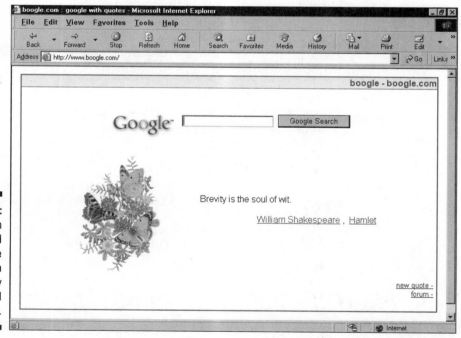

**Figure 14-21:**
Boogle is an
unenhanced
Google
engine, with
a pretty
picture and
a quote.

# Chapter 15

# Twisted Googling and Google Games

## In This Chapter

▶ Googlewhacking

▶ Random searching

▶ Finding out about everything through the Googlism

▶ Keyword fighting

▶ More random searching and page bouncing

▶ Reversing Google

▶ Creating Google art

Google users and third-party developers are an imaginative, playful bunch. And some of the most Google-happy activities that sweep faddishly through the Internet are represented in this chapter.

Forthwith, a collection of Google games that whack and skewer the great index in deliriously time-wasting ways.

# In Pursuit of the Googlewhack

It started a few years ago, and has grown as an underground-cum-mainstream time-waster. The game is called Googlewhacking, and its goal is to obtain just one Google result for a two-word keyword string. A few recent triumphs (they're not mine) follow:

    ambidextrous scallywags

    squirreling dervishes

    fetishized armadillo

    anxiousness scheduler

There is nothing official about Googlewhacking, so rules might seem excessively officious, but you won't get a whack recorded on the Googlewhack site unless it conforms to certain guidelines:

- **No quotes:** Using the exact phrase operator (see Chapter 2) makes it too easy to get a whack. Forcing unrelated words to exist right next to each other, as a phrase, instantly reduces results. Letting the words exist anywhere on the Web page brings in many more hits, toughening the game.

- **No other search operators:** Although not listed as a Googlewhacking rule, it makes sense. Any of the operators described in Chapter 2, standard or specific to Google, narrow results artificially and should be considered cheating. Use pure, unfettered keywords thrown into the entire Web index.

- **No scripts allowed:** If you're resourceful enough to write a little software program that automatically queries Google with randomly combined words, don't use it. It violates the spirit of the game, but more important, this sort of quasi-cheating takes the fun out of cudgeling your brain for almost-impossible search strings.

- **Web searches only:** You might want to experiment with image searches, Groups searches, or news searches (Directory searches are too easy), but as of now, results of these variants are not considered true whacks.

- **Real keywords only:** The Googlewhack arbiter is Dictionary.com.

- **Real result(s) only:** If you manage to produce a single result (which is harder and more gratifying than finding a four-leaf clover), that result page must be legitimate and meaningful. Pages that contain mere lists of words, or gibberish, don't constitute a whack.

Play the game at Google, but visit the Googlewhack site for inspiration, history, and to read successful whacks and their humorous definitions:

```
www.googlewhack.com
```

The inventive definitions of whack strings are almost the best part of Googlewhacking. In one particularly brilliant set of whackinitions, the site fabricated all-Enron explanations for recent whacks (see Figure 15-1). Reading through the whacktionary is both amusing and inspiring.

If you are so lucky (talented?) as to successfully whack Google, go to the Googlewhacking site and click the Record Your Whack! link. Googlewhack provides Google search boxes to verify your success. Don't use these boxes to try out new whacks. Their only purpose is to verify whacks already established through Google.

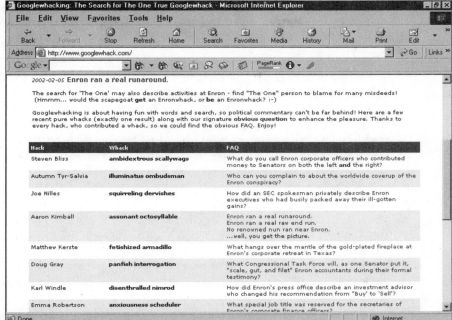

**Figure 15-1:** Google-whack definitions are almost the best part of the game.

Unfortunately, whacks are rarely permanent. Their transience is not due to the ever-changing Google index, but the urge to brag. If you promote your own whack, or record it on the Googlewhack site, that instantly creates a second page with your two keywords. Google will probably find it eventually. The Googlewhack site is already in the index, of course, so within a month (roughly, Google's major update cycle) your whack will be ruined.

Googlewhackers are a strict bunch, but they look kindly on artificially ruined whacks as described in the previous paragraph. In fact, the name Heisenwhack has been applied to such disruptions in the quantum whack-field, after the physicist Werner Heisenberg. He, along with Niels Bohr, theorized that nothing exists without measurement, and the sheer act of measuring a phenomenon alters it. Hence, there is no objectivity. (This, however, is not the Heisenberg Uncertainty Principle, despite what some Googlewhacking sites tell you. The Uncertainty Principle is about the impossibility of measuring both the position and momentum of a particle.) The lack of objectivity relates to the unwhacking of keywords through the simple act of observing (mentioning the whack on a Web page) them.

You can cut through a ruined whack by searching for the two keywords with the added negative keyword `-googlewhack` (using the *NOT* operator). That should deliver the original single search result, verifying the un-Heisenwhacked whack.

Here's a question. If finding one result with two words is a Googlewhack, what is finding two results with one word? (Try searching the keyword *gastrolytic*.) A Googlesplit?

# The Random Googlelaar

In the previous section on Googlewhacking, I mentioned that using automated, random-word search generators was cheating. Googlelaar, which generates one-word, two-word, and three-word searches in English or Dutch, provides perfect examples of why these things don't yield legitimate whacks. Here's the home page:

```
www.northernlake.com/googlelaar/
```

When I first encountered Googlelaar, I got a whack in my first random search: *pained pentanone*. I've shown the search results in Figure 15-2, for the fun of seeing a Googlewhack, albeit an illegitimate one. Cheating or not, it's amazing to see that "1 of 1" in the summary bar.

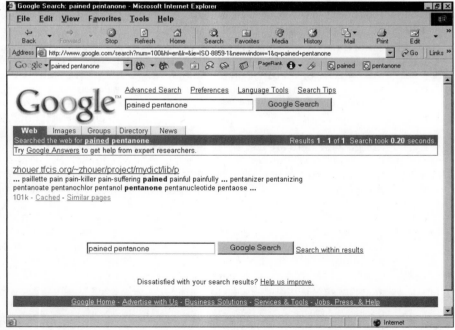

**Figure 15-2:**
A Google-whack! Except it's not legitimate. This search results was generated through a Googlelaar random search.

Googlelaar, and other random-word Google interfaces, are frivolous to the extreme. But there's something trivially satisfying about making Google chase its tail. Figure 15-3 shows Googlelaar's page — it's simple enough to use. Click the drop-down menus to select the number of words and language, and then click the Hit me! button. Google delivers the search results. Click the Back button to try another search.

Googlelaar prowls through the Webster's *Second International Dictionary* to find its keywords, and presumably the entire dictionary is in its memory. Most of the words I get are unfamiliar to me — and I know a lot of words. This means that either English has more exotic words than I realized or Googlelaar skews the keyword selection toward obscurities. In any event, a common results total for two- or three-word searches through Googlelaar is 0.

Now, using Googlelaar for one-word random searches is more diverting. And this is where a little keyboard tip gives the exercise some rhythm. Googlelaar launches a search with a press of the Enter key — you don't need to click the Hit me! button. So you can bounce back and forth between Googlelaar and the search results page with repeated Enter-Back-Enter-Back sequences. There's never a need to type a keyword, of course.

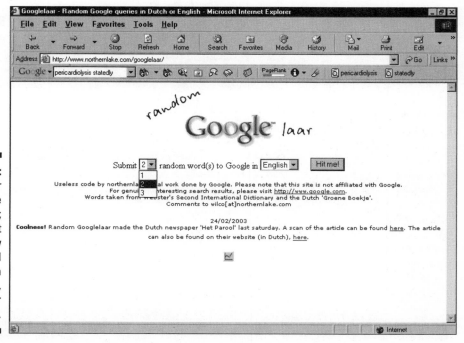

**Figure 15-3:**
Googlelaar provides the keywords; you just choose how many and which language, English or Dutch.

# *Googlism*

Googlism uses tricky (and undivulged) keyword manipulations to ascertain what Google "thinks" about people, places, and things. Although the keyword chicanery is hidden, the results are clearly scraped from actual Web pages Google finds in relation to your keyword(s). But don't mistake this site for an information resource — it's entertainment only. Googlism swept through the Usenet newsgroups when it was introduced, as everyone delighted in discovering the supposed revelatory truth about their online acquaintances.

Googlism works in plain fashion. Go to the home page (Figure 15-4):

```
www.googlism.com
```

**Figure 15-4:**
Googlism finds out everything about people, places, and things.

Type a keyword, click the appropriate option (Who, What, Where, or When), and click the Googlism! button. What follows is a list of sentence fragments and occasional complete phrases scraped from Google search results. The amusement factor is due to taking the phrases out of context, as if they were always meant to be as declamatory as they appear in Googlism. Take, for example, this short sample from the Googlism on Microsoft:

Microsoft is calling you

Microsoft is losing its grip

Microsoft is calling you a lab rat

Microsoft is

The last one seems complete unto itself.

Run a Googlism on yourself, but remember that results must come from Web pages that include your name. Of course, getting hits on your name that belong to an identically named stranger is fun, too.

Want to know where a particular Googlism comes from? Even the silliest sounding ones are not made up; they come from some Web page. Simply type the Googlism into Google (not into Googlism) and check the results. Put quotes around the Googlism if the original search results show any confusion.

# Squabbling Keywords

Google's reputation as an arbiter of cultural relevance makes it the perfect source for a game that pits keywords against each other. Who is more important, Sean Connery or Harrison Ford? And if one gets more Google results than the other, does that really tell us something? The question seems ludicrous on the face of it, but considering the size and scope of Google's index, and the depth with which it catalogues human interest as expressed on the Web, there might be something to the idea.

Anyway, nobody is trying to write a doctoral dissertation on the thesis. Again, the point here is entertainment. Here are the three sites in question:

- ✔ GoogleFight at `www.googlefight.com`
- ✔ Google Smackdown at `www.onfocus.com/googlesmack/down.asp`
- ✔ Google Duel at `www.sfu.ca/~gpeters/cgi-bin/pear/`

The three sites are more similar than different, but each has strong and weak points. Figure 15-5 illustrates the home page of Google Smackdown. As with the others, the interface invites you to enter two keywords, phrases, or names. The engine then scrapes the results totals and throws away the actual results, leaving you with a count of the number of hits for each of the competing keywords or keyword strings.

This is great fun. During a political season, pit one *American Idol* candidate against another. Who is really more popular, Clay Aiken or Ruben Studdard? (Hint: Count those telephone votes again.) Plug in any two names, concepts, expressions, objects, or locations. Put your home town against your friend's home town. Let Plato and Socrates fight it out in the Google index.

Astute Google users might be tempted to put quotes around their keyword phrases to keep them intact, yielding more accurately competitive results. No need. Each of these three sites automatically adds quotes to your phrases (though you don't see the quotes) when they throw the search into Google. If you add your own quotes, around the invisible quotes, Google ignores the whole mess and treats your keywords individually. Then you get more results, but less accurate ones.

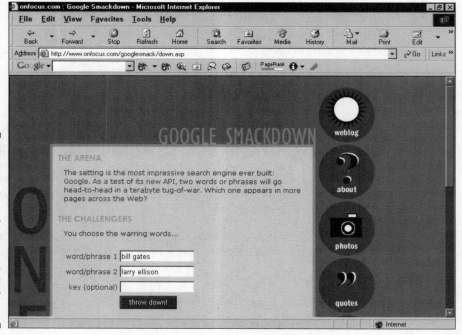

**Figure 15-5:**
Google Smack-down, one of three popular keyword battle sites. In this shot, Bill Gates fights Larry Ellison.

Figure 15-5 shows Google Smackdown and its keyword boxes. This one (and also Google Duel) requests that you use your own Google developer's key; it's only polite to provide your own key when a site provides space to enter it. (See Chapter 14 for information about getting a key.) Googlefight has a pleasing interface that puts your two keyword phrases in different colors.

When it comes to displaying results, my favorite is Google Duel, which renders an illustrative graph of the results, in addition to dishing up the raw numbers (see Figure 15-6). Notice the link to an advanced version of Google Duel. The page is actually called Google Duel for Writers, and it encourages users to enter up to ten synonyms or like-meaning phrases, to see which is the most Googly popular. As a writer, I can tell you that this "tool" is more entertaining than productive. The result (see Figure 15-7) continues the graph format.

Overall, when in the mood for a keyword fight, I find myself going to Googlefight more than the others. The interface is the least pleasant, in my opinion, but I like the archive of interesting and amusing keyword matchups.

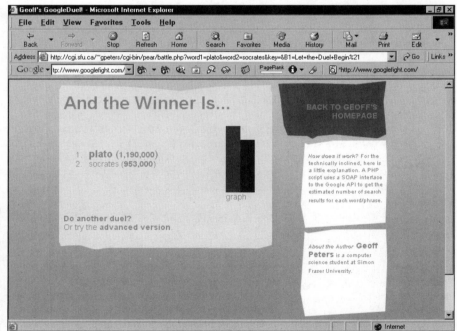

**Figure 15-6:** Google Duel displays keyword fights in graphical format.

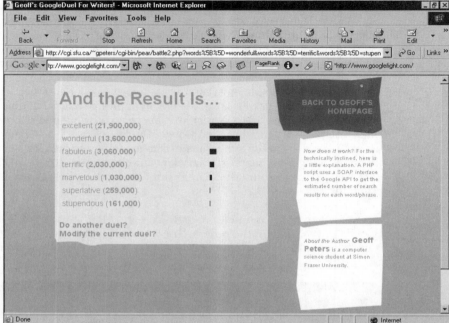

**Figure 15-7:**
Google Duel
for Writers
compares
the
popularity of
up to ten
words or
phrases.

# *More Random Searching*

Earlier in this chapter I describe Googlelaar, which randomly generates keywords and shows you Google's search results for those words. In this section,
I introduce three engines that also randomly contrive keywords but take the
happy meaninglessness of random searching to the next level by leaping
directly to the first result site for those words.

Two main features distinguish the best of these sites from the not-as-good:

✔ **Keyword customization:** Even though it's the engine's job to generate
random keywords, they all allow the user to specify the number of keywords used. Clearly, the greater flexibility in this department, the more
fun the engine is. One of the sites described here even lets you set the
maximum length of the keywords, by number of letters.

✔ **Frames:** Frames on Web pages can be a disagreeable design choice, but
in this case they really help. Some sites throw the target page into your
browser window without an anchor frame, forcing you to backtrack if
you want to try a new random search. The better designs display the
randomly found page below a horizontal frame containing the means to
launch a new search.

The danger of random searches — besides being a stultifying waste of time — is that you're likely to stumble into site types that you'd ordinarily avoid. If you don't like opening PDF files, for example, you might be upset when one comes screaming in, unannounced. Adult sites are not out of bounds, either, unless you click the Safesearch box — provided the search engine furnishes one.

## Mangle

Mangle — nice name for a site, isn't it? And not really descriptive: Mangle doesn't destroy keywords; it invents them. First, go to the Mangle site:

```
www.mangle.ca
```

Hoping to please everyone, Mangle offers a choice of interfaces — frames or no frames. On the search page (see Figure 15-8), you can choose up to five keywords (the default setting is three). You can also select a country and language, or leave the gates wide open for everything. (Random searches become particularly useless if conducted in a language you don't understand.) The engine is naturally biased toward English, and generally delivers English-language sites in default mode.

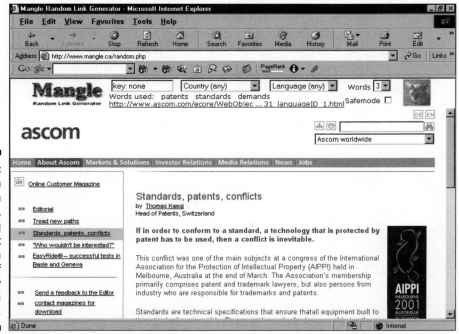

**Figure 15-8:** Mangle in search mode, displaying the first search result of randomly chosen keywords.

Note a few features of the Mangle search frame:

- ✔ The keywords used by the engine are displayed just below the drop-down menus.
- ✔ The displayed page's link is below the keywords.
- ✔ Check the Safemode box to apply Google filtering to Mangle's search results.
- ✔ Use the drop-down menu to change the number of keywords. You may choose between one and five keywords.
- ✔ Click the cat picture (upper-right corner) to launch a search. Pressing the Enter key doesn't do it.

For truly empty-headed searching, click the archive search link on Mangle's home page. You get a random page from Mangle's storehouse of previously randomized results. So not only are you searching in the dark, you're taking random results from other people's blind searches. Good times!

## Random Bounce Me

Like Mangle, Random Bounce Me provides a framed interface for easy multiple searches:

```
random.bounceme.net
```

Disconcertingly, the site presents you with your first result the moment you set foot on the home page. Don't be fooled — you haven't mistakenly clicked to the wrong site. (Or maybe you have; what do I know?) It just looks like an unrelated site because your first search result is displayed in most of the browser window. The engine's frame awaits your adjustment.

Interestingly, Random Bounce Me invites you to select a maximum word length in addition to the number of keywords. Use the drop-down menus for those settings. The Max word size menu is based on letters — up to 32 of them! The longer your words and the more keywords you allow, the fewer your results. It's easy to get zero results. Here are the keywords for three consecutive zero-results searches that this site delivered for four keywords with up to nine letters each:

> grace overeye unpaper straitl
>
> dachshund hypaspist freckling po
>
> cockpit strial sleepward epigeal

That is one obscure dictionary being used to generate keywords. Anyway, shorten your words and ask for fewer of them to widen the results. The keywords chosen for your search are displayed in the left corner of the search frame. Click the Random Bounce Me button to request a new page.

# Random Google page

One of the simplest random search pages is appropriately named the Random Google page and is located here:

```
www.bleb.org/random
```

Two distinguishing features mark this site. First, you can select up to ten keywords to be generated randomly. That many keywords, more often than not, leads to zero results, but what's more fun than trying over and over until you find a page that matches ten keywords? The second feature is a list of recent search results (including yours) at the bottom of the home page. Each link allows you to recreate the search, in the excitement of real time. Or click the Normal link to see Google search results instead of a random page from those results.

# Random imagery

The Random Google Image Finder does to Google's Image index what the other randomizing engines to do the Web index. The site is located here:

```
ianwatt.dingojunction.com/ri/
```

The dead-simple interface offers a choice of one or two keywords and any of Google's three levels of image filtering (see Chapter 2). Click the Show me the pics! button to see results. The Random Google Image Finder doesn't skip to a single result as do other engines described here. You get a standard Google Image search results page.

Searching randomly for images is more rewarding, genuinely serendipitous, and even almost productive. The improvement over random Web searching is due to the generally poor labeling of image files on the Internet. Even when you're trying to find certain images, Google is often stumped or confused. So the difference between targeted and random searching is less significant.

I prefer searching with just one randomly generated keyword. And I've browsed through some terrific results — though I rue the day the Random Google Image Finder assigned me the keyword *butt*.

# The ultimate random Web search page

If there's one site that puts together all the important features of the others, and adds some of its own, for a thoroughly time-wasting and gloriously unproductive Google experience, it's the Random Web Search page, at this location:

www.randomwebsearch.com

The figure shows the options available on the home page. This site can act as a standard Web-search interface to Google. Just type your keywords and click the Google Search button. For random searching, click the Generate Random Word(s) button. You get one word most of the time, but the engine will throw you a phrase when you least expect it. And you can add your own keywords to the randomly generated word. Click the Google Search button for

standard results or the I'm Feeling Lucky button to see the first result site. Frames are not used when displaying target sites, so click the Back button to return for another search.

Click the Add Word tab to contribute a brilliant keyword to the site's archive. That word will begin appearing, randomly, on other people's screens.

Best of all, click the Found tab to see randomly found Web pages with short descriptions. This collection justifies the entire random-search movement. Maybe. At the very least, when using Random Web Search, you will be — as the site proclaims — "Wasting your time more efficiently."

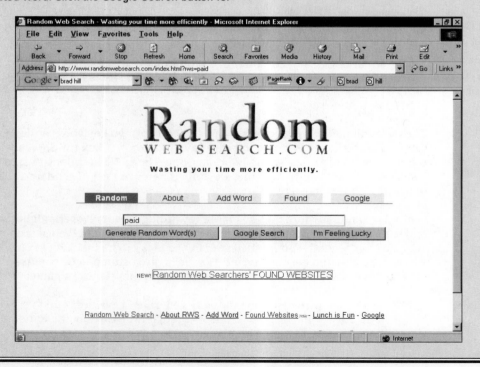

# Google Backwards

The elgooG site emulates Google in every respect, but in reverse. This site puts a literal spin on the concept of *mirror site*. Most mirror sites replicate their originals in every detail, but elgooG replicates Google as a mirror image. Go to the elgooG page (Figure 15-9) to see what I'm talking about:

```
www.alltooflat.com/geeky/elgoog/
```

The reversal is thorough. Keywords delivered through this page make no sense to Google unless they're typed backwards. So, to search the keyword *internet*, you need to type *tenretni*. Good luck.

The elgooG site carries this conceit through all Google's interface pages — Advanced Search, Preferences, Language Tools, the whole lot. News, Groups, Directory — all backwards. (In the Directory and Google Groups, pages that are at the second level and lower revert to a normal display.) Oh, and search results are reversed, too. When you click any result to leave Google, your screen reverts to its normal display.

Of what possible use is elgooG? The same might be asked of neutrinos — what purpose could they serve? In both cases, science has not yet found an answer.

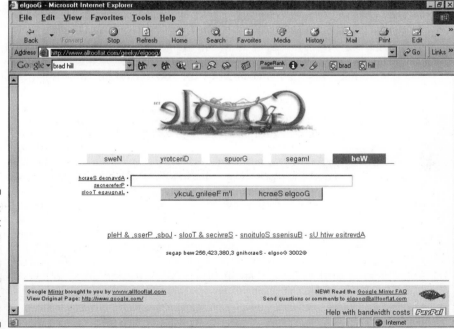

**Figure 15-9:** This is not a printing mistake! The elgooG site mirrors Google, literally.

# Google Art

Google Art creator hosts one of the most obscure Google games in circulation. Google Art is founded on a helpful quirk in the search results of Google Groups: search keywords are highlighted. Somebody at kryogenix.org took advantage of this results display to contrive a method of creating art that would appear only as a Google Groups search result. The result is like ASCII art (images created from keyboard characters and symbols) but with colors generated by Google's highlight. Figure 15-10 shows an example. You can get started on a Google art project by visiting the Google Art creator site:

```
www.kryogenix.org/code/browser/aqgoogle/
```

Google Art creator assigns two-letter vowel clusters to colors, according to the color order with which Google Groups highlights keywords. The clusters are aa, ae, ai, ao, au, ea, ee, ei, and so forth. Google Art creator provides a graphical interface so you don't have to memorize color assignments, allowing you to draw (so to speak) by clicking small blocks of color into a grand design. (See a decidedly inartistic example in Figure 15-11).

When you're finished, Google Art creator generates an ASCII message body for posting to Google Groups. It looks something like this:

```
..  ..  ..  ..  ..  ..  aa  aa  ae  ae  eu  eu  eu  ai  ..  ..  ..  ..  ea  ea  ea
ao  ao  ao  ei  ei  ei  ei  ..  ..  ..  ..  ..  ee  ee  ee  ae  ae  ae  ..  ..  ..
aa  ae  ai  ao  au  aa  aa  ..  ..  ..  ..  ei  ei  ei  ei  ei  ..  ..  ..  aa  aa
```

Anything remotely artistic would be much longer than this example. The double dots represent blank, uncolored spaces. Again, Google Art creator manufactures the message body for you, based on your drawing efforts with blocks of color.

Click the Make post to Google button to generate the message body. Despite the button's implication, clicking it doesn't really make a post to Google Groups; it merely generates the message body. You must copy and paste it into a Google Groups message body. You may also use a dedicated newsgroup reader to make the post. (See Chapter 4 for more on all this Groups business.)

After the post is made, allow a few hours for Google to catalog it on the Google Groups server. After it arrives, anybody stumbling across it without searching for it in a certain manner sees only the ASCII text, as in the preceding example. To highlight the vowel clusters, you must search *with those clusters as keywords*. That's right — you must actually conduct a Google Groups search with a keyword string like *aa ae ei eo*, and possibly a much longer one. Google Art creator comes to the rescue again, though: When it furnishes your message body text, it also gives you the necessary search string.

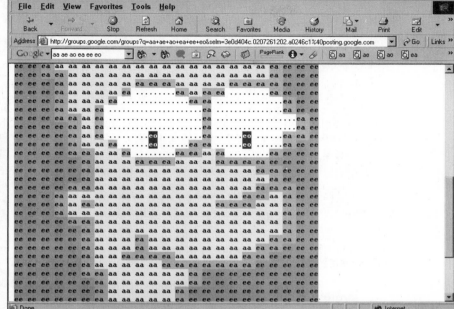

**Figure 15-10:**
More colorful than shown here, Google art displays only in a Google Groups search result.

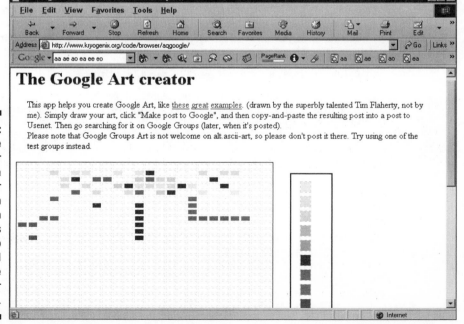

**Figure 15-11:**
The Google Art creator provides a palette for your design and then converts your work to an ASCII message ready for highlighting.

Here, then is a rundown of steps necessary to create and view Google art:

1. **Go to the Google Art creator site:**

   `www.kryogenix.org/code/browser/aqgoogle/`

2. **Create art.**

   Click a color, and then click inside the art frame to deposit that color in a grid. To erase any colored box, click the blank color and click the colored box again.

3. **Click the Make post to Google button.**

   You may also type a message title in the provided space (but you don't need to). If you don't, simply enter the title when you post to Google Groups. But typing it now gives you a more precise search string, which you might need to find your artwork later. After a minute, Google Art creator displays your message body and search string at the bottom of the page.

4. **Copy and paste the search string to another location on your screen, such as Windows Notepad.**

5. **Copy and paste the message body to the same location as the search string.**

6. **Go to Google Groups.**

7. **Search for and display the *misc.test* newsgroup.**

   See Chapter 4 for information about navigating Google Groups. You want to post your art to a test group, not to any newsgroup. Most social groups would flame you hotly for dumping a bunch of ASCII gibberish onto the board.

8. **Click the <u>Post a new message to misc.test</u> link.**

9. **On the Compose your message page, paste the message body and subject title in their respective boxes, and click the Post message — No preview button.**

   You could preview the message, but it would not show up as colored art. If you copied and pasted correctly, there are no mistakes.

10. **Wait.**

    It takes Google Groups three to eight hours to capture and catalog posted messages.

11. **Anywhere in Google Groups, copy and paste the search string provided by Google Art creator.**

12. **Click the search result representing your posted message.**

    You're finally there. With the correct search string provided by Google
    Art creator, your message appears colored with highlights representing
    your keywords.

The value of Google Art creator? Marginal, at best. This is definitely an exercise in personal fulfillment, because the likelihood of anybody else finding
your art with the correct search string is virtually nonexistent. But if you get
good at this, you could always put up a Web page with instructions, thereby
opening a sort of ephemeral art gallery, hosted entirely by Google Groups.

# Part V
# The Part of Tens

## The 5th Wave
By Rich Tennant

"He saw your laptop and wants to know if he can run a quick Google search."

# In this part . . .

The book draws to a reluctant close here. Unless you've come to this part first, in which case the book explodes in joyful commencement here.

Three chapters are stuffed with short tips, reminders, exotic tricks, personal habits I deem worth sharing, and destinations that help you better understand the irrevocable and deep relationship you have forged (must forge, will forge) with Google.

If you read this book from start to finish, these pages will top off the renovation of your Googling mindset. If you are taking this book out of order, perhaps the items in these chapters will motivate you to explore other chapters. Either way, drink plenty of coffee and remember: Don't let an entire day happen without Google. [Editors' note: Brad has slipped into a fitful slumber, tormented by caffeine-generated dreams of battling the ferocious Google index, its tentacles thrashing. We must pity him and hope for regained coherency before he writes his next book.]

# Chapter 16

# Ten Google Tricks

*In This Chapter*

▶ Searching within the search results

▶ Mapping addresses

▶ Using the Google phone book

▶ Opting out of the phone book

▶ Seeing (and erasing) previous searches

▶ Finding word meanings

▶ Using negative search operators

▶ Searching by date

▶ Getting quick stock and company information

▶ Double- and triple-clicking keywords

This chapter is where you can find tips and Google discoveries that don't fit elsewhere in the book. The following sections explore the Google phone book, how to use search operators in an unusual way, assigning a date range to a Google Web search, mapping street addresses, and more. Happy browsing!

## Searching within Search Results

Like a compact telescope, Google can keep looking within itself to narrow a search. From any search results page, you can conduct a secondary search that uses your first search results as a mini-index. Your second set of search results exist in the sites that make up the first set.

This feature is nearly hidden at the bottom of each search results page. Keyword boxes containing your search terms are located at the top and bottom of results pages, but only the bottom one sports the <u>Search within results</u> link, as shown in Figure 16-1.

When you click the <u>Search within results</u> link, Google presents a new search page with an empty keyword box, as shown in Figure 16-2. It would be preferable if Google let you launch a new search within the results of a previous search, directly from the bottom of the results page. Alas, you must trudge through the new page with its blank keyword box, enter your new keywords there, and press Enter.

Figures 16-1 and 16-2 show the first two legs of a three-part search that started with *england cottage rentals*, telescoped downward to *cotswolds*, and finally narrowed to *bed and breakfast* (Google automatically removed the *and*). By this process, the search results were narrowed from about 29,000 to about 1100, and from there to 477.

Google's keyword syntax regarding searches within searches is simple: Google simply adds the second set of keywords to the first set and the third set to the combined first and second sets. So, I could have accomplished the preceding example in one step with the following keyword string:

```
england cottage rentals cotswolds bed breakfast
```

I'm not likely to think ahead in such detail, though, so the Search within results feature is useful.

Google enforces a ten-word limit on keyword entries for any single search, and searches within results count cumulatively. So you may continue narrowing downward up to ten times, given one keyword per search. Google starts eliminating keywords after you've reached ten.

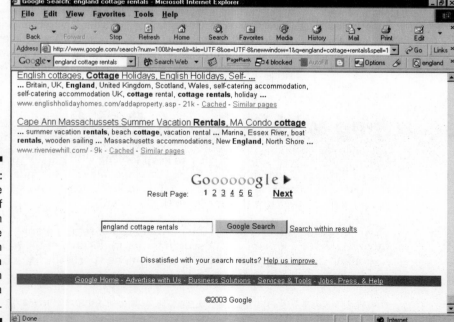

**Figure 16-1:**
At the bottom of each search results page you can start a search within a search.

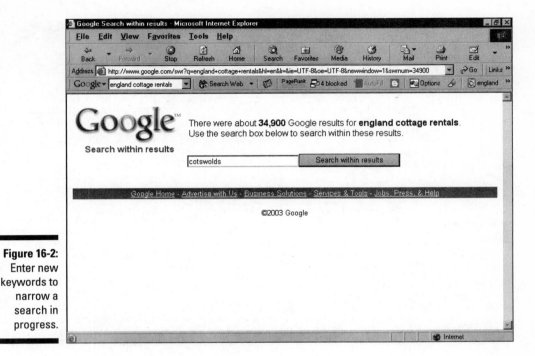

**Figure 16-2:**
Enter new
keywords to
narrow a
search in
progress.

# *Mapping It*

Maps (like stock prices) represent a type of information Google doesn't own but does point to. This means that with the right keywords, you can get one click away from an on-screen map of an address — even a vague address. Google partners with Yahoo! Maps and MapQuest when you give it a hint that you're seeking an address.

Typing an entire address in the keyword box definitely does the trick. When you type an address as your keyword, Google delivers a standard search results page, at the top of which is an invitation to click over to one of the two map providers. (See Figure 16-3.) The two links are configured to display a map of your input address.

Google springs helpfully to action whenever it senses that you have geography on your mind. Entering just a postal zip code brings up the mapping offer, as does mixing a zip code with other keywords. Try a street name with its zip code — no house or apartment number — and Google gets the hint.

**Figure 16-3:**
Google
responds to
an address
by offering
two map
links.

# The Google Phone Book

One of the great underrecognized features of Google is the built-in phone and address book. This is not a link-over deal like maps (see the preceding section) or stock prices. The Google index embodies address and phone-number information, like the White Pages. In my experience, Google does a better job culling this information from its index than do the high-profile online directories (Yahoo!, Switchboard, WhoWhere, and others).

Activating the Google phone and address book is a somewhat hit-and-miss affair, but Google takes the hint as easily here as it does with the mapping function. Type a first name, a last name, and a ZIP Code in the keyword box, and if that person's address is in the index, Google displays it above the regular search results (along with the phone number). Don't know the zip code? Who does? Replace it with the U.S. state abbreviation — that works fine. No commas are necessary in the keyword string.

Google provides a specialized search operator (a keyword modifier) that hooks into the phone book. Unsurprisingly, it's the *phonebook* operator. Use it without any spaces between the colon and the first keyword (see Chapter 2 for more on using Google's operators), like this:

```
phonebook:smith ny
```

Figure 16-4 shows the results of this search. As you can see, the volume of results sometimes requires multiple pages, just as with a Web search. Another difference in this results page is just below the keyword box. After Google dips into its phone book, it presumes that you might want to stay there for a while, and gives you a choice of applying your next keywords to the phone book or to a Web search.

By the way, you can narrow your phone book searches to residential only or business only by using variants of the plain *phonebook* operator:

- ✔ Use *rphonebook* for residential listings
- ✔ Use *bphonebook* for business listings

Using the *bphonebook* operator, Google turns into one heck of a fast Yellow Pages directory. Looking for a Chinese restaurant in your neighborhood? Lay down the keyword string with your ZIP Code:

```
bphonebook:chinese restaurant 10010
```

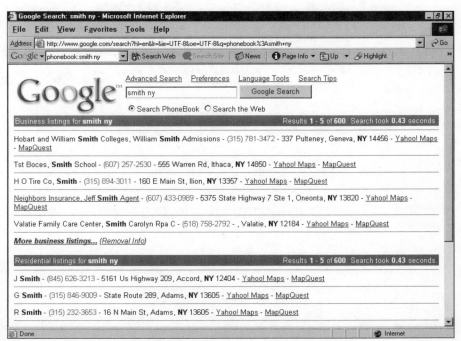

**Figure 16-4:** The Google phone book in action.

# Opting Out of the Phone Book

Isn't the *phonebook* operator, just described, nifty? Don't you love using it? Aren't you glad . . . hey, wait a minute. This means that *your* address can be outed as easily as somebody else's. Even more provocative, Google provides a reverse function in its address and phone book, whereby a person can get your address by typing your phone number.

Of course, these functions are easy to find outside Google. But Google is the site everyone uses for nearly every basic information bit, and it's only increasing in popularity. For whatever reason, you might decide you don't want your address and phone number in the index.

Removing a personal listing requires only filling out an on-screen form (see Figure 16-5). Removing a business listing requires sending your request on company letterhead to a postal address. You can start either by clicking the Removal Info link on the results page. Or go straight to the page here:

```
http://www.google.com/help/pbremoval.html
```

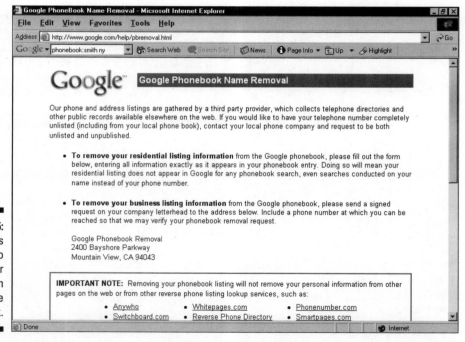

**Figure 16-5:** Use this page to remove your listing from the Google phone book.

# Seeing (and Erasing) Previous Searches

If you use Microsoft's Internet Explorer browser (most people do), you might notice that Google seems to anticipate certain keyword entries. As you type a word, a list drops down below the keyword box, suggesting a completed word or words. This can be helpful. It can also be a flaming annoyance that you'd give anything to be rid of.

Actually, Google is not doing a thing — the autocompletion feature is part of Internet Explorer, version 5 and later. If you're determined to shut it off, you must do so in the browser. Here's how:

1. **In Explorer, choose Tools⇨Internet Options.**
2. **Click the Content tab.**
3. **Under Personal Information, click the AutoComplete button.**
4. **In the AutoComplete Settings window, click the Clear Forms button.**
5. **If you want to disable Explorer from completing future forms, uncheck the Forms box and then click OK.**
6. **In the Internet Options window, click its OK button.**

Unchecking the Forms box prevents Explorer from tracking your form fill-ins at *all* sites, not just at Google. This means eliminating the convenience of Explorer autocompleting your name, e-mail address, postal address, and other personal information at shopping sites and when registering at some Web sites. I get annoyed when it tries to complete my keywords, but I live with it on Google because I want that feature elsewhere.

Autocompletion is not always annoying in Google, either. Sometimes I repeat past searches. In particular, I like seeing previous searches that begin with a search operator, such as *phonebook*. In that case, Explorer's autocompletion delivers a long list of previously searched phone numbers — kind of like an instantly available online address book.

Explorer's autocompletion feature is different than the History function on Google's Toolbar, which is unequivocally handy.

# Word Meanings

Chapters 1 and 2 discuss Google's built-in dictionary. The dictionary contributes to search results when prompted by a misspelling — or what it perceives as a misspelling according to the aggregated knowledge of the Google index. Furthermore, Google shunts you over to Dictionary.com when you click one of your keywords in the blue search summary bar on the results page. (Chapter 2 covers these topics in depth.)

Google is superlative at defining words I know how to spell but whose meaning eludes me. By simply pairing the *glossary* or *definition* keyword with the word I want defined, I can often get the gist of the word's meaning — without clicking through the search results page. Even if that happy consolidation of information doesn't happen, the results certainly link me to several solid definitions.

Figure 16-6 shows how much information you can glean from a search results page for the keyword string *glossary peer-to-peer*. Having Google by your side is helpful when reading a technical manual.

You can modify Google's use of your keywords when searching for glossary information just as with any other search. Using the *site* operator (see Chapter 2) might prove useful to narrow glossary hits of medical terms to educational domains, for example. Try this keyword string to see what I mean:

```
encephalitis definition site:.edu
```

But then, I also find that consumer-level information is generally easier to understand — and no less informative — than information from professional sources.

**Figure 16-6:**
When searching for word definitions, you might not need to click search results.

# Negative Search Operators

I discuss Google's special search operators in Chapter 2. Here, I want to point out that you can make Bizarro commands of Google by turning its search operators into negative operators. A simple minus sign does the trick:

```
searching google index -site:google.com
```

This string displays hits about searching Google from all over the Web except at the Google site — a good way to escape in-house Google Help pages.

The same search tactic applies to the *inurl* and *intitle* operators. Using the negative *intitle* operator helps dig beneath the surface. The biggest, loudest sites in a Google results page usually contain your keywords in the page title as well as in the page's text. Forcing the keywords out of the title tends to bring secondary page up toward the top of the results list.

As of this writing, the negative trick doesn't work with the *allintitle* and *allinurl* operators. In both cases, the negative command works only with the first keyword following the command, not with all keywords as the positive command does.

# Searching by Date

Although Google Groups enables painless searching of Usenet within date ranges (see Chapter 4), Web searching is not so easily placed along a time-line. There are two reasons for this. First, Web pages are not as anchored in time as Usenet newsgroup posts. Usenet documents every message posted to the system, to the second. (The exact time varies by newsgroup server, but the point is that Google's server can assign an exact time to each of the nearly one billion bits of Usenet history in its index.) Web pages are updated and posted to their servers, but they're not perceived as time-specific documents and are certainly not part of ongoing conversations. To complicate matters, the page's update time might be separated from Google's indexing time by days.

Google does allow date-range Web searching, using the time that the page was added to the index as the defining point of the timeline. But the second reason Google is hard to search in this manner involves the date format used, which is Julian, not the standard Gregorian we're accustomed to. Julian dates look like random-number strings, and figuring out how to set a searchable date range isn't worth the trouble, even with the help of Julian-Gregorian converters you can find online. If you write Google programs that allow dated searching, you must master the Julian format, which actually makes such programming easier. But at the front end of Google (searching from the home page), Julian date jockeying is out of the question.

Fortunately, those programmers who have written alternate Google interfaces come to the rescue. I keep one such site bookmarked for the occasions when I want to narrow my Web searches by date range:

```
www.faganfinder.com/engines/google.shtml
```

The Fagan Finder page, as you can see in Figure 16-7, is an alternate Advanced Search page that includes date ranges. It's a great example of how Google's open index lets independent programmers improve certain portions of the Google service. Use the drop-down menus to set your date range, enter keywords into one or more boxes, and clock the Go button. Besides the Date features, the options on this page are identical to options on Google's Advanced Search page.

Click the Google Ultimate Interface link on the Fagan Finder page shown in Figure 16-7 for the most complete alternate Google Advanced Search page around. See my description in Chapter 14.

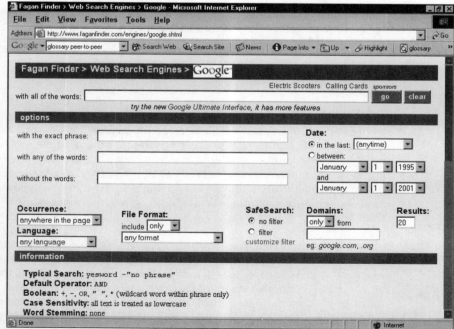

**Figure 16-7:**
Searching
within a
date range
is easier
at Fagan
Finder than
at Google.

# Quick Stock and Company Information

In Chapter 2, I discuss how to use the *stocks* operator to link seamlessly from Google to selected financial sites to get stock prices. Here, I want to explain how Google can search on stock ticker symbols, as well as unabbreviated company names, giving distinct results for each type of search.

Stock ticker symbols are understandable keywords to Google. When not preceded by the *stocks* operator, the first result of such a search gives the company name and a link to a price quote at Yahoo! Finance. (Using the *stocks* operator takes you directly to Yahoo! Finance, bypassing the search results page.) Typical Google search results follow below the link, as shown in Figure 16-8. Above the results is also a link to the Google Directory page holding that company's listing.

Searching on the true company name shows a Directory category (not necessarily the same one as when searching on the ticker symbol), followed by a selection of headlines related to that company, if available. Below those information blurbs are the regular Web search results. Figure 16-9 illustrates this search results page, using Microsoft as the company name.

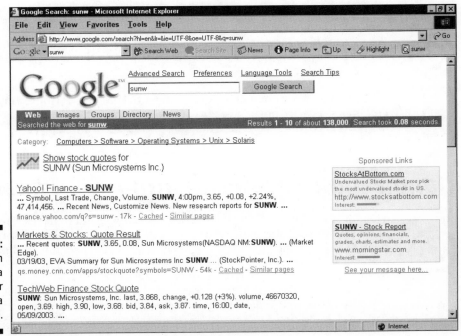

**Figure 16-8:** Search results for a stock ticker symbol as a keyword.

**Figure 16-9:**
Searching
on a
company
name (not
its stock
symbol)
yields a
directory
category
and news
headlines.

When searching for a company whose name has two words, use quotation marks around them (for example, *"General Motors"*), enforcing the exact phrase operator.

When you merge a company name with its ticker symbol (for example, *"general motors" gm*), Google gives precedence to the company name and doesn't instantly recognize any desire on your part to see a stock price.

# Double- and Triple-Clicking Keywords

This tip is a small point, but one so consistently useful to me that I can't close out this chapter without including it. Often, new searches are launched on the search results page, on the heels of a previous search. In those instances, your previous keywords appear in the keyword box and you need to supplant them with one or more new keywords. In Windows, double-click a single word to highlight it, and type a new word right over it or delete the word by pressing the Delete key. This tip works even with words that are mashed up against search operator with no spaces, like this — *intitle:kayak*. Double-clicking *kayak* highlights that word alone.

Just as useful, triple-clicking in the keyword box highlights the entire search string. I do this all the time to delete the string and replace it with new keywords.

Highlighting previous keywords in the Google Toolbar works differently. A single-click in the keyword box highlights the entire string. (This happens on only the first single-click; subsequent single-clicks deselect the string and then do nothing.) A double-click selects a single word. Triple-clicking does nothing.

# Chapter 17

# Ten More Google Tricks

*In This Chapter*

▶ Seeing the Google Zeitgeist

▶ Including "stop words" in your search

▶ Using the Google Toolbar as a spellchecker

▶ Putting operators first, for the history list

▶ The post-factum toolbar

▶ Searching for academic papers

▶ Talking with other Googlers

▶ Using the Google Toolbar as a headline generator

▶ Buying me gifts in the Google Store

▶ Viewing altered Google logos

Ten Google tricks (see Chapter 16) aren't nearly enough. Forthwith (I don't really know what that word means), ten more Google tricks.

## The Google Zeitgeist

Don't you wonder how other people use Google? And given Google's awesome popularity, don't you wonder what the big trends are? Google isn't the average search engine. Googling is a social force, and Google trends say important things about society and culture. Well, maybe not important things, but things.

Fortunately, Google isn't too modest to track its own usage and package the results in an entertaining format. The Google Zeitgeist presumes to be a mirror of virtual society — its interests, passions, desires, infolusts, technical specifications, and national demographics. Google puts all this together every month in a page of charts and graphs. Find the Google Zeitgeist at this location:

```
www.google.com/press/zeitgeist.html
```

The highlight of the monthly Zeitgeist is the double list of the top ten gaining and declining search queries, as shown in Figure 17-1. These charts are compiled weekly, and tend to represent emerging and fading trends and fads.

Click the Archived information <u>available here</u> link (on the left) to access stored gaining and declining query charts for the life of the Zeitgeist, back to early 2001.

Of particular interest to geekish users are the charts revealing the operating systems and browsers used to access Google. Scroll down the page a bit to see that data. The language chart is likewise fascinating and shows a long-term trend in which English is gradually losing its dominance.

Click any link in any Zeitgeist list to launch a search on that keyword.

**Figure 17-1:**
The Google
Zeitgeist.
Scroll down
to see more
charts and
graphs for
the previous
month.

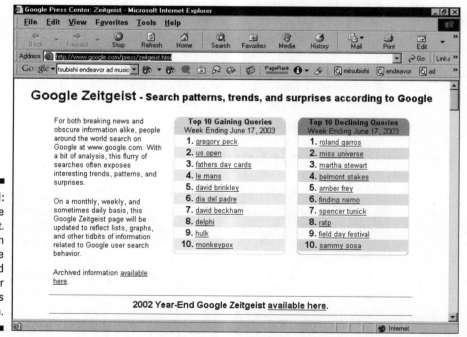

# Including "Stop Words"

Google consolidates search strings by automatically eliminating certain pronouns, articles, and other short, common words. *Or* and *and* are examples of these so-called *stop words*. The exclusion of stop words keeps search results clean but is a frustration when you want those words included in the string and matched to a Web page.

The answer is to include search operators which treat all keywords equally. (Search operators are introduced in Chapter 2.) The preeminent operator for grouping keywords is the exact phrase operator, which uses quotation marks around a keyword string to match it exactly to text on Web pages. For example:

```
"bacon and eggs"
"smokey the bear"
"trick or treat"
```

The exact phrase operator goes beyond just forcing Google to accept stop words. The operator also forces Google to keep its hands off the search string entirely, matching the word order to Web text.

# The Google Toolbar as Spellchecker

The great convenience of the Google Toolbar (introduced in Chapter 9) is that it's always with you. That makes searching a one-click experience. It also makes Google a one-stop dictionary. Google's tendency is to correct misspelling in the gentlest, most polite way: "Did you mean...?" Google does not contain a dictionary, per se, but its vast accumulated understanding of words through the compilation of billions of text pages makes Google an authority on spelling common words, names, and places.

Normally, Google's nudging toward proper spelling is performed in the service of better search results. But Google's lexicographic knowledge can be deployed for its own sake, and I have found the Toolbar to be a perfect means of quickly checking the spelling of a name or place. If Google doesn't suggest a new spelling on the search results page, chances are you've got it right. To be more sure, I sometimes deliberately spell a name or place wrongly and let Google correct me. I've used this method innumerable times in the writing of this booke, um, book.

# Operators First, for History's Sake

To use this tip, it's important to understand how Google and your browser keep track of your search queries. Keep in mind these two facts:

- ✔ On the Google home page, your browser keeps a history of search requests. The Google keyword box is a form, and most browsers can keep track of everything typed into forms. Look in your browser's settings to clear or disable the history of all the forms you fill out, including Google search requests.

- ✔ On the Google Toolbar, Google keeps a history of your search requests. You can turn off this feature in the Toolbar Options (see Chapter 9).

Assuming that you have both features turned on, you see a list of previous search requests pop down from the keyword box — on both the Google site and the Toolbar — when you begin typing. This list corresponds to the letters you're typing and shortens as you type more letters. This feature drives some people to distraction, but I like it and always have both histories enabled.

The point of all this relates to search operators (see Chapter 2 for an introduction to and list of search operators), especially the ones unique to Google. Many of these Google-specific operators can be placed anywhere in the keyword string, like this:

```
"google for dummies" site:bradhill.com
site:bradhill.com "google for dummies"
```

These examples deliver the same search results. The advantage to putting the operator first, and doing so every time you use that operator, is that the history feature displays a list of all your site searches when you begin typing that operator. That list makes a convenient record of sites that you've Googled in the past. (See Figure 17-2.)

I find this technique particularly useful with the *site*, *cache*, *link*, *intitle*, and *inurl* operators.

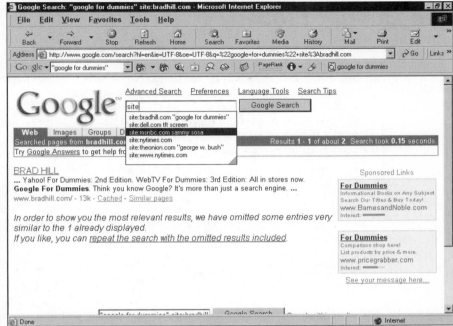

**Figure 17-2:**
Putting
Google
operators
first creates
an operator-
specific
history list.

# *Post Factum Toolbar*

If you have the Google Toolbar installed (and you should), you might notice a curious fact. The Toolbar's keyword box displays the keywords you most recently entered at the Google site. Even though you didn't use the Toolbar, it behaves as if you did. Not only are the keywords displayed in the search box, they appear as toolbar icons for highlighting, just as they do when you search using the Toolbar. (See Chapter 9 for a rundown of all Toolbar features.) In other words, the Toolbar behaves egotistically, as if it were always the means of your Google search, even when you launch your keywords from the Google site.

This Toolbar behavior is worth remembering because those highlight icons are so darn handy — one of the Toolbar's best features, really. Clicking a keyword icon repeatedly skips the highlight from one instance of the keyword on a Web page to the next instance. Clicking the Highlight button (it looks like a yellow marker on the Toolbar) highlights all instances of all keywords on the Web page.

Of course, the synergy between Google's site and the Toolbar works in reverse, too: Keywords entered in the Toolbar are displayed in Google's keyword box on the search results page.

# The Google Library

Google is not a replacement for dedicated online research facilities such as ProQuest and eLibrary. But the range and depth of academic material you can find through Google is truly amazing. Two operators help narrow searches to academic realms and certain types of result:

- ✔ **filetype:** The *filetype* operator can isolate the PDF format, which is commonly used to post academic papers.

- ✔ **site:** The *site* operator narrows search results to a particular site (such as a university) or an entire top-level domain. In this tip I'm focusing on the *.edu* domain.

Combining these two operators yields fantastic and fascinating results. Whatever your interests, you can give your searching an academic slant by forming search requests for academic PDF files. A few examples:

```
filetype:pdf site:.edu "black holes"
filetype:pdf site:.edu rebuilding iraq
filetype:pdf site:.edu movie stars
```

This type of searching narrows results considerably. To broaden the search, you can always remove one of the two operators — try that if you get no results at all. To narrow a search even further, try putting a specific college URL after the *site* operator. You can also use Google's university search, as described in Chapter 6.

I suggest narrowing to the *.edu* domain as a natural method of targeting academic papers. But leaving that operator out of the picture brings in interesting white papers and business documents posted to dot-com addresses. And narrowing to government sites with the *site:.gov* operator gives great results too, for political, social, governmental, and military topics.

You don't need to have Adobe Acrobat Reader to see PDF files through Google. That reader keeps the PDF formatting intact, and it's a free download. But PDF files do take longer to load than HTML files, and Google handily converts all PDF documents to HTML documents on demand — just click the <u>View as HTML</u> link in any PDF search result.

# Talking with Other Googlers

Google encourages discussion among its users. To that end, Google has set up several (11, to be exact) Usenet newsgroups in Google Groups (see Chapter 4). Google is especially interested in generating conversation around the Google Labs experiments (see Chapter 8). In those groups dedicated to Webquotes, Google Sets, and other lab mutations, you can occasionally log a rare sighting of a Google representative taking suggestions and answering questions.

Following is a list of newsgroups about Google, as of this writing:

```
google.public.labs.compute
google.public.labs.glossary
google.public.labs.google-viewer
google.public.labs.keyboard-shortcuts
google.public.labs.sets
google.public.labs.voice-search
google.public.labs.webquotes
google.public.programming-contest
google.public.support.general
google.public.public.translators
google.public.labs.web-apis
```

You might find these groups in a stand-alone newsgroup reader, depending on your Usenet provider. But you won't find any discussions in those groups and you'll wonder why I pointed you to them. Google doesn't distribute the content of its public groups throughout Usenet, so you must access them through Google Groups. See Chapter 4 to find out how to search for newsgroups in Google.

Figure 17-3 illustrates the google.public.support.general newsgroup as seen in Google Groups. This group is the place to turn for general discussion and help with Google features not found in Google Labs.

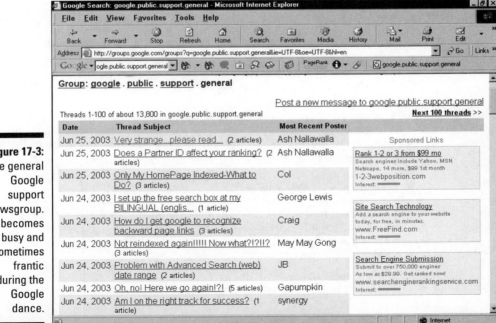

**Figure 17-3:** The general Google support newsgroup. It becomes busy and sometimes frantic during the Google dance.

# The Toolbar Headline Generator

Google's Web search results are hooked into Google News in a subtle but distinct way. When you search with keywords that relate to news items gathered by Google News, Google displays headlines on top of your regular Web search results (see Figure 17-4).

Using the Google Toolbar deliberately to generate headlines in this manner results in a fast way to check out a news story or current events subject. Of course, going to Google News and searching there leads to more comprehensive results. But when you want a quick rush of headlines in seconds, try the Toolbar. Just type your newsy subject or specific story keywords into the Toolbar and press Enter.

If you use Google News more than the Google Web search — in other words, if Google has become primarily a news service for you — make sure you use the Combined Search button in the Google Toolbar Options, and set it to always search the most recently-searched Google realm every time you press Enter. Confused? Good; my work here is done. Kidding, kidding — let me unpack this for you. Follow these steps for easy, repetitive news searching from the Google Toolbar:

1. **Install the Google Toolbar.**

   See Chapter 9.

2. **Click the Google button, and then click the Toolbar Options selection.**

3. **Scroll down the page and click the <u>experimental features</u> link.**

4. **Click to select the Combined Search button option.**

5. **Click the box next to "Keep the last search done with the Combined Search button as the default."**

6. **Click the OK button at the bottom of the page.**

7. **Back on the main Toolbar Options page, click the OK button at the bottom of that page.**

Now, when you first search for news headlines in the Toolbar, use the Combined Search button to launch a Google News search, not a Google Web search. After that first search, the Google Toolbar remembers your preference and automatically puts subsequent keywords into Google News, not Google Web. Pressing the Enter key launches the world's best news search, right from your browser.

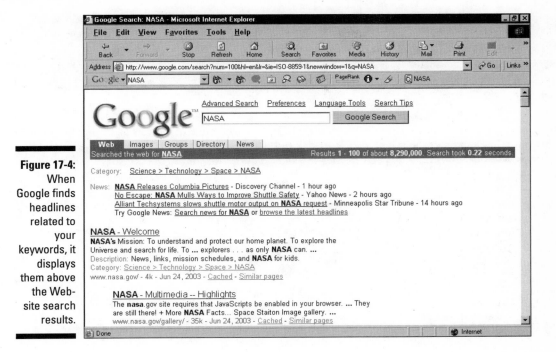

# The Google Store

As brainy as Google is, the company isn't above making money. The Google Store doesn't generate revenue like Google's advertising does, but there it is. Pens, mouse pads, wearables, wristwatches, CD cases, mugs, even a Google golf umbrella.

Two facts of profound importance must be mentioned. First, authors love gifts. Second, the CD case (Figure 17-5) is utterly cool. I'm just saying.

The Google Store is here:

```
www.googlestore.com
```

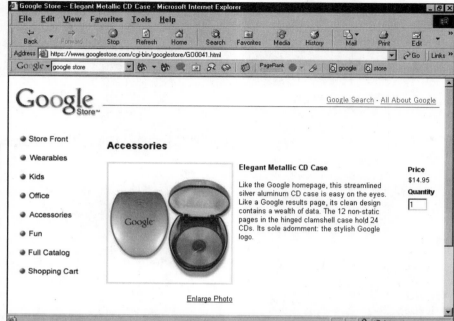

**Figure 17-5:**
The Google
Store, for
merchan-
dise that
advertises
your slavish
relationship
with the
Google-
beast.

# Google Logos

You have probably noticed that Google celebrates holidays and various current events by altering its logo. These days, most of Google's inspired and
witty alternate logos are created by Dennis Hwang. Google maintains an
archive of altered logos, as well as early-history logos before Hwang's reign
and fan-created logos. Figures 17-6 and 17-7 show off small portions of these
collections.

If you want to place a Google logo on your Web site, Google asks that you use
an official logo, and you are given a choice of sizes and colored backgrounds.
The official logos are located here:

```
www.google.com/stickers.html
```

The altered and fan logos are located on separate pages:

```
www.google.com/holidaylogos.html
www.google.com/customlogos.html
```

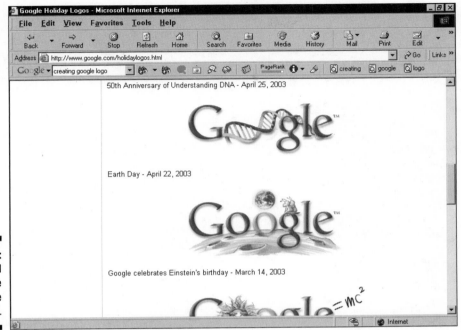

**Figure 17-6:**
Altered
Google
logos are
archived.

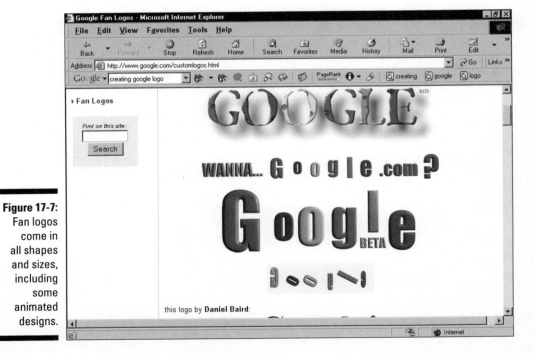

**Figure 17-7:**
Fan logos
come in
all shapes
and sizes,
including
some
animated
designs.

# Chapter 18

# Ten Sites about Google

*In This Chapter*

▶ Google Watch

▶ Webmaster World

▶ PageRank

▶ Google Weblog

▶ Elgoog

▶ The Founders' home pages

▶ Googlepress

▶ Google Review

▶ gooGuide

▶ Something Awful

*T*here are three broad areas of Google obsession:

✔ The search engine itself, and all of Google's related services

✔ Alternate Google sites and interfaces, described in Chapters 14 and 15

✔ Analysis and discussion of Google and its extraordinary effect on our online lives

This book is mostly concerned with hands-on, heady interaction with the Google index through all its interfaces, both official and unofficial. This one chapter points to sites in the third group. These sites *about* Google range from the technical to the journalistic, from the critical to the laudatory.

# Google Watch

www.google-watch.org/

This extremely critical and well-researched site offers a tonic to blind Google mania. Google Watch believes, in its words, "There's a struggle going on for the soul of the web, and the focal point of this struggle is Google itself."

Google Watch has problems with Google's dominance and the influence it wields. The site also takes issue with the PageRank system, claiming that it unfairly adds to the prominence of popular sites that don't necessarily deserve their popularity. Further, Google Watch dislikes Google's use of cookies to track user behavior through the site. Google Watch even believes that Google's cached copy of Web sites is illegal, not to mention problematic for Webmasters. Google's general secretiveness is raked over the coals at Google Watch.

Google Watch is an investigative site, a scathing indictor of Google's operations, an explainer of technical arcana, and a loud whistleblower. In May of 2003, when it became apparent to Webmasters that something strange was happening in the index, and the results of April's deep crawl had seemingly been discarded, Google Watch provided the most objective (and, of course, highly critical) voice amid the swirling speculation.

Judging by Google Watch's high PageRank, many people are reading. You should too, if you're interested in the dark side of the Google phenomenon.

# Webmaster World: Google

www.webmasterworld.com/forum3

Along with Google Watch, Webmaster World's Google forum is one of the most visited sites for serious Google watchers. Naturally, this forum is populated by Webmasters — site owners trying to maximize their exposure in the Google index and on search results pages. Much of the conversation is fairly advanced and technical, as you can see even from a glance at the discussion headers shown in Figure 18-1.

Topics in this forum include bettering one's PageRank, understanding and coping with the Google dance, anticipating the deep crawl and preparing a site for it, and the best ways to lure the Google spider, make it happy, and endure its occasional wrath.

Recently, Webmaster World started two new forums, one for the Google Toolbar and one for Google AdWords.

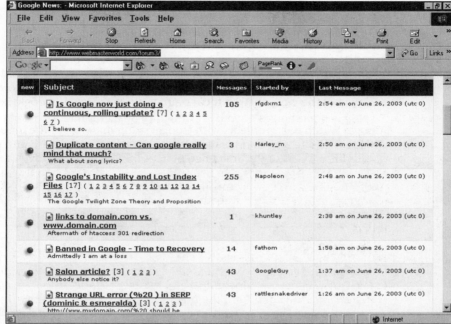

**Figure 18-1:**
The Google
forum at
Webmaster
World is the
place for
advanced
discussion
of Google
positioning
issues.

# Google PageRank

pr.efactory.de

PageRank is arguably the most important search technology to hit the Web in years. The ranking of Web pages based on popularity, as defined by the amount of back-linking directed toward them, lies at the heart of Google's effectiveness. Yet determining PageRank is not a simple matter of counting links. Google deploys algorithms that are both highly technical and partly secret.

This site explains PageRank with a depth only a truly ambitious Google fanatic can appreciate. Here you find a mathematical description of the Google algorithm as taken from the university papers of Google's founders. Eight other sections delve into the details of how PageRank is implemented, the role of incoming and outgoing links, ranking distribution issues, and quite a bit more, the description of which would make me appear quite foolish.

# *Google Weblog*

google.blogspace.com

The Google Weblog provides a simple, nontechnical update of Google news. There's nothing controversial or difficult here. Even the typeface is childishly huge (see Figure 18-2). Pro-Google perhaps to a fault, the Google Weblog is nonetheless objective enough to be a credible news source.

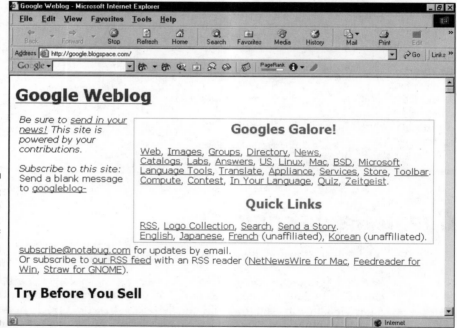

**Figure 18-2:**
The Google Weblog. Simple, brief news updates about all things Google.

# Elgoog.nl

www.elgoog.nl

This site is not be confused with the Elgoog described in Chapter 15. *That* Elgoog is a mirror image of the real Google. *This* Elgoog is a potent directory to Google-related sites. Prefaced as an "ode to Google," the site is less poetic than methodical and is possibly the most comprehensive directory of online Googlish destinations.

Figure 18-3 shows how Elgoog.nl breaks down its directory subjects. The inner workings of the directory exhibit a somewhat slapdash organization, with considerable duplication among the subjects. But never mind that. Many riches lurk within.

**Figure 18-3:**
The Elgoog.nl directory of Google-related destinations.

# The Founders' Home Pages

```
www-db.stanford.edu/~sergey
www-db.stanford.edu/~page
```

Sergey Brin and Larry Page founded Google on the back of their student research at Stanford University. Their college Web pages are still posted (and enjoying pretty good PageRanks, too). It's rather fun to see what they were involved with when they last updated their sites, before the fast-growing corporate Google swept them away from school. Brin's site features the famous paper written by the two students, "The Anatomy of a Large-Scale Hypertextual Web Search Engine." Both pages were more or less abandoned in early 1998.

# Googlepress

```
groups.yahoo.com/group/googlepress/
```

Google distributes press releases to anyone who wants them. These bulletins contain news about Google's services and features, and are, of course, free.

Curiously, Google uses a Yahoo! Group to collect memberships in the distribution list. Normally, Yahoo! Groups are used to build online communities around a certain topic, and they enable message-board discussions, chat rooms, shared calendars, posted pictures, and other fun features. Google has all those features turned off and uses the group strictly for e-mailing newsletters.

You sign up for Google's press releases by joining the Googlepress group. If you have a Yahoo! ID already, follow these steps:

1. **Go to the following URL:**

   ```
   groups.yahoo.com/group/googlepress/
   ```

2. **Click the <u>Join This Group!</u> link.**

3. **Complete the Edit My Membership page.**

   Here, you choose a Yahoo! ID (if you own multiple IDs), an e-mail address (if Yahoo! has more than one on file for your ID), the message delivery style, and the message format. It might take up to a day for your Yahoo! ID to be added to the group membership. During that time, you are classified as a Pending member.

4. **Click the Save Changes button.**

If you don't have a Yahoo! ID, follow these steps:

1. **On the Googlepress home page, click the Join This Group! button.**

2. **On the Sign In page, click the <u>Sign up now</u> link.**

3. **On the Welcome to Yahoo! page, fill in all the required information fields, and then click the Submit This Form button.**

   This page is a typical site registration page, but more complex than many. When you click the Submit button, Yahoo! sends a verification e-mail to the address you provided.

4. **Find the verification e-mail and click the link provided in the message body.**

   A browser window appears with the information required to complete your membership to the Googlepress group.

5. **On the Join This Group page, make the choices required and then click the Join button.**

   Check to make sure your provided information is correct. Decide how you would like to receive Google's newsletters. Select the Individual emails option — in this particular group it's the only option that makes sense. Then select whether you'd like your newsletter to arrive in HTML format or non-HTML (plain text). I prefer receiving the HTML format.

At this point you have joined the Googlepress group, and you see a Membership Pending page. The entire process is completed fairly quickly, and a confirmation e-mail is sent within a few minutes in most cases.

A lot of work to receive an occasional newsletter? You bet! Google is quite foolish to use a Yahoo! Group (which is designed for community interaction) for the simple task of sending press releases. There should be a one-step sign-up form within Google for this thing. This editorial comment has been brought to you free of charge.

# Google Review

notess.com/search/features/google

Staking a claim to pure objectivity, the Google Review presents a thorough rundown of Google's features, strengths, and weaknesses. After a short historical summary of Google's birth and emergence, the front page launches into a detailed inventory of Google's operating features.

This one-page review makes a good reference and is worthy of being printed. Related articles linked in the sidebar (see Figure 18-4) are dated.

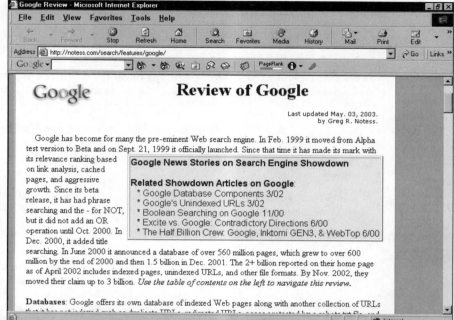

# gooGuide

www.googuide.com

Perhaps the most professional of the Google information sites, gooGuide is timely, decently written, and dedicated to keeping its ear on the ground. Rumors are explored, but sensationalism is avoided.

At the heart of gooGuide (see Figure 18-5) lies the Google Gazette, a weekly electronic newsletter posted to the site and distributed through e-mail. No site registration is necessary. The Google Gazette contains site optimization tips and articles about whatever is currently transpiring in the Google universe. Helpfully, gooGuide also carries links to articles about Google from far and wide.

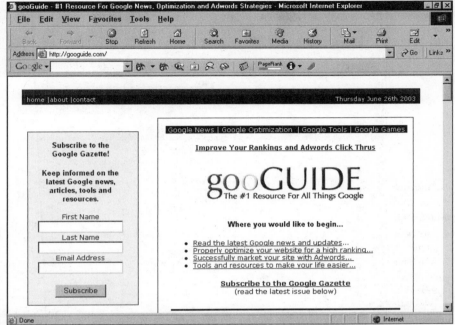

**Figure 18-5:**
gooGuide,
home of the
Google
Gazette.

# Something Awful (Logos)

www.somethingawful.com/article.php?id=382

The preceding URL points to a Weblog page that, in turn, leads to several
pages of maverick Google logo designs. Don't go in here with delicate sensibilities. Figure 18-6 shows a couple of harmless examples, but some of them
are in deliberate bad taste. But funny? Let's just say that you should view at
your own risk.

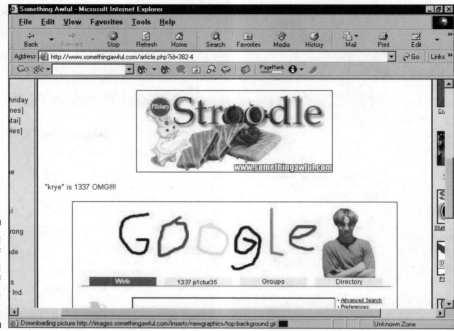

**Figure 18-6:**
A couple of
Something
Awful rips of
the Google
logo.

# Index

## • Symbols •

* (asterisk wildcard), 71, 72
: (colon), 40
-group operator, 70
- (minus sign)
  Froogle and, 71
  negative search operator
    and, 305
  overview of, 39
+ (plus sign)
  Froogle and, 71
  overview of, 39

## • A •

About Google Compute
  option (Google
  Compute), 140
academic searching, 316
accessing
  Directory, 49
  newsgroups, 66
account
  AdWords, creating, 201–206
  Blogger, creating, 228–229
  Google Answers, creating
    and logging in, 116–117
  Web API section for license
    key, 242
accuracy of search results, 1
ad group, 200–201
Add a Comment button
  (Google Answers),
  128, 129
Add URL button
  (TouchGraph
  GoogleBrowser), 251

address book, 12, 300–301
address, mapping, 299–300
Advanced button
  (TouchGraph
  GoogleBrowser), 251
Advanced Groups Search
  page, 84–86
Advanced Image Search
  page, 43–45
Advanced Search page. *See
  also* Advanced Search
  page (Google)
  FaganFinder page, 306
  Froogle, 98–99
  Google Alert, 257, 258
  Google Catalogs, 105–106
Advanced Search page
  (Google)
  Date setting, 37
  Domain setting, 37
  File Format setting, 37
  freshness filtering and, 245
  Google Ultimate Interface
    compared to, 264
  keywords, multiple, using,
    35–36
  Language setting, 36
  Links feature, 38
  Occurrences setting, 37
  overview of, 34–35
  SafeSearch setting, 37
  Similar feature, 38
advertisement
  banner, 197
  placement of on search
    results page, 200
  writing, 203–206
advertising business, 198

AdWords program
  account and first ad,
    creating, 201–206
  activating account, 206–207
  ad group, 200–201
  control center, 201,
    205–206, 207–212
  daily budget, creating, 205
  editing campaign, 210–211
  keyword modifiers, 213
  Keyword Suggestion tool,
    213–216
  keywords, 212
  login page, 205
  managing campaign,
    207–212
  overview of, 15–16, 198–200
  Power Posting tool, 216
  starting new campaign,
    211–212
  Traffic Estimator table, 215
  viewing campaign reports,
    208–209
alias, 65. *See also* screen
  name
All products feature
  (Froogle), 93
All results from the store
  feature (Froogle), 93
allintext operator (Froogle),
  94, 97
allintitle operator
  Froogle and, 94, 97
  Google Groups and, 71
  overview of, 42
  UncleSam search and, 111
allinurl operator, 42
*alt.* newsgroups, 66

alternative interfaces
bare-bones, 243–244
Boogle, 274
Floogle, 272–273
GAPS (Google API Proximity
Search), 266–268
GARBO (Google API
Relation Browsing
Outliner), 268–270
GAWSH (Google API Web
Search by Host), 270–271
GooFresh, 245–246
Google Dance Tool, 262–263
Google Tool, 264
Google Ultimate Interface,
264–266
Google-Dance-Tool, 263
instant messaging, 271–272
My Google-Dance-Machine,
259–262
overview of, 241–242
Recipe Search, 273–274
TouchGraph
GoogleBrowser, 246–255
AND operator
Froogle and, 71
overview of, 39
AOL
Instant Messenger, 272
message boards, 62
API (application
programming interface),
16, 242
Apple Macintosh
searches, 112
Archive Index Date Format
(blog), 238
archiving blog, 237
article, 64, 78
* (asterisk wildcard), 71, 72
authenticity, question of,
13–14
Author link (Google Groups),
75, 76
author operator, 79

Author setting (Advanced
Groups Search page), 85
Author's e-mail link (Google
Groups), 75
autocompletion feature,
turning off, 303
AutoFill (Google Toolbar 2.0),
172, 177–178
Automatic Removal Tool, 78
autotranslate feature,
191–194

## • B •

Back button
browser and Google Viewer,
145–146
TouchGraph
GoogleBrowser, 251
Back Color button
(TouchGraph
GoogleBrowser), 251
back links feature, 17
banner advertising, 197
bare-bones search interface,
243–244
beta version, 89, 171
binaries, 64
Blog This! button (Google
Toolbar 2.0), 172,
176–177, 233
Blogger
account, creating, 228–229
BlogSpot, creating blog at,
229–231
editing screen, 231
FTP server, creating blog
on, 231–232
overview of, 14, 227
Blogger Pro, 232
blogs. See also Blogger
creating at BlogSpot,
229–231
creating at FTP server,
231–232

editing, 232–233
formatting, 238–239
overview of, 14, 227–228
settings, adjusting, 235–238
template, changing, 239
writing, posting, and
publishing, 233–235
BlogSpot Plus, 232
bold typeface, 233
Boogle, 274
Boolean operators, 35, 39–40
Boolean search string, 36
bot, 16. See also spider
bphonebook operator, 301
brackets, square, 213
brand name, recognition of, 1
Brin, Sergey, Web site of, 328
browser
Back button and Google
Viewer, 145–146
Find feature, 30
Google Zeitgeist and, 312
history of search
requests, 314
right-click context menu,
adding Google-related
items to, 164, 167
TouchGraph
GoogleBrowser, 246–255
transliterated language
and, 190
browser buttons
getting, 180
overview of, 15, 159
requirements for, 160
browser enhancements. See
also browser buttons;
Google Toolbar
Google as default search
engine, 160, 182–183
requirements for, 160
browsing
Directory, 48–49
Froogle, 91–92
Google Groups, 66–69

BSD searches, 111–112
bulletin board system, 62

● **C** ●

cache, 31, 33
cache operator, 41
Cached link, 31–32, 33
cached search result and
    Google notice, 32, 33
Cape Clear (company), 256
case-insensitivity, 27
catalogs, online. *See* Google
    Catalogs
Category button (Google
    Toolbar), 166
Category link, 31
cell phone, Web-enabled, and
    wireless Google, 14
Clarify Question button
    (Google Answers),
    120, 128
Clear button (TouchGraph
    GoogleBrowser), 251
clickthrough
    ad placement and, 200
    billing by, 198, 201
    description of, 15, 197
cloaking, 223
Close Question button
    (Google Answers),
    120–121, 125
closing question (Google
    Answers), 125, 126
colon (:), 40
Coloration setting (Advanced
    Image Search page), 45
Combined Search button
    (Google Toolbar)
    adding, 109
    Google News and, 319
    overview of, 170, 171
community and newsgroups,
    63, 84
company name, searching
    on, 307–308

Complete Thread link
    (Google Groups), 75,
    77, 78
Configuration Page (Google
    Compute), 140
content of Web page,
    dividing topically, 222
Convert line breaks
    (blog), 238
cookie
    preferences and, 21
    purpose of, 116
copyright and images, 45
cost-per-click (CPC), 201
crawler, 218. *See also* deep
    crawl; fresh crawl;
    spider
Create New Ad Group
    link, 211
Create New Ad link, 210
creating
    AdWords account, 201–206
    blog at BlogSpot, 229–231
    blog on FTP server, 231–232
    Blogger account, 228–229
    Google Answers account
        and logging in, 116–117
    hyperlink in blog, 233
cross-post, 64

● **D** ●

date
    Advanced Groups Search
        page, 86
    Advanced Search page, 37
    Google Groups and, 73, 79
    Julian format, 305–306
    searching by, 305
Date Header Format
    (blog), 238
daterange operator, 245
deep crawl, 218, 220, 259
default search engine, Google
    as, 160, 182–183
definition keyword, 304

Deja News, 12, 61
Delete Ad Group link, 210
Delete (ad) link, 201
Delete Campaign link, 210
deleting keyword, 308–309
Dictionary.com, 29
Digital Songstream Web
    site, 227
Directory
    accessing, 49
    add URL link, 54, 55
    Become an Editor link, 53
    browsing, 48–49
    categories of, 30–31
    home page, 50
    index compared to, 220
    News category page, 50
    overview of, 11, 47, 49–52
    PageRank system, 47, 48, 51
    search results and, 54
    subcategory page, 52
    Submit a Site link, 53–55
    submitting Web page to,
        52–55
    Yahoo! Directory compared
        to, 48
Directory tab, 28
distributed computing,
    136, 139
document repository, 13
domain
    Advanced Search page, 37
    description of, 34
    .edu, 316
Domain setting (Advanced
    Image Search page), 45
doorway page, 221
double-clicking keyword, 309
dynamic page, 221

● **E** ●

Edit (ad) link, 210
Edit Campaign Settings
    link, 210

Edit Question Parameters
button (Google
Answers), 120, 128
editing
ad campaign, 210–211
blog, 232–233, 235, 236
.edu domain, 316
elgooG, 289
Elgoog Web site, 327
Elmer Fudd language, 22
e-mail
alerts, 256–258
searching by, 256
Encoding (blog), 238
etiquette and newsgroups, 84
Everflux, 218
exact phrase operator, 35, 39,
313. *See also* quotes
operator
Excite (search engine), 26
expertise and newsgroups, 63
expired message, 64

● *F* ●

FaganFinder page, 306
FAQ (Frequently Asked
Question) file, 64
fee
activating AdWords
account, 207
Blogger Pro, 232
BlogSpot Plus, 232
Google Answers tipping
system, 128–129
posting question to Google
Answers, 118, 133
file format
Advanced Search page, 37
PDF, finding files in, 110
PDF, reading and
loading, 316
filetype operator
academic material and, 316
PDF and, 110

Filetypes setting (Advanced
Image Search page), 44
filter, 24, 37, 45, 86
Find feature of browser, 30
Find results (Advanced
Image Search page), 44
flame, 64, 84
Flash, 272–273
Floogle, 272–273
formatting blog, 233, 238–239
frames, 222, 284
free download, 45
fresh crawl, 218, 220, 259
freshness settings, 244–246
Froogle
Advanced Search page,
98–99
beta version of, 89–90
home page, 91
overview of, 13
price comparisons, 96
product page, 92–94
search operators, 94–95,
97–98
search results, 92–94
searching and browsing,
91–92
second-level page, 92
FTP server, creating blog at,
231–232

● *G* ●

games
elgooG, 289
Google Art, 290–293
Googlelaar, 278–279
Googlewhack, 275–278
Googlism, 280–281
Mangle, 285–286
Random Bounce Me,
286–287
Random Google, 287
Random Google Image
Finder, 287

Random Web Search, 288
squabbling keywords,
281–284
GAPS (Google API Proximity
Search), 266–268
GARBO (Google API Relation
Browsing Outliner),
268–270
GAWSH (Google API Web
Search by Host), 270–271
glossary keyword, 304
glossary search engine,
148–149
GooFresh, 245–246
Google Alert, 256–258
Google Answers
account, creating and
logging in, 116–117
adding comment, 129, 130
Ask a Question page,
118, 119
clarifying and modifying
question, 128
comments and
conversations, 124–126
dialogue between
researcher and poster,
121–124
directory, surfing,
131–132, 133
fine-tuning and rating
answer, 128–129
formulating question,
130–133
home page, 118
interacting with, 127
locked questions, 122
My Account link, 117
overview of, 14, 115
posting and canceling
question, 118–124
refund and reposting
question, 129
setting price for, 133

staff of researchers for, 115–116
Terms of Service, 117
tipping system, 128–129
value of, 127
View Question page, 119, 120–121
Google API Proximity Search (GAPS), 266–268
Google API Relation Browsing Outliner (GARBO), 268–270
Google API Web Search by Host (GAWSH), 270–271
Google Art, 290–293
Google as brand name, 1
Google Catalogs
Advanced Search page, 105–106
beta version of, 89–90
control bar, 100, 102, 103, 104
directory page, 100, 101, 102
home page, 100, 101
More results from this catalog link, 103
overview of, 13, 99–100
search results page, 100, 102, 103
searching, 100–105
Google Compute
Configuration page, 140, 141
FAQ, 140, 141
installing, 138, 139
Max Processor Usage setting, 140, 141
overview of, 136–138
running on multiple computers, 139
Standard and Conservative modes, 140
tweaking, 138–141
uninstalling, 142
work unit, 140
Google dance, 244, 259

Google Dance Tool, 262–263
Google Directory
accessing, 49
add URL link, 54, 55
Become an Editor link, 53
browsing, 48–49
categories of, 30–31
home page, 50
News category page, 50
overview of, 11, 47, 49–52
PageRank system, 47, 48, 51
search results and, 54
subcategory page, 52
Submit a Site link, 53–55
submitting Web page to, 52–55
Yahoo! Directory compared to, 48
Google Duel, 281, 283, 284
Google Glossary, 148–149
Google Groups
about Google, 316–317
Advanced Groups Search page, 84–86
Author link, 75, 76
author operator, 79
Author's e-mail link, 75
browsing and searching, 66–69
Complete Thread link, 75, 77, 78
Google Art and, 290–291
group operator, 69–71
home page, 67
keyword box, 74
limitations of, 66, 74
message dates, 86
message header, 74–75
message page, 76
Newsgroups link, 75
No frame link, 78
Original Format link, 75, 77
overview of, 61–62
PageRank system, 67, 68, 72
password, 82, 83

Post a follow-up to this message link, 75
posting message through, 80–83
quote-back, 83
reading message and thread, 74–79
registration, 80
Related groups list, 72–73
reply page, 83
restricting post from archive, 78
search results, 68–69, 73
searchable archives, 66
Sort by date link, 73, 79
Sort by reply link, 79
time stamp, 74
View thread link, 73
View with frames link, 78
Google interface, 187–188
Google Labs. *See also* Google Compute; Google Viewer
Discuss with others link, 155
Google Glossary, 148–149
Google Sets, 150–151, 252–255
Keyboard Shortcuts, 135–136, 153–155
overview of, 13, 135–136
Voice Search, 152–153
WebQuotes, 135–136, 146–148
Google News
features, 55–58
front page, 55, 56
headlines, 56
national editions of, 59
news categories, 56
overview of, 12, 47
preferences and, 57
related link, 57, 58
search results, 59, 318
searching, 58–59
searching feature, 55

Google News *(continued)*
  searching from Google
    Toolbar, 319
  submitting news source, 59
  Text Version link, 57, 58
  top story categories, 56
  updating of, 48
Google notice, 32, 33
Google PageRank Web
    site, 325
Google Review Web site,
    329–330
Google Search button, 180
Google Sets
  overview of, 150–151
  TouchGraph viewer and,
    252–255
Google Smackdown, 281,
    282–283
Google Store Web site,
    319–320
Google Tool, 264
Google Toolbar. *See also*
    Google Toolbar 2.0
  amount of text on button,
    choosing, 165, 166
  browser requirements
    for, 160
  button options, 165–169
  experimental features,
    170–171
  headline generator, 318–319
  highlighting keyword, 309
  history of search
    requests, 314
  installing, 160–163
  keyword box on, 315
  national Google, choosing,
    164, 165
  news searching from, 319
  non-English, 194–195
  Options page, 163–165
  overview of, 15
  PageRank feature, 162

specialty searching
    and, 109
spellchecking and, 313
stocks operator, 40
Google Toolbar 2.0. *See also*
    Google Toolbar
  AutoFill, 172, 177–178
  Blog This! button, 172,
    176–177
  google-set-vista and, 255
  installing, 172–173
  Options panel, 172
  overview of, 171–172
  pop-up blocker, 172,
    179, 255
  Search Country button, 172,
    175–176
  Toolbar Options dialog box,
    174–175
Google Ultimate Interface,
    264–266
Google Viewer
  Back button of browser
    and, 145–146
  control bar, 143–144, 145
  high-speed Internet
    connection and, 143
  overview of, 135–136
  results page, 143, 145
  search page, 143, 144
Google Watch Web site, 324
Google Weblog Web site, 326
Google Zeitgeist, 311–312
Googlebot, 224
Google.com button, 180
Google-Dance-Tool, 263
GoogleFight, 281, 283
Googlelaar, 278–279
Googlematic, 272
GooglePress Web site,
    328–329
google.public.support.general
    newsgroup, 317
GoogleScout button, 180

google-set-vista tool, 252–255
Googlewhack, 275–278
Googlism, 280–281
Googolator, 272
gooGuide Web site, 330–331
government tracker. *See* U.S.
    government searches
group operator, 69–71
Groups tab, 28, 86

• *H* •

Hacker language, 22, 23
Handspring PDA and wireless
    Google, 14
headline, 200, 318
Headlines feature (Google
    News), 56
Heisenwhack, 277
Highlight button (Google
    Toolbar), 167, 169, 315
highlighting keywords, 181,
    308–309
Hill, Brad (author)
  *Internet Searching For
    Dummies,* 61
  *Yahoo! For Dummies,* 10,
    48, 162
history of search
    requests, 314
home page. *See also* home
    page (Google)
  Directory, 50
  Froogle, 91
  Google Alert, 256
  Google Answers, 118
  Google Catalogs, 100, 101
  Google Dance Tool, 262
  Google Groups, 67
  Google Sets, 150
  Google Smackdown, 282
  Google Ultimate
    Interface, 265
  Googlelaar, 279

google-set-vista, 253
Googlism, 281
My Google-Dance-
   Machine, 260
Open Directory Project
   database, 53, 54
Random Web Search, 288
WebQuotes, 147
Yahoo! site, 26
home page (Google)
   Advanced Search link,
      34–35
   Directory link, 49
   I'm Feeling Lucky button, 27
   Images tab, 43
   overview of, 26, 27
   Preferences link on, 20
   tabs atop keyword box, 28
HotBot (search engine), 26
hyperlink
   creating in blog, 233
   search results page and, 29

• *I* •

I'm Feeling Lucky button
   Google home page, 27
   Google Toolbar, 166
image finder
   Google as, 12
   Random Google Image
      Finder, 287
image searching, 42–45
Images tab
   Advanced Image Search
      link, 43
   Google home page, 28
impression, billing by, 198
index. *See also* Google dance;
   spider
   continual shifting of, 218
   description of, 31
   Directory compared to, 220
   freshness settings, 244–246

getting site into, 218–222
public API and, 16
purity of, 221
size of, 17
info operator, 41
information engine, 10
installing
   Google Compute, 138, 139
   Google Toolbar, 160–163
   Google Toolbar 2.0, 172–173
   Java plug-in 1.3, 247–248
instant messaging, 271–272
intellectual property, online,
   45
Interest Bar, 200
interface language
   preference, setting,
      21–23, 186–187
interfaces. *See also*
   alternative interfaces;
   random-word Google
   interfaces
   API (application
      programming interface),
      16, 242
   bare-bones search, 243–244
   Google, 187–188
   Google Ultimate Interface,
      264–266
Interlingua, 22
Internet and World Wide
   Web, 11
Internet Explorer
   autocompletion feature, 303
   Google as default search
      engine for, 160, 182–183
   Google Toolbar and, 173,
      174
*Internet Searching For
   Dummies* (Brad Hill), 61
intitle operator
   Froogle and, 71
   negative, 305
   overview of, 42
   UncleSam search and, 111

inurl operator
   negative, 305
   overview of, 42
italic typeface, 233

• *J* •

Java plug-in 1.3, 247–248
journalists and blogging, 228
Julian date format, 305–306
Jump to page feature (Google
   Catalogs), 103

• *K* •

Keyboard Shortcuts,
   135–136, 153–155
keyword box
   Froogle, 92
   Google Groups, 74
   Google, tabs atop, 28
   Google Toolbar, 164
keyword loading, 223
Keyword Suggestion tool,
   213–216
keywords. *See also* Google
   Sets; keyword box;
   operators; random-word
   Google interfaces
   ad group, 200
   Advanced Search page,
      35–36
   AdWords and, 203, 212–216
   competing, 281–284
   Dictionary.com and, 29
   double- and triple-clicking,
      308–309
   Froogle, 92
   glossary and definition, 304
   Google Groups, 67, 71
   google-set-vista and, 255
   highlighting, 181, 308–309
   number of, 28
   proximity searching,
      266–268

keywords *(continued)*
  searches within
      searches, 298
  searching on highlighted,
      181–182
  selection of and Google
      Sets, 150–151
Klingon language, 22

## • L •

language. *See also* non-
      English content
  Advanced Groups Search
      page setting for, 85
  Advanced Search page
      setting for, 36
  AdWords and, 201, 202
  blog, 238
  Google Zeitgeist and, 312
  machine translation, 13,
      191–194
  preferences, setting, 21–23,
      186–187
  requesting for search,
      189–191
Language Tools page,
      186–189, 190, 191
learning and newsgroups, 63
letters, uppercase and
      lowercase, 27
license key, 242, 243, 266, 283
license to software
      developers, 242
link exchange, 197
link loading, 223
link operator
  checking status of incoming
      links with, 219
  GARBO and, 268
  overview of, 41
link structure of Web site, 222
Links setting (Advanced
      Search page), 38
Linux searches, 111–112
logging in to Google Answers,
      116–117

logos, 320–321, 331–332
lurking, 64, 84
Lycos (search engine), 26, 51

## • M •

Macintosh searches, 112
managing ad campaign,
      207–212
Mangle, 285–286
mapping address, 299–300
MapQuest, 299
message, 64. *See also* Google
      Groups
message board. *See* Usenet
Message dates setting
      (Advanced Groups
      Search page), 86
message excerpt, 73
message header (Google
      Groups), 74
Message ID setting
      (Advanced Groups
      Search page), 85
Microsoft Internet Explorer.
      *See* Internet Explorer
Microsoft Windows
      searches, 112
Min Inbound button
      (TouchGraph
      GoogleBrowser), 251
minus sign (-)
  Froogle and, 71
  negative search operator
      and, 305
  overview of, 39
mirror site, 289
modem speed
  Froogle results page and, 94
  Google Catalogs and, 105
  number of results and, 25
Modify Price or Keywords
      link, 210–211
More results from
      domain.com link, 33

MSN Messenger, 272
My Google-Dance-Machine,
      259–262

## • N •

Narrow by price feature
      (Froogle), 93
Narrow results feature
      (Froogle), 93
navigating back to Google, 25
negative keyword, 213
negative search
      operators, 305
Netscape
  browser/e-mail/newsgroup
      program, 66
  Google as default search
      engine for, 160
  Open Directory Project
      and, 51
  as search engine, 26
news. *See* Google News
News button (Google
      Toolbar), 167
News categories feature
      (Google News), 56
news searching from Google
      Toolbar, 319
news source, submitting, 59
News tab, 28
Newsgroup link (Google
      Groups), 75
newsgroup name, 73
newsgroup reader, 12, 65, 66
newsgroup server, 64–65
Newsgroup setting
      (Advanced Groups
      Search page), 85
newsgroups. *See also* Google
      Groups
  about Google, 316–317
  accessing, 66
  benefits of, 63
  description of, 65

etiquette, 84
Google Answers compared
  to, 127
google.public.support.
  general, 317
posting message to, 80–83
responding to message "off
  the board", 75
translators, 189
newsletters, e-mailed,
  328–329, 330–331
Next button (Google
  Toolbar), 170
No frame link (Google
  Groups), 78
Node label shows button
  (TouchGraph
  GoogleBrowser), 251
non-English content
  areas of, 185
  Google toolbar, 194–195
  Language Tools page,
    186–189
  searching for, 23
NOT operator
  Froogle and, 71
  overview of, 39
notice, Google, 32, 33
number keys and Keyboard
  Shortcuts, 154
number of results, setting,
  24–25

**• O •**

objectionable material, 24
objectivity, 277
Occurrences setting
  (Advanced Search
  page), 37
online bulletin board
  system, 62
online shopping. *See* Froogle;
  Google Catalogs
onUnloadJavaScript
  event, 170

Open Directory Project
  database
  description of, 47, 48, 51
  home page, 53, 54
  Submit a Site link and, 53
open source software
  movement, 51, 111
operating system
  information, 312
operators
  allintitle, 42, 71, 94, 97, 111
  allinurl, 42
  AND, 39, 79
  author, 79
  Boolean (standard), 35,
    39–40
  bphonebook, 301
  cache, 41
  daterange, 245
  exact phrase, 35, 39, 313
  filetype, 110, 316
  Froogle, 94–95, 97–98
  GooFresh and, 245
  Google, 40–42
  Google Groups, 71
  group, 69–71
  -group, 70
  info, 41
  intitle, 42, 71, 111, 305
  inurl, 42, 305
  link, 41, 219, 268
  minus sign (-), 39, 71, 305
  negative, 305
  NOT, 39, 71
  OR, 39, 71
  overview of, 38
  phonebook, 300–301
  placement of, 314–315
  plus sign (+), 39, 71
  quotes, 39–40, 71, 213,
    268, 313
  rphonebook, 301
  site, 34, 41–42, 113, 271,
    304, 316
  site:.gov, 110, 316
  specialty search engines,
    110

stocks, 40–41, 307–308
store, 94–95
Options panel (Google
  Toolbar 2.0), 172
OR operator
  Froogle and, 71
  overview of, 39
Original Format link (Google
  Groups), 75, 77
Outlook Express as
  newsgroup reader, 12,
    65, 66

**• P •**

Page button (Google
  Catalogs), 103
page description, 30
Page indicator feature
  (Google Catalogs), 103
Page Info menu display
  button (Google
  Toolbar), 167
Page, Larry, Web site of, 328
page rank, 17
page title, 30
Page view button (Google
  Catalogs), 103, 104
PageRank display button
  Google Toolbar, 166, 167
  Google Toolbar 2.0, 173
PageRank system
  Directory and, 47, 48, 51
  Google Groups and, 67,
    68, 72
  integrity of, 223
  Web site about, 325
Palm handheld computer
  and wireless Google, 14
Pause Ad Group link, 210
PDF format
  finding files in, 110
  reading and loading, 316
phone book
  opting out of, 302
  overview of, 12, 300–301

phonebook operator, 300–301
Pig Latin, 22
plus sign (+) operator
 Froogle and, 71
 overview of, 39
pop-up blocker (Google Toolbar 2.0), 172, 179, 255
portals
 all-purpose information, 26
 shopping, 13, 89–90
Post a reply link (Google Groups), 75
posting
 entry to blog, 233, 234
 message through Google Groups, 80–83
 message to newsgroup, 65
 question to Google Answers, 118–124
Power Posting tool, 216
power searching, 28
preferences
 cookie and, 21
 Directory and, 53
 Froogle and, 94
 Google Catalogs and, 105
 Google News and, 57
 Google Toolbar and, 162, 164
 Google Viewer and, 145
 interface language, setting, 21–23, 186–187
 number of results, 24–25
 Results Window setting, 25
 SafeSearch filter, 24
 Search Language, 23
 setting, 19–21
Preferences page, 20, 24
Previous button (Google Toolbar), 170
price comparisons in Froogle, 96
privacy issues and Google Compute, 137

privacy policy
 Google Answers and, 116
 Google Toolbar and, 162
 preferences and, 21
processing chip, 136
Product description feature (Froogle), 93
Product name feature (Froogle), 93
proximity searching, 266–268
public API, 16
public domain, 45
publishing blog, 233, 234

### • Q •

quote-back, 65, 82, 83
quotes operator
 AdWords and, 213
 Froogle and, 71
 GAPS and, 268
 overview of, 39–40
 stop words and, 313

### • R •

Radius button (TouchGraph GoogleBrowser), 251
Random Bounce Me, 286–287
Random Google, 287
Random Google Image Finder, 287
Random Web Search, 288
random-word Google interfaces
 Googlelaar, 278–279
 Mangle, 285–286
 overview of, 279, 284–285
 Random Bounce Me, 286–287
 Random Google, 287
 Random Google Image Finder, 287
 Random Web Search, 288
Rate Answer button (Google Answers), 128

reality TV, 32
Recipe Search, 273–274
recreation and newsgroups, 63
Related stories feature (Google News), 57
relation browsing, 268–270
removing archived post from Google Groups, 78
Request Answer Clarification button (Google Answers), 128
reset Google Toolbar button, 168, 169
restricting post from Google Groups archive, 78
results page. See also search results
 ad placement on, 200
 company name search, 308
 Directory, 54
 French interface, 188
 freshness of results, 244–246
 Froogle, 92–94
 GARBO, 270
 Google Catalogs, 100, 102, 103
 Google Glossary, 148–149
 Google Groups, 68–69, 73
 Google News, 59
 Google Sets, 151
 Google Viewer, 143, 145
 Google-Dance-Tool, 263
 image search, 43
 Keyboard Shortcuts, 153, 154
 My Google-Dance-Machine, 261
 phone book, 301
 promotional link on, 197–198
 Search within results link, 297–299
 stock ticker symbol search, 307

translating Web pages from, 193–194
WebQuotes, 148
Results Window setting, 25
reusing image, 45
robots.txt file (Robots Exclusion Protocol), 223–224
rphonebook operator, 301

## • S •

SafeSearch filter
  Advanced Groups Search page, 86
  Advanced Image Search page, 45
  Advanced Search page, 37
  overview of, 24
screen name, 65, 73
scrolling off, 64
search box. *See* keyword box
Search Country button (Google Toolbar 2.0), 172, 175–176
Search Directory button (Google Toolbar), 166
search engine
  default, Google as, 160, 182–183
  Excite, 26
  GAPS (Google API Proximity Search), 266–268
  GARBO (Google API Relation Browsing Outliner), 268–270
  GAWSH (Google API Web Search by Host), 270–271
  glossary, 148–149
  Google Dance Tool, 262–263
  Google Tool, 264
  Google-Dance-Tool, 263
  history of, 10
  HotBot, 26
  index for, 16
  Lycos, 26, 51

My Google-Dance-Machine, 259–262
  Netscape, 26
search engine listing, 217, 222–223
Search feature (Google Catalogs), 103
Search for Extra-Terrestrial Intelligence (SETI), 136
Search Groups button (Google Toolbar), 166
search history, keeping and preserving, 164–165
Search Images button (Google Toolbar), 166
Search Language preference, 23
search operators. *See* operators
search page (Mangle), 285
search queries, top ten gaining and declining, 312
search results. *See also* results page
  accuracy of, 1
  Cached link, 31–32, 33
  Category link, 31
  Directory category, 30–31
  indented results, 33–34
  overview of, 28–30
  page description, 30
  searching within, 297–299
  Similar Pages link, 32–33
Search Settings page (Google Alert), 257, 258
Search Site button (Google Toolbar), 166
search string, 36
Search Web button (Google Toolbar), 166
searching. *See also* operators; random-word Google interfaces; specialty search categories

advanced, 34–38
basic, 25–28
Cached link, 31–32, 33
by date, 305
Directory category, 30–31
by e-mail, 256
Froogle, 91–92
Google Catalogs, 100–105
Google Directory and, 54
Google Groups, 66–69
Google News, 58–59
Groups tab and, 86
on highlighted keywords, 181–182
by host, 270–271
images, 42–45
improving skills in, 127
indented results, 33–34
by instant messaging, 271–272
language and location, 190, 191
narrow subcategory of directory, 51
page description, 30
requesting language for, 189–191
results page, 28–30
within search results, 297–299
Similar Pages link, 32–33
Searching feature (Google News), 55
Security Warning window, 247–248
Send Feedback option (Google Compute), 140
servers
  freshness and, 244
  Google dance and, 259
  Google Dance Tool, 262–263
  Google Tool, 264
  Google-Dance-Tool, 263
  My Google-Dance-Machine, 259–262
  newsgroup, 64–65

SETI (Search for Extra-Terrestrial Intelligence), 136
shopping portal, 13, 89–90. *See also* Froogle; Google Catalogs
Show (blog), 238
Show first button (TouchGraph GoogleBrowser), 251
Show Singles button (TouchGraph GoogleBrowser), 251
Show title field (blog), 238–239
Similar Pages feature (Google Toolbar), 180
Similar Pages link (search results), 32–33
Similar setting (Advanced Search page), 38
site operator
  academic material and, 316
  GAWSH and, 271
  glossary and, 304
  overview of, 41–42
  searching large Web site and, 34
  university searches, 113
site:.gov operator, 110, 316
size of Web page, 29
Size setting (Advanced Image Search page), 44
software kit, 242
Something Awful Web site, 331–332
Sort by date link (Google Groups), 79
Sort by reply link (Google Groups), 79
spam, 65
specialty search categories
  Apple Macintosh and Microsoft Windows, 112
  finding, 108

Google Toolbar and, 109
Linux and BSD, 111–112
overview of, 107
universities, 13, 113–114
URLs, 108
U.S. government, 13, 109–111
spellchecking, 313
spider. *See also* deep crawl; fresh crawl
  attracting, 219–220, 221–222
  description of, 218
  Google dance and, 244
  keeping out of site, 223–224
  manipulating, 222–223
splash page, 221
sponsored links (Google Groups), 74
sponsorship, 199
square brackets, 213
Stanford University protein folding project, 138
starting
  new AdWords campaign, 211–212
  thread, 65
stock ticker symbol, searching on, 307
stocks operator, 40–41, 307–308
Stop Computing option (Google Compute), 140
stop words, 313
store operator, 94–95
strengths of Google, 12–13
Subject setting (Advanced Groups Search page), 85
submitting
  catalog addition request, 105
  news source to Google News, 59
  Web page to Directory, 52–55, 220
  Web site to index, 219

subscribing to newsgroup, 65
Summary bar feature (Froogle), 92
summary of results, 29
Suppress the onUnload JavaScript event button (Google Toolbar), 170
Switch to Conservative Mode option (Google Compute), 140

● *T* ●

template for blog, changing, 239
text, descriptive, 30
third-party development, 16
thread, 65
thread title, 73
threaded, 65
threading, 62
thumbnail, 43
time stamp, 74
Time Zone (blog), 238
Timestamp Format (blog), 238
Title bar feature (Google Catalogs), 103
toolbar. *See* Google Toolbar; Google Toolbar 2.0; Yahoo! Companion toolbar
Top story categories feature (Google News), 56
TouchGraph GoogleBrowser
  nodes, 248, 249
  toolbar, 251
  visualizing related sites, 246–252
  Zoom bar, 251, 252
TouchGraph viewer, 252–255
traffic, competition for, 197, 217
Traffic Estimator table, 215

translation on the fly, 13, 191–194
translators, amateur, 189
triple-clicking keyword, 309
troll, 65

## • *U* •

Uncertainty Principle, 277
UncleSam search. *See* U.S. government searches
uninstalling Google Compute, 142
university searches, 13, 113–114
Up button (Google Toolbar), 167, 168
URL
  blog and, 237
  description of, 247
  search results page and, 29
U.S. government searches, 13, 109–111
Usenet. *See also* Google Groups
  Deja News and, 61
  description of, 12, 62–63, 65
  Google Answers compared to, 125
  terminology for, 64–65

## • *V* •

View Blog tab, 235
View My Stats option (Google Compute), 140
view thread link (Google Groups), 73
View with frames link (Google Groups), 78
viewing
  AdWords campaign report, 208–209
  blog in edit screen, 235, 236
visual keyword sets, 252–255

Voice Search, 152–153
Voting buttons (Google Toolbar), 167

## • *W* •

Web crawl, 218
Web page. *See also* home page; results page
  dividing content topically, 222
  excluding from Google, 224
  getting into Google index, 217, 218–222
  submitting to Directory, 52–55, 220
Web searching. *See* searching
Web sites
  AdWords login page, 205
  Boogle, 274
  Brin, Sergey, 328
  browser buttons, 180
  default search engine, Google as, 182–183
  Digital Songstream, 227
  Elgoog, 327
  elgooG, 289
  FaganFinder page, 306
  Floogle, 272
  GAPS, 266
  GARBO, 268
  GAWSH, 270
  GooFresh, 245
  Google Alert, 256
  Google Art, 290
  Google Dance Tool, 262
  Google Duel, 281
  Google Glossary, 248
  Google Labs, 136
  Google PageRank, 325
  Google Review, 329–330
  Google Sets, 150
  Google Smackdown, 281
  Google Store, 319
  Google Tool, 264
  Google Toolbar, 161

  Google Toolbar 2.0, 172
  Google Ultimate Interface, 264
  Google Viewer, 143
  Google Watch, 324
  Google Weblog, 326
  Google Zeitgeist, 312
  Google-Dance-Tool, 263
  GoogleFight, 281
  Googlelaar, 278
  GooglePress, 328–329
  google-set-vista, 252
  Googlewhack, 276
  Googlism, 280
  gooGuide, 330–331
  Keyboard Shortcuts, 153
  Language Tools page, 186
  logos, 320–321, 331–332
  Mangle, 285
  My Google-Dance-Machine, 260
  Open Directory Project database, 51
  Page, Larry, 328
  Random Bounce Me, 286
  Random Google, 287
  Random Google Image Finder, 287
  Random Web Search, 288
  Recipe Search, 274
  removing listing from phone book, 302
  searching in large, 34
  Something Awful, 331–332
  specialty search categories, 108
  Stanford University protein folding project, 138
  TouchGraph GoogleBrowser, 247
  translators, amateur, 189
  Voice Search, 152
  Webmaster World: Google forum, 324–325
  Welcome to AdWords page, 202

Web tab, 28
Weblogs. *See also* Blogger
  creating at BlogSpot,
    229–231
  creating at FTP server,
    231–232
  editing, 232–233
  formatting, 238–239
  overview of, 14, 227–228
  settings, adjusting, 235–238
  template, changing, 239
  writing, posting, and
    publishing, 233–235
Webmaster World: Google
    forum Web site, 324–325
WebQuotes
  home page, 147
  overview of, 135–136,
    146–147
  results page, 148
wildcard (*), 71, 72

windows
  navigating back to
    Google, 25
  opening to display search
    results, 164
Windows searches, 112
wireless Google, 14
word meaning, finding,
    303–304
Word-find buttons (Google
    Toolbar), 168
World Wide Web, 11

• X •

X-News, 66

• Y •

Yahoo! Companion toolbar,
    40, 162
Yahoo! Directory, 48
Yahoo! Finance, 40, 41, 307

*Yahoo! For Dummies* (Brad
    Hill), 10, 48, 162
Yahoo! Groups, 328
Yahoo! Maps, 299
Yahoo! Messenger, 272
Yahoo! News, 12, 56
Yahoo! Shopping, 13, 90
Yahoo! site
  history of, 10
  home page, 26
  integrated searching and
    browsing, 11
YIMGoogle, 272

• Z •

Zoom bar
  google-set-vista, 255
  TouchGraph
    GoogleBrowser, 251, 252
Zoom button (Google
    Catalogs), 103